# www.wadsworth.com

*www.wadsworth.com* is the World Wide Web site
for Wadsworth and is your direct source to dozens of
online resources.

At *www.wadsworth.com* you can find out about
supplements, demonstration software, and student
resources. You can also send email to many of our
authors and preview new publications and exciting
new technologies.

**www.wadsworth.com**
Changing the way the world learns®

**GERALD COREY** is a Professor Emeritus of Human Services at California State University at Fullerton, an Adjunct Professor of Counseling and Family Sciences at Loma Linda University, and a licensed psychologist. He received his doctorate in counseling from the University of Southern California. He is a Diplomate in Counseling Psychology, American Board of Professional Psychology; a National Certified Counselor; a Fellow of the American Psychological Association (Counseling Psychology); and a Fellow of the Association for Specialists in Group Work.

Jerry received the Outstanding Professor of the Year Award from California State University at Fullerton in 1991. He teaches both undergraduate and graduate courses in group counseling, as well as courses in experiential groups, the theory and practice of counseling, and professional ethics. He is the author or co-author of 15 textbooks in counseling currently in print, 3 student videos with workbooks, and about 60 articles in professional publications. *Theory and Practice of Counseling and Psychotherapy* has been translated into the Arabic, Indonesian, Portuguese, and Chinese languages. *Theory and Practice of Group Counseling* has been translated into Chinese, Russian, and Spanish.

Along with his wife, Marianne Schneider Corey, Jerry often presents workshops in group counseling. In the past 25 years the Coreys have conducted group counseling training workshops for mental health professionals at many universities in the United States as well as in Mexico, China, Germany, Belgium, Scotland,

Canada, and Ireland. The Coreys also frequently give presentations and workshops at state and national professional conferences. In his leisure time, Jerry likes to travel, hike and bicycle in the mountains, and drive his 1931 Model A Ford.

Other textbooks, student manuals and workbooks, and educational videos by Gerald Corey from Brooks/Cole Thomson Learning include:

- *Case Approach to Counseling and Psychotherapy*, Sixth Edition (2005)
- *Theory and Practice of Group Counseling*, Sixth Edition (and *Manual*) (2004)
- *Group Techniques*, Third Edition (2004, with Marianne Schneider Corey, Patrick Callanan, and J. Michael Russell)
- *Clinical Supervision in the Helping Professions: A Practical Guide* (2003, with Robert Haynes and Patrice Moulton)
- *Issues and Ethics in the Helping Professions*, Sixth Edition (2003, with Marianne Schneider Corey and Patrick Callanan)
- *Becoming a Helper*, Fourth Edition (2003, with Marianne Schneider Corey)
- *Groups: Process and Practice*, Sixth Edition (2002, with Marianne Schneider Corey)
- *I Never Knew I Had a Choice*, Seventh Edition (2002, with Marianne Schneider Corey)
- *The Art of Integrative Counseling* (2001)

Jerry is co-author, with his daughters Cindy Corey and Heidi Jo Corey, of an orientation-to-college book entitled *Living and Learning*, published by Wadsworth. He is also co-author (with Barbara Herlihy) of *Boundary Issues in Counseling: Multiple Roles and Responsibilities* and *ACA Ethical Standards Casebook*, Fifth Edition, both published by the American Counseling Association.

He has also made three videos on various aspects of counseling practice: (1) *CD-ROM for Integrative Counseling* (2005, with Robert Haynes); (2) *Ethics in Action: CD-ROM* (2003, with Marianne Schneider Corey and Robert Haynes); and (3) *The Evolution of a Group: Student Video and Workbook* (2000, with Marianne Schneider Corey and Robert Haynes). All of these student videos and CD-ROM programs are available through Brooks/Cole Thomson Learning.

## Have an *INTERACTIVE, PERSONAL EXPERIENCE* with counseling theories and skills!

Introducing the
**Seventh Edition**
of Gerald Corey's
***Theory and Practice
of Counseling and Psychotherapy***
and its integrated suite
of teaching and learning tools

* Theory and Practice of
  Counseling and Psychotherapy,
  Seventh Edition
* Student Manual, Seventh Edition
* Case Approach to Counseling
  and Psychotherapy, Sixth Edition
* CD-ROM for Integrative
  Counseling
* The Art of Integrative
  Counseling

# Student Manual for
# Theory and Practice of Counseling and Psychotherapy

## SEVENTH EDITION

### Gerald Corey

California State University, Fullerton

Diplomate in Counseling Psychology,

American Board of Professional Psychology

THOMSON
™
BROOKS/COLE

Australia • Canada • Mexico • Singapore • Spain
United Kingdom • United States

**WADSWORTH**

**THOMSON LEARNING**™

Executive Editor: *Lisa Gebo*
Acquisitions Editor: *Marquita Flemming*
Assistant Editor: *Shelley Gesicki*
Editorial Assistant: *Amy Lam*
Technology Project Manager: *Barry Connolly*
Marketing Manager: *Caroline Concilla*
Marketing Assistant: *Mary Ho*
Advertising Project Manager: *Tami Strang*
Project Manager, Editorial Production: *Katy German*

Print/Media Buyer: *Judy Inoyue*
Permissions Editor: *Stephanie Lee*
Production Service: *The Cooper Company*
Text and Cover Designer: *Cheryl Carrington*
Copy Editor: *Kay Mikel*
Cover Image: *Corbis*
Compositor: *Thompson Type*
Printer: *West Group*

Library of Congress Control Number: 2004100349

ISBN 0-534-53606-9

**Brooks/Cole—Thomson Learning**
**10 Davis Drive**
**Belmont, CA 94002**
**USA**

**Asia**
Thomson Learning
5 Shenton Way #01-01
UIC Building
Singapore 068808

**Australia/New Zealand**
Thomson Learning
102 Dodds Street
Southbank, Victoria 3006
Australia

**Canada**
Nelson
1120 Birchmount Road
Toronto, Ontario M1K 5G4
Canada

**Europe/Middle East/Africa**
Thomson Learning
High Holborn House
50/51 Bedford Row
London WC1R 4LR
United Kingdom

**Latin America**
Thomson Learning
Seneca, 53
Colonia Polanco
11560 Mexico D.F.
Mexico

**Spain/Portugal**
Paraninfo
Calle Magallanes, 25
28015 Madrid, Spain

# CONTENTS

**PART 1  Basic Issues in Counseling Practice**

   1   Introduction and Overview / 3

   2   The Counselor: Person and Professional / 12

   3   Ethical Issues in Counseling Practice / 30

**PART 2  Theories and Techniques of Counseling**

   4   Psychoanalytic Therapy / 41

   5   Adlerian Therapy / 52

   6   Existential Therapy / 70

   7   Person-Centered Therapy / 81

   8   Gestalt Therapy / 92

   9   Behavior Therapy / 105

   10   Cognitive Behavior Therapy / 122

   11   Reality Therapy / 138

   12   Feminist Therapy / 153

   13   Postmodern Approaches / 168

   14   Family System Therapy / 181

**PART 3  Integration and Application**

   15   An Integrative Perspective / 197

   16   Case Illustration:
        An Integrative Approach in Working With Stan / 212

**Appendix I Scoring Key for Chapter Quizzes** / 216

**Appendix 2 Other Books and Videos by the Author** / 217

# PART 1

# Basic Issues in Counseling Practice

**1** Introduction and Overview

**2** The Counselor: Person and Professional

**3** Ethical Issues in Counseling Practice

# Chapter 1

# Introduction and Overview

 INTRODUCTION

This manual is designed to accompany *Theory and Practice of Counseling and Psychotherapy,* Seventh Edition, and *Case Approach to Counseling and Psychotherapy,* Sixth Edition (both Brooks/Cole Thomson Learning, 2005). The manual is aimed at helping you and your instructor personalize the process by which you learn about counseling theories and therapeutic practice. It emphasizes the *practical application* of various therapeutic approaches to your personal growth. And it stresses the critical evaluation of each therapy as you are called on to use the skills of the approach in exercises, activities, and consideration of case examples and problems. The manual demands that you become an *active learner,* both inside and outside the classroom, in your growth as a person and as a future counselor.

The manual is appropriate for courses in counseling theory and practice, intervention strategies, and human services and also for internship experiences. It is well suited to practicum courses during which you apply your knowledge of the helping process to specific, practical field experiences. Key features of the manual are:

- Self-inventories to assess your attitudes and beliefs about counseling theory and practice, the counselor as a person, and ethical issues
- A summary overview of each major theory of counseling
- A review of the highlights of each theory
- Questions for discussion and evaluation
- A prechapter self-inventory for each approach
- A list of addresses of major professional organizations
- Sample forms and charts for some chapters
- Assessment forms for the appraisal of life patterns
- Case examples and cases for practice
- The case of Ruth for each of the theory chapters
- Experiential activities for inside and outside of class
- Ethical and professional issues for exploration
- Issues basic to your personal development
- A glossary of key terms for each theory
- A quiz on each theory

# HOW TO USE THE MANUAL WITH THE TEXTBOOK

Let me suggest some ways of deriving the maximum benefit from the combined use of the textbook and the manual. These suggestions are based on student input and my experiences in teaching counseling courses.

1. Begin with the manual. Skim the entire manual to get some "feel" for the program.

2. Then complete the survey questionnaire in this chapter. (You may find it useful to take it again at the end of the course to assess any changes in your attitudes toward counseling and the helping process.)

3. Before you read and study a textbook chapter on one of the 11 theories, complete the manual's corresponding prechapter self-inventory, which is based on the key concepts of the approach discussed in the textbook. The purpose of the inventory is to assess your degree of agreement or disagreement with the concepts of the theory, *not* to seek the "right answer." My students have said that the inventories give them a clear focus as they read the chapter material.

4. Also before reading each theory chapter, carefully study the manual's overview of the theory treated in the chapter. The overview provides a framework, in capsule form, for the entire textbook chapter. A glossary of key terms and several questions for discussion and evaluation are also included in the manual to assist you in considering important issues before you read the textbook chapter. Students report that the overviews give an organizational framework from which to better grasp the textbook material.

5. After reading and studying a textbook chapter, turn again to the manual.

    a. Review the questions (for critique and personal applications).

    b. Retake (or at least review) the self-inventory.

    c. Look at the overview and focus on key ideas of the theory once again.

    d. Review the key terms defined in the glossary.

    e. Select a few key questions or exercises that are most meaningful to you, and clarify your position on the issues underlying the questions.

    f. Circle the questions or exercises you chose, write down additional questions you would like to pursue, and bring both sets to class for further discussion.

    g. Apply to the theory the list of questions found in the next section of this chapter, entitled Reviewing the Highlights of a Theory.

    h. Formulate your own critique of the approach, and think about aspects that you would most like to incorporate in your own personal style of counseling.

    i. Take the quizzes at the end of each theory chapter and score them, referring to the key in Appendix 1.

6. For most of the chapters in this manual, I have intentionally provided an abundance of exercises and questions, more than can be expected to be integrated within one course. Look over all the material in a chapter and select the questions and exercises that seem the most relevant, stimulating, and interesting to you. I hope that at the end of the course you will review the material in this manual. At that time you may want to consider questions or activities that you omitted in your initial reading.

7. In reading and thinking about Chapter 2 ("The Counselor: Person and Professional") do your best to relate to the issues in a personal manner. This chapter will set the tone for the book by raising issues that you can explore as you study each of the theory chapters. Students have found that they get a lot more from this course (and from the textbook and manual) by relating to what they read in a *personal* way. Thus, in studying each theory you have some excellent opportunities to apply what you are learning about the theory to your own life. By bringing yourself into this reading, you make

ning sessions of the course and compare your viewpoints with those of other students. Take the inventory again at the end of the course to see whether any of your beliefs, attitudes, and values have changed.

1. I think the purpose of counseling and psychotherapy is to
   a. assist clients in creating solutions to their problems.
   b. tell others how best to run their life.
   c. make clients happy and contented.
   d. always provide an answer or solution to the client's problem.
   e. _____

2. My view of clients who seek counseling is that they
   a. can be trusted to find creative solutions to their problems.
   b. are generally in need of advice on how to proceed.
   c. will progress only if I am highly active and structured.
   d. will generally be resistant to change unless doing so is easy.
   e. _all above____

3. Regarding the issue of human freedom, I believe that we
   a. create our own destiny by making choices.
   b. possess *limited* degrees of freedom.
   c. are almost totally the products of conditioning.
   d. are what our genetic makeup and environment make us.
   e. _b and d____

4. I believe that selecting the goals of counseling
   a. is primarily the client's responsibility.
   b. is primarily the therapist's responsibility.
   c. is a collaborative venture of client and therapist.
   d. can interfere with the spontaneity of counseling.
   e. _____

5. Psychotherapy should be aimed primarily at
   a. assisting clients in creating a new life story.
   b. making the unconscious conscious.
   c. providing symptom relief in as brief a time as possible.

   d. learning realistic and responsible behavior.
   e. _____

6. Counseling should mainly focus on
   a. what people are thinking.
   b. what people are feeling.
   c. what people are doing.
   d. each of these, depending on the stage of therapy.
   e. _____

7. Counseling is a process of
   a. reeducation.
   b. helping clients make life decisions.
   c. learning to integrate one's feeling and thinking.
   d. learning more effective coping behaviors.
   e. _all of above___

8. Counseling and therapy should focus on
   a. the client's past experiences.
   b. the client's experience in the here-and-now.
   c. the client's strivings toward the future.
   d. whatever the client decides.
   e. _all of above___

9. Counseling and therapy should focus primarily on
   a. changing behavior.
   b. providing insight.
   c. changing attitudes and feelings.
   d. challenging values.
   e. _all of above___

10. In thinking about practicing counseling in a multicultural society, it is essential to
    a. have specialized course work on various cultures.
    b. get fieldwork experience in multicultural settings.
    c. come to terms with my own culture.
    d. develop skills in working with culturally different clients.
    e. _b and d___

11. Specific knowledge about cultural differences is

    a. essential for effective counseling.
    b. dangerous because of the tendency to stereotype.
    c. impossible to acquire because of the number of cultures.
    d. useful in providing a conceptual framework.
    e. _____ a and d

12. A person's early childhood experiences are

    a. not really important material for therapy.
    b. the determinants of the person's present adjustments.
    c. experiences that must be explored in therapy.
    d. of interest but not of much significance for who one is today.
    e. _____

13. The most important function of a therapist is

    a. being present for and with the client.
    b. interpreting the meaning of the client's symptoms.
    c. creating trust that allows the client to freely explore feelings and thoughts.
    d. giving the client specific suggestions for things to do outside the therapy sessions.
    e. _____ all of above

14. I believe that counselors should be

    a. active and directive.
    b. relatively nondirective, allowing the client to direct.
    c. whatever the client wants them to be.
    d. directive or nondirective, depending on the client's capacity for self-direction.
    e. _____

15. The power of a therapist

    a. should be used to manipulate the client in the direction the therapist deems best for the client.
    b. should be minimized because of its danger.
    c. can be a vital force that the therapist can use in modeling for a client.
    d. is always a sign of a therapist's need to reinforce his or her own ego.
    e. _____

16. To help a client, a therapist

    a. needs to have had a problem similar to the client's problem.
    b. must be free of any conflicts in the area he or she is exploring with the client.
    c. must share similar life experiences and values with the client.
    d. must like the client personally.
    e. _____

17. I believe that for those wishing to become therapists, undergoing therapy

    a. is an absolute necessity.
    b. is not an important factor in a therapist's capacity to work with others.
    c. is necessary only when a therapist has severe personal problems.
    d. should be encouraged strongly but not required.
    e. _____

18. Regarding the client–therapist relationship, I think

    a. the therapist should be a friend to the client.
    b. the therapist must remain relatively anonymous.
    c. a personal and warm relationship is not essential.
    d. the therapist needs to function as an expert.
    e. _____

19. A counselor should

    a. select one theory and work strictly within that framework for the sake of consistency.
    b. ignore theory because it is not related to practical applications.
    c. strive to combine a couple of theoretical approaches.
    d. integrate all the theories by applying the appropriate concepts and techniques to each client.
    e. _____

20. Of the following, the most important feature of effective therapy is

    a. knowledge of the theory of counseling and behavior.
    b. skill in using techniques appropriately.
    c. genuineness and openness on the therapist's part.
    d. the therapist's ability to specify a treatment plan and evaluate the results.
    e. _____ all of above

**Directions:**   *T = true. F = false.* For items 21 through 50 circle the answer (T, F, or both) that best fits your belief. Then, on the line provided, give a reason for your answer.

**Example:**   T   (F)   Giving advice is an important function of therapists.

*This is the easy way out, but it is not therapy.*

T   F   21. Therapists should work only with clients whom they really like and care for.
_They should provide help to everyone_____

T   F   22. As long as I counsel others, it is essential that I be open to the idea of receiving therapy myself.
_____I am not_____

T   F   23. I have goals for my clients in advance of seeing them.
_____

T   F   24. It is critical that my values be kept out of the therapy process.
_____

T   F   25. To work with a client effectively, the therapist must first be aware of the person's cultural background.
_____

T   F   26. I should model certain behaviors that I expect my clients to learn.
_____

T   F   27. My own levels of self-awareness and psychological health are probably the most important variables that determine the success or failure of counseling.
_____

T   F   28. It is therapeutically useful for me to be completely open, honest, and transparent with my clients.
_____

T   F   29. It is appropriate for me to discuss my personal conflicts at length with my clients, for they can apply my solutions to problems they are facing.
_____

T   F   30. The kind of person I am is more important than my theoretical orientation and my use of techniques.
_____

T   F   31. Knowledge of my own cultural background is as important as knowing about the cultural background of my client.
_____

T   F   32. Intellectual insight is a necessary and sufficient condition for change.
_____

T   F   33. Therapy must be aimed at social and political change if any real personal change is to occur.
_____

T   F   34. My job as a therapist is basically that of a teacher, for I am reeducating clients and teaching them coping skills.

_____

T   F   35. I view my client as being an expert in his or her own life.

_____

T   F   36. Because confrontation might cause great pain or discomfort in a client, I think it is generally unwise to use this technique.

_____

T   F   37. My own needs are really not important in the therapeutic relationship with a client.

_____

T   F   38. Because silences during a therapy session are generally considered a sign of boredom, care should be taken to avoid them.

_____

T   F   39. It is essential that I form a collaborative relationship with my client.

_____

T   F   40. The therapeutic relationship should be characterized by the same degree of sharing by both client and therapist.

_____

T   F   41. I must be careful to avoid mistakes, for my clients will lose respect for me if they observe me faltering.

_____

T   F   42. Therapy need not be a personal relationship, for it can be effective if the therapist possesses technical skill.

_____

T   F   43. Therapy can have either a positive or a negative effect on a client.

_____

T   F   44. There is no personal change or growth unless a person is open to anxiety and pain.

_____

T   F   45. As a counselor, I want to be flexible and modify the techniques I use, especially in counseling culturally diverse clients.

_____

T   F   46. As a counselor, I strive to be objective and not to become personally involved with my clients.

_____

T   F   47. As a therapist, I should not judge my client's behavior, for therapy and value judgments are incompatible.

_____

T    F    48. If I experience intense feelings toward my client (anger or sexual attraction, for example), I have lost my potential effectiveness to counsel that person, and I should terminate the relationship.

_____

T    F    49. It is inappropriate to touch clients, under any circumstances.

_____

T    F    50. I would not accept an involuntary client.

_____

# Chapter 2

# The Counselor: Person and Professional

 A SURVEY OF YOUR ATTITUDES AND BELIEFS ABOUT THE COUNSELOR AS PERSON AND PROFESSIONAL

**Directions:** This self-inventory is designed to clarify your thinking on issues raised in the textbook concerning the counselor as a person and a professional. You may want to select more than one answer; notice also that line "e" is for any qualifying responses you want to make or any other answer you would like to provide.

1. Which of the following do you think is most important as a determinant of the outcome of therapy?
   a. the skills and techniques the counselor possesses
   b. the particular theoretical orientation of the counselor
   c. the kind of person the counselor is
   d. the quality of a collaborative client–therapist relationship
   e. _____ all of what ___

2. What is the most important component of therapist authenticity?
   a. respectful curiosity
   b. caring and compassion for the client
   c. willingness to confront the client when necessary
   d. modeling those qualities the therapist expects of the client
   e. _____

3. Which of the following is the most important attribute, or personal characteristic, of effective therapists?
   a. having an appreciation of their own culture
   b. being open to change
   c. being present and making connections

   d. having resolved any pressing personal problems
   e. _____

4. What is your position with respect to you receiving personal therapy before you begin working with clients?
   a. I don't feel the need because I have few pressing problems.
   b. I am very eager to get involved in my own therapy as a client.
   c. I am ethically obligated to experience my own therapy before I expect to counsel others.
   d. I would do it only if I were required to do so.
   e. _____

5. If you were to become a client, on what issue(s) might you most focus in your therapy sessions?
   a. re-authoring the story of my life
   b. unfinished situations from my past, especially relationships with my parents
   c. my fear of overidentifying with my clients' problems
   d. my anxieties over my ability to work effectively with various types of clients
   e. _____

6. Over which of the following issues do you have the greatest degree of *anxiety* when you think about beginning as a counselor?

   a. not having the knowledge or skills to be effective
   b. making a mistake (or mistakes) that will damage the client
   c. having clients demand too much from me and being unable to meet those demands
   d. finding that I was never really cut out to be a therapist in the first place
   e. _____

7. How would you determine what constitutes *appropriate* and *facilitative* self-disclosure as a counselor?

   a. by doing whatever feels comfortable to me at the time
   b. by observing the reactions of my client to my disclosures
   c. by observing the degree to which the client engages in deeper self-exploration
   d. by monitoring my motivations for engaging in self-disclosure
   e. _____

8. When do you think it is important to disclose yourself to your clients?

   a. when they ask for it or when I sense that this is what they need
   b. whenever I have persistent reactions, thoughts, perceptions, or feelings
   c. when I want to influence clients to choose a certain course of action
   d. when nothing much seems to be happening in the sessions
   e. _____

9. How does the issue of *perfectionism* apply to you as a counselor?

   a. I am sure that I will demand perfection of myself, which means that I cannot tolerate making any mistakes in my sessions.
   b. I will view my mistakes as an opportunity and learn from them.
   c. If I failed with a client, I think I would be devastated.
   d. Although I will strive to be the best I can, I will not burden myself with the demand that I never make mistakes.
   e. _____

10. What is your policy on being honest with your clients?

    a. I believe in being completely frank and totally open with clients regarding any impressions I may have toward them.
    b. I believe I need to carefully weigh what I say for fear of damaging our relationship.
    c. If I did not think I were competent to deal with a particular client, I would want to tell the person so.
    d. If I expect them to be honest with me, I had better be honest with them.
    e. _____

11. How do you think you would tend to deal with *silences* during a counseling session?

    a. I would be threatened and tend to think I had done something wrong.
    b. I would ask the client questions to get him or her going again.
    c. I would discuss with the client my own reactions to the silence.
    d. I would sit it out and wait for the client to take the initiative.
    e. _____

12. What is your view on the role of *giving advice* in counseling?

    a. Because I see the counseling process as guiding clients, I would freely give advice if I thought this was what the client wanted.
    b. I would rarely, if ever, give advice, for even if the advice was good, it may make the client dependent on me.
    c. Because I view the client as an expert on him- or herself, I would refrain from dispensing advice.
    d. I think I would give advice to a client when I had a strong preference for a direction I hoped he or she would choose.
    e. _____

13. What are your views concerning the use of *humor* in therapy?

    a. Whenever I deemed it appropriate, I would interject humor in a session, because I see laughter as potentially very therapeutic.
    b. I might use humor when I had a solid relationship with a client and doing so seemed appropriate to the situation.

c. I would avoid humor, as I think it can easily distract a client from dealing with the serious matters of therapy.

d. I would use humor when my client got into "heavy feelings" to lighten things up a bit so that neither of us would get depressed.

e. _____

14. How do you expect that you will go about developing your own counseling style?

a. by working within the framework of one theory initially

b. by modeling myself after a supervisor

c. by combining techniques from several therapeutic approaches

d. by keeping a journal of what I do and experience as I work with clients

e. _____

15. How do you think you can best *prevent burnout*?

a. by not blaming people or things outside of me for my feelings of devitalization and helplessness

b. by taking the time to play and engage in hobbies

c. by making sure that my personal needs are being met in my life away from work

d. by quitting a job as soon as I find that I am losing interest or when I am feeling ineffective

e. _____

16. As a counselor, I expect that my values will affect the counseling process

a. in those cases in which I have values strongly divergent from my client's.

b. only in cases in which I attempt to sway the client to my way of thinking.

c. at all times, because I cannot separate my values from my work as a counselor.

d. when I have strong negative reactions to certain behaviors or values of my client.

e. _____

17. My position on the ethics involved in the role of values in therapy is that

a. therapists should never impose their values on a client.

b. therapists should teach the client proper values.

c. therapists should openly share their values when appropriate.

d. therapist values should be kept out of the relationship.

e. _____

18. Of the following motivations, the one that best expresses my reason for wanting to be in a helping profession is

a. my desire to nurture others.

b. my desire to give advice to those who have problems.

c. my desire to get confirmation of my value as a person.

d. my need to be needed and to feel that I am helping others.

e. _____

19. I won't feel ready to counsel others until

a. my own life is free of problems.

b. I've experienced counseling as a client.

c. I feel very confident and know that I'll be effective.

d. I've become a self-aware person and developed the ability to continually reexamine my own life and relationships.

e. _____

20. If a client evidenced strong feelings of attraction or dislike for me, I would

a. help the client work through these feelings and understand them.

b. enjoy these feelings if they were positive.

c. refer my client to another counselor.

d. direct the sessions into less emotional areas.

e. _____

## Suggestions on How to Use This Inventory

1. Now that you have finished this inventory, go back over it and circle a few of the items that had the greatest meaning to you. Bring these issues to class and compare your

reactions with those of fellow students. You might also discuss why these issues held special meaning for you.

2. Discuss with others in class what it was like for you to go through this inventory. What did it stir up in you? What did you learn about yourself?

3. Go back to the initial Survey of Attitudes and Values Related to Counseling and Psycho-therapy: A Self-Inventory and Pretest in Chapter 1 of this manual. Look over your responses to determine the degree of consistency between these two surveys. I strongly recommend that you also circle several of the items that you would *most* like to bring up for class discussion. It is a good idea to review your initial responses at the end of the semester in small groups. This process can help you examine any shifts in your thinking.

 ## COUNSELOR VALUES AND THE THERAPEUTIC PROCESS

Read the section in Chapter 2 entitled "The Counselor as a Therapeutic Person" and reflect on your role as a change agent. When you think about what you most want to accomplish in counseling people, what do you hope for? I take the position that who you are as a person is the critical variable in determining the outcomes of your professional work with clients. Of course, you need to master theories of counseling, you need to have a wide range of knowledge, and you must acquire and hone many counseling skills. But being an effective counselor is far more than mastering a body of knowledge and possessing skills.

### Using Yourself as an Instrument for Change

When I think of counseling, I think of the art of reaching others. This prayer of Saint Francis of Assisi embodies for me the heart of the counselor's role in making a significant difference in the lives of others.

Lord, make me an instrument of thy peace.
Where there is hatred, let me sow love;
Where there is injury, pardon;
Where there is doubt, faith;
Where there is despair, hope;
Where there is darkness, light;
Where there is sadness, joy;
O divine Master, grant that I may not so much seek
To be consoled as to console;
To be understood as to understand;
To be loved, as to love;
For it is in giving that we receive;
It is in pardoning that we are pardoned;
It is in dying to self that we are born to eternal life.

From *Meditation* by Eknath Easwaran, founder of the Blue Mountain Center of Meditation, copyright 1991; reprinted by permission of Nilgiri Press, P.O. Box 256, Tomales, CA 94971, www.nilgiri.org.

The counselor is instrumental in assisting clients to become more of the persons they were meant to be. For me, counseling is about teaching people: the price of hatred, both toward self and others; the importance of forgiveness, both of self and others; developing the faith to believe in oneself, others, and a higher power; being able to see some light at the end of a dark tunnel; finding hope admist tears and sadness; coming to appreciate the value of loving others and oneself; seeing the power of understanding and acceptance;

and finding meaning in life by giving to others. Easwaren suggests that we use the lines of this prayer as the basis for meditation. He believes the words of the prayer have an almost universal appeal. Regardless of one's religious affiliation or spiritual beliefs, there is a deep message in this prayer. Take time now to reflect on what this prayer means to you.

- In what ways might you apply the words of Saint Francis to yourself?

  _____

  _____

- What insights does this prayer suggest that you can apply to your role as a counselor?

  _____

  _____

- What values are embedded in this prayer?

  _____

  _____

- How might this prayer help you focus on some core values that could guide your counseling practice?

  _____

  _____

- How can you best assist clients in reflecting on qualities described in this prayer without imposing your vision on your clients?

  _____

  _____

- How will you measure the degree to which you are making a significant difference in the lives of clients?

  _____

  _____

- What other thoughts do you have as you reflect on this prayer?

  _____

  _____

## The Role of Values in Counseling

Read the section in Chapter 2 entitled "The Counselor's Values and the Therapeutic Process" and reflect on how certain of your values might be an asset or a liability in your work with clients. Which values are likely to help you connect with a client? Which of your values might make it difficult for you to objectively assist clients in finding their own way? These questions are designed to help you search yourself for answers about the role of values in counseling. After you have responded to these questions, talk with other students about your thoughts on these value issues.

- To what degree do you think it is best not to reveal your values to clients lest you bias the direction your clients are likely to take?

  _____

  _____

- What is one way that you can help clients clarify their own values?

  _____

  _____

- To what degree is it possible for you to disagree with a client's values and still accept him or her as a person?

  _____

  _____

- Is the purpose of counseling to teach values to clients or to teach clients how to discover their own values?

  _____

  _____

- What difference do you see between exposing or imposing your values on clients?

  _____

  _____

- Is it possible to separate a discussion of values from the therapeutic process? To what extent do you view counseling as a process of exploring values?

  _____

  _____

■ How can you retain your own sense of values and remain true to yourself, yet at the same time allow your clients the freedom to select values and behaviors that differ sharply from yours?

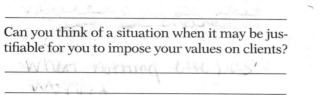

_____

_____

■ Can you think of a situation when it may be justifiable for you to impose your values on clients?

_____

_____

■ What course of action might you take when you become aware of a sharp value conflict with a client?

_____

_____

## Dealing With Value Conflicts

At times you and a client may experience value clashes that make it difficult for you to work together. To help you identify such circumstances, complete the following inventory, and determine when you might refer a client to someone else because of a conflict of value systems. Use this code:

    1 = I would definitely work well with this type of person.

    2 = I would probably find working with this type of person difficult or challenging.

    3 = I am quite certain that I would not work well with this type of person.

_____ 1. an adolescent girl who wants to explore her feelings about whether to have an abortion

_____ 2. an adolescent boy who is convinced that living *for drugs* and *on drugs* is the way to live

_____ 3. a gay or lesbian couple who want to explore their relationship problems

_____ 4. a lesbian couple who want to discuss their desire to adopt a child

_____ 5. a man who is deeply troubled over an extramarital affair but is not ready to give up this relationship

_____ 6. a woman who is deeply troubled over an extramarital affair but is not willing to give it up

_____ 7. a very dogmatic individual who is convinced that all of his problems would be solved if he did God's will and made the Lord the center of his life

_____ 8. a woman who has a great deal of hostility toward any form of religion and who wants to explore her negative feelings in this area

_____ 9. a person who has extremely strong fundamentalist religious beliefs

_____ 10. a man whose basic value system includes the attempt to use and exploit others for his own gain

_____ 11. a person who has tested HIV-positive and has no intention of informing his partner

_____ 12. a teenager who is having unsafe sex and sees no problem with this behavior

_____ 13. a high school student who seeks counseling to discuss conflicts she is having with her adopted parent from a different culture

_____ 14. a man who is convinced that his way is "right" and who wants to impose his values on everyone with whom he has contact

_____ 15. a married woman who wants to leave her family so that she can "be free from the burdens of responsibility"

_____ 16. a high school student who thinks she may be lesbian and wants to explore her sexual orientation

_____ 17. an interracial couple wanting to adopt a child and being faced with their respective parents' opposition to the adoption

_____ 18. a female client from a culture that does not value autonomy or independence for women

_____ 19. an elderly man who is very conflicted about the meaning of his life and wants to talk about how his religious beliefs are not helping him find purpose in life

_____ 20. a depressed young man who expresses a desire to talk about persistent thoughts of ending his life because he sees little hope for his future

## Some Questions You Might Explore

1. What specific kinds of clients might you have difficulty working with because of a clash of values?

2. How would you handle the situation if you discovered that you were not being effective with a client because of a difference in values?

3. What are some of your central values and beliefs, and how do you think they will either inhibit *or* facilitate your work as a counselor?

4. Interview some practicing counselors about their experiences with values in the counseling process. You could ask questions such as these: What kinds of clients have you had difficulty working with because of your value system? How do you think your values influence the way you counsel? How are your clients affected by your values? What are some of the main value issues that clients bring into the counseling process?

I suggest that you bring the results of this inventory to class and form small groups to discuss ways to deal with situations in which you have a divergent value system from your client's. There are some excellent possibilities for role-playing these situations in a small group. As much as possible, role-play the situation first, and then discuss the issues and your experience in the exercise.

## CASES DEALING WITH VALUE ISSUES

In your practice you are likely to be faced with ethical issues involving sharp differences between your own values and certain values of your clients. In some situations these value conflicts do not become apparent until the therapeutic alliance is well established. Thus, it is not simply a matter of referring clients in cases of value clashes. Consider referral as your option of last resort and focus on how you might work with value conflicts between you and your client without resorting to referral.

This section provides cases on various topics for you to role-play in class and for discussion. One person can assume the client's role, and several students can take turns role-playing various alternative ways of dealing with each situation. Discussion generally proves to be lively following a brief role enactment in class. Focus on your own values, and identify any areas where you might tend to impose your values on a client. Discuss how you see your values either helping or hindering your intervention in each of these cases.

The first four cases are illustrated in the education video *Ethics in Action: Institutional Version* (Gerald Corey, Marianne Schneider Corey, & Robert Haynes, 1998). These cases deal with religion, abortion, sexual orientation, and end-of-life decisions.

## Religious and Spiritual Concerns

In this role play, "Religion as Answer," the issue is a conflict of values between the client and the counselor. The client (LeAnne) thinks prayer should be her answer to her personal problems. She thinks she is not hearing the Lord clearly. The counselor (Suzanne) has some trouble understanding what the client's religion means to her. Instead, Suzanne comments that she feels that she is in competition with God and the client's religion. Suzanne wants LeAnne to put more faith in the counseling process as a way to find an answer to her problems. Assume you are counseling LeAnne. How would you answer these questions?

1. How would you expect your spiritual and religious values to affect the manner in which you counsel LeAnne? Would you be inclined to introduce the topic of spirituality or religion if LeAnne did not specifically mention this if you believed that doing so would be helpful?

2. Is it ethical for you to challenge LeAnne's belief in the power of prayer and her reliance on God to solve her problems? Explain.

3. If you thought LeAnne was avoiding personal responsibility by relying on reading scripture and praying, what might you say to her?

4. Are you forcing your values on LeAnne if you are unwilling to explore religious or spiritual themes when she introduces them in a therapy session?

5. Under what conditions would you be inclined to refer LeAnne because of her spiritual or religious beliefs?

## Contemplating an Abortion

In the role play "Contemplating an Abortion," there is a value clash between client and counselor. The client (Sally) is considering an abortion, and the therapist (Lucia) has difficulty with this possible decision. Lucia says that she is feeling uncomfortable because of her belief that life begins at conception. Lucia tells Sally that she will have to get some consultation to sort out her thinking. Sally is anxious and wants to talk about what she might do and is somewhat taken aback by her counselor's response. How would you answer these questions?

1. Was the counselor's disclosure that she had trouble with Sally's possible abortion helpful to her? How might this disclosure be burdensome to the client?

2. Lucia said that she wanted Sally to consider her options objectively and make the best decision for herself. Do you think it would be likely that Sally would be able to do this, knowing what her counselor thinks about abortion?

3. Assume that you have been counseling Sally for several months for her bouts with depression. At one session Sally tells you:

   "I just found out I am pregnant. I am really not ready to have a child and I'm not sure what to do. I don't want to give my child up for adoption. And I'm not sure that I am open to having an abortion. My religious values and moral convictions would make it extremely difficult to choose abortion. Really, I can see no option, yet I know I must make some choice. Can you help me?"

4. Let's assume that you are personally opposed to abortion on moral or religious grounds. If so, would you be in a position to encourage Sally to explore all of her alternatives? Would you see it as your task to persuade Sally to accept another option besides abortion? Given the fact that you have been counseling Sally for several months, if you were to refer her to another counselor because of your beliefs and values on

abortion, would this constitute abandonment? Would a referral be in her best interest? Can you respect your client's right to have a different value system from yours and help her decide what course to follow?

## Sexual Orientation

In this role play, "Coming Out," the client (Conrad) brings out his homosexual orientation. Conrad states that he is struggling with this mainly because it is not accepted in his culture or in his religion. Conrad admits that he trusts his counselor (John) and that it feels good to be able to make this disclosure. Conrad wants his counselor's help in coming out to his friends and family. Conrad wants to explore his thoughts and feelings about his sexual orientation in light of his cultural and religious values.

Conrad finds that John is unreceptive at best. John says, "Are you sure this is the best thing for you?" Then John discloses that he does not approve of the "homosexual lifestyle" and adds that he does not see it as "being very healthy." Conrad has negative reactions to John's judgmental attitude and lack of acceptance of who he is as a person. Assume you are counseling Conrad; how would you answer these questions?

1. How might the values you hold either help or hinder your ability to establish effective relationships with lesbians or gay men?

2. In working with gay or lesbian clients, how might your values influence what you say or do?

3. What are the main ethical issues that you think need to be addressed pertaining to counseling gay and lesbian clients?

4. If you are not able to support Conrad's sexual orientation, would you seek consultation? Would the ethical action be a referral?

5. If Conrad didn't disclose his sexual orientation to you until months after the beginning of therapy, what would you do if you did not approve of gay/lesbian relationships?

6. If a gay client accepted his sexual orientation, would you still be able to work with him on meeting his personal goals for therapy? Would you be inclined to refer him? Why or why not?

## End-of-Life Decisions

In this role play, "Talk of Suicide," the client (Gary) is HIV-positive and is seriously considering suicide. The counselor (Natalie) tells Gary that she can't believe what she is hearing from him. Natalie is doing her best to persuade him not to take his life. She tells him that he is taking the easy way out by choosing to end his life. She asks him if he has a plan. She asks him to think about his family and other options. She lets him know that he may be in a crisis state and not able to make a good decision. Natalie has a definite agenda for her client. She doesn't want Gary to take his life. She wants him to explore other options. She is concerned about Gary's welfare and the welfare of his family. This vignette raises both ethical and legal issues. Consider these questions:

1. What is the central ethical issue involved in this role play? What are the legal issues involved?

2. Where do you stand with respect to key questions on end-of-life decisions? What religious, ethical, and moral beliefs do you hold that might enable you to support Gary's decision about ending his life due to the circumstances of the case? What beliefs do you hold that might make it difficult for you to support Gary's decision?

3. If Gary were your client, would you respect his self-determination, or would you influence him to search for alternatives to suicide? Do you have an ethical right to block

Gary if he insists that he wants to choose death over life? Do you have an ethical duty to respect Gary's decision, assuming that he thinks this issue through thoroughly?

4. Do you have the responsibility to forcefully protect Gary from the potential harm his own decisions may bring to both himself and his family?

The next three cases (dealing with divorce, sexual promiscuity, and the affair) are illustrated in *Ethics in Action: CD-ROM*. This interactive program is designed for home study.

## The Divorce

The client (Janice) has made a decision to leave her husband and get a divorce. She says she doesn't want to work on her relationship anymore. The counselor (Gary) says he hates to hear that. Janice hasn't been happy for a long time, and she is tired of her husband's temper and his moods. Gary brings up the kids and asks who will be the advocate for them. Janice thinks that if she is happy they will be happy. She says she will take care of the kids but that she has to do something with her life. Gary concludes by asking, "Is divorce the best way to take care of them?" Explore these questions:

1. Do you think it is the counselor's job to make the decision for the client?

2. What values do you hold pertaining to divorce? How might your values influence the way you would counsel Janice?

## Sexual Promiscuity

Suzanne is single and engages in unprotected premarital sex with multiple partners. The counselor (Richard) expresses concern for Suzanne, who reports meeting a guy in a bar and having sex with him, which she says is the best she has had in a week. He asks if she is protecting herself from pregnancy and HIV. Suzanne says, "I'm not going to get HIV. People are blowing it totally out of proportion." She says she doesn't know why he is so worried about it, for after all, it's her life. Richard then focuses on how Suzanne's behavior plays out the recurring theme of abandonment by her father. She thinks there is no connection. Assume Suzanne is your client; how would you answer these questions?

1. What interventions would you make in this situation?

2. Do you think it is appropriate to convince Suzanne that her behavior is harmful? Is it ethically acceptable for you to use persuasion? Explain.

3. Under what circumstances, if any, might you try to convince or persuade Suzanne to change a particular behavior?

4. Would you attempt to educate Suzanne about the risks of unprotected sexual activity? If so, how would you go about this so that she might be open to being educated?

5. What are your values pertaining to promiscuous behavior? Would you attempt to change her behavior, depending on your value orientation?

6. If she were using preventive measures and restricting her sexual behavior to one man, would this make a difference in the way you might counsel her?

## Relationship Issues

The client (Natalie) is struggling with her marriage and the fact she is having a long-term affair. She feels alive, youthful, and beautiful when she is with this other person. At home she feels depressed and sees her purpose as being just to serve her husband. For years she has been there for others, but now she has to think about herself. The counselor (Janice) says: "Having an affair is not a good answer for someone—it just hurts everyone. I just don't think it is a good idea." Assume you are counseling Natalie; how would you answer these questions?

1. What are your values about being faithful in a committed relationship, and how would your values affect the way you counsel Natalie?

2. As Natalie's counselor, what would you most want to pay attention to and why? What does this tell you about your values?

3. If your values were in conflict with Natalie's, what would you do to resolve the conflict?

4. Do you see any potential sources of countertransference on your part that would make it difficult for you to objectively and ethically work with Natalie?

5. Under what circumstances, if any, might you consider a referral for Natalie? Why?

## Another Relationship Issue

The client (Joyce) is a married woman in her late 30s with three children. She has been in weekly individual therapy for 6 months. She is struggling to decide whether she wants to remain married to her husband, whom she perceives as boring, uninvolved with their children, complacent, and overly involved in his work. Although Joyce has urged him to join her in marriage counseling or undertake some form of therapy for himself, he has consistently refused. He maintains that he is fine and that she is the one with the problems. She tells the therapist that she would divorce him immediately "if it weren't for the kids" and that when the children finish high school, she will surely leave him. For now, however, she is ambivalent; she cannot decide whether she wants to accept the security she now has (along with the deadness of her relationship with her husband) or whether she is willing to leave this security and risk making a better life for herself. She has been contemplating having an affair so that someone other than her husband can meet her physical and emotional needs. She is also exploring the possibility of finding a job so that she will be less dependent on her husband. By getting a job, she could have outside opportunities for personal satisfaction and still remain in the marriage by deciding to accept what she has with him. Consider these questions, and decide what value judgments can be made:

1. One of Joyce's reasons for staying married is "for the sake of the children." What if you, as her therapist, accept this value and believe she should not challenge her marriage because children need both parents and a divorce is damaging? Might she be using the children as an excuse? What if your judgment is that she would be better off by divorcing now? What do your beliefs about divorce, marriage, and children have to do with her possible decisions?

2. Joyce is talking about an affair as a possibility. What are your values concerning monogamy and extramarital sex? Do you believe having an affair would be helpful or destructive for your client? Would you be able to allow her to make this decision? What influence might your views have on her? Could you objectively counsel her if your values differed from hers in this area?

# BECOMING AN EFFECTIVE MULTICULTURAL COUNSELOR

Working ethically with culturally diverse client populations requires that you possess the awareness, knowledge, and skills to deal effectively with their concerns. Although it is unrealistic to expect you to have an in-depth knowledge of all cultural backgrounds, it is feasible for you to have a comprehensive grasp of the general principles for working ethically and sensitively with clients who are different from you. Try to understand the worldview of the culturally different client, and develop appropriate intervention strategies and techniques to become an effective multicultural counselor.

This would be a good time to take an inventory of your current level of awareness, knowledge, and skills. Complete the following self-examination of multicultural counseling competencies.

## Multicultural Counseling Competencies: A Self-Examination

This self-examination on how well you are able to demonstrate multicultural counseling competencies is based on standards proposed by Sue, Arrendondo, and McDavis (1992). It is for your own use in evaluating how well you are doing in becoming competent as a counselor of clients whose cultural background differs from yours.

This self-assessment is not intended as a research instrument and is certainly not intended to compete with other excellent research protocols.

Give yourself a grade for each question based on the following criteria.

A = always    B = often    C = sometimes    D = seldom    F = never

If you wish to use numbers to calculate an average to arrive at a grade, use the following scores: A = 4, B = 3, C = 2, D = 1, F = 0.

### I. Counselor Awareness, Knowledge, and Skills

_____ 1. I actively work on becoming more aware of my own cultural heritage.

_____ 2. I constantly seek to become more aware of different cultural heritages.

_____ 3. I strive to understand and value cultural heritages that differ from my own.

_____ 4. I work at understanding how my own cultural background influences my beliefs, values, attitudes, and biases about psychological processes.

_____ 5. I regularly evaluate the limits of my competencies and expertise in counseling persons from different cultural backgrounds.

_____ 6. I question my comfortableness with differences that exist between me and my clients in regard to race, ethnicity, culture, and beliefs.

_____ 7. I strive to understand how my own racial and cultural heritage affects my personal and professional definitions and biases about what is normal and abnormal.

_____ 8. I seek to understand how oppression, racism, discrimination, and stereotyping affect me personally.

_____ 9. I regularly question how I may have benefited or been adversely affected directly or indirectly by individual, institutional, or cultural racism.

_____ 10. I diligently work at uncovering my own beliefs, attitudes, and feelings regarding racism.

_____ 11. I seek to gain greater knowledge about how I socially impact others.

_____ 12. I strive to become ever more knowledgeable about my communication style and how it may facilitate or hinder working with clients who are culturally different from me.

_____ 13. I regularly seek out educational, consultative, and training experiences that enrich my understanding of culturally different populations.

_____ 14. I constantly engage in the process of understanding myself as a racial and cultural being.

_____ 15. I actively strive to achieve a nonracist identity.

## II. Understanding the Worldview of the Culturally Different Client

_____ 16. I work at becoming aware of my negative emotional reactions toward racial and ethnic groups that may prove detrimental to my clients.

_____ 17. I willingly and regularly contrast my own beliefs and attitudes with those of culturally different clients with whom I work in a way that is nonjudgmental.

_____ 18. I question myself constantly about any stereotypes and preconceived notions I hold toward other racial and ethnic minority groups.

_____ 19. I study to obtain specific knowledge and information about particular culturally different groups before trying to work with them individually or collectively.

_____ 20. I work to more thoroughly incorporate competencies that will help me in understanding the literature on minority identity developmental models.

_____ 21. I update myself regularly (at least every 3 months) in understanding how race, culture, and ethnicity may affect personality formation, vocational choices, manifestations of psychological disorders, help-seeking behavior, and the appropriateness of counseling approaches.

_____ 22. I actively engage in processes (such as reading, supervision, and discussions) that help me gain a greater awareness of how sociopolitical influences impinge upon the life of racial and ethnic minorities.

_____ 23. I interact with people of different cultures in striving to understand how immigration issues, poverty, racism, stereotyping, and powerlessness all leave major scars that may influence the counseling process.

_____ 24. I familiarize myself as often as possible (but at least quarterly) with relevant and up-to-date research regarding the mental health and disorders of various ethnic and racial groups.

_____ 25. I actively seek out educational experiences that enrich my knowledge, understanding, and cross-cultural skills.

_____ 26. I am actively involved with individuals, outside of counseling settings, whose cultural heritage differs from mine in order to more fully appreciate and understand their lives and lifestyles.

## III. Developing Appropriate Intervention Strategies and Techniques

_____ 27. I seek to recognize as well as respect my clients' religious and spiritual beliefs and values about physical and mental functioning.

_____ 28. I strive to understand and respect indigenous helping practices and minority community intrinsic help-giving networks.

_____ 29. I value and appreciate bilingualism.

_____ 30. I do not view another language as an impediment to counseling.

_____ 31. I seek to know and understand how generic characteristics of counseling (e.g., culture- or class-bound) may clash with cultural values of various minority groups.

_____ 32. I strive to recognize institutional barriers that prevent minorities from using mental health services.

_____ 33. I examine potential bias in assessment instruments on a regular basis.

_____ 34. I use assessment procedures and interpret assessment findings in regard to the cultural and linguistic characteristics of my clients.

_____ 35. I regularly study about minority family structures, hierarchies, values, and beliefs.

_____ 36. I seek out knowledge about the community characteristics and resources where I live.

_____ 37. I make it my business to become aware of relevant discriminatory practices at the social and community level that may be affecting the psychological welfare of my clients and minority culture populations.

_____ 38. I work constantly at becoming skilled and able to engage in a variety of verbal and nonverbal helping responses, including the accurate and appropriate sending and receiving of verbal and nonverbal messages.

_____ 39. I resist becoming tied down to any one method or approach to helping.

_____ 40. When I sense that my helping style is limited and potentially inappropriate, I work at anticipating and ameliorating its negative impact.

_____ 41. I question myself periodically as to when I should exercise institutional intervention skills on behalf of clients.

_____ 42. I help clients determine whether a problem stems from racism or bias in others so that they do not inappropriately blame themselves.

_____ 43. I seek consultation from traditional leaders or religious and spiritual leaders and practitioners when it is appropriate in the treatment of culturally different clients.

_____ 44. I take responsibility for interacting in the language requested by my clients even if it means making a referral to outside resources, such as a bilingual counselor, or finding a translator with cultural knowledge and an appropriate professional background.

_____ 45. I regularly engage in training and becoming more of an expert in the use of traditional assessment and testing instruments and in understanding their technical aspects as well as their cultural limitations.

_____ 46. I work toward eliminating biases, prejudices, and discriminatory practices.

_____ 47. I strive to become increasingly cognizant of the sociopolitical contexts in conducting evaluations and providing interventions.

_____ 48. I sensitize myself through various means to issues of oppression, sexism, and racism.

_____ 49. I take responsibility in educating my clients about the processes of psychological intervention, such as goals, expectations, legal rights, and my counseling orientation.

Scores on this self-administered instrument range from "A" to "F." There are three areas in which to assess yourself:

1. Counselor Awareness, Knowledge, and Skills, Items 1–15

   My Grade _____

2. Understanding the Worldview of the Culturally Different Client, Items 16–26

   My Grade _____

3. Developing Appropriate Intervention Strategies and Techniques, Items 2–49

   My Grade _____

   My Total Grade _____

Since all three areas are related, a low grade in any one will impact the other two. Therefore, in evaluating your score, look at both your area grades and your total grade. Ways to constructively improve your grades include:

- Examining your own cultural heritage and background
- Attending workshops and classes on multicultural counseling
- Obtaining supervision from a skilled multicultural counselor
- Reading books and journal articles
- Joining a group that studies multicultural issues
- Viewing videos on multicultural counseling

- Participating in interactive computer software focused on multicultural counseling
- Becoming a member of a professional group that deals with multicultural counseling issues, such as the Association for Multicultural Counseling and Development
- Participating in minority culture events in your community, and working in the sociopolitical arena to bring about needed changes

*Source:* Adapted from S. T. Gladding, P. Pedersen, and D. Stone, "Multicultural Counseling Competencies: A Self-Examination," *ACES Spectrum Newsletter,* Winter, 1997, Vol. 58, No. 2. Reprinted with permission of authors.

### SUGGESTED ACTIVITY
### Cultural Diversity in Counseling Practice

**Directions:** Fill in the blanks with the answers you think are appropriate for you. Remember that in this kind of activity there are no "correct" answers and that the point of the exercise is to stimulate you to think about what it will take for you to become a culturally effective counselor.

1. How effective do you think you would be in counseling clients who are culturally different from you?

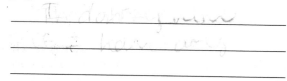

2. What is one specific way in which your cultural background could help you understand clients from different cultures?

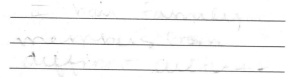

3. What is an example of a belief, attitude, or assumption of yours that could block your effectiveness in working with diverse client populations?

4. What is an example of a belief, attitude, or assumption of yours that will enhance your effectiveness in working with diverse client populations?

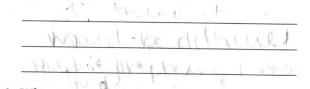

5. What can you do to increase your awareness and knowledge in the area of cultural diversity?

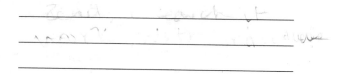

6. What specific knowledge do you think you need to effectively counsel someone who is different from you in ethnic background, age, gender, sexual orientation, or socioeconomic status?

7. What is one skill that you would most like to acquire to make you more effective in counseling those from different cultures?

8. How could you encourage and allow a client who is culturally different from you to teach you about his or her culture?

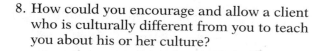

9. When and why might you decide to refer a client who differs from you with respect to culture, ethnicity, socioeconomic background, religion or value system, age, sexual orientation, or gender?

_____

_____

_____

10. What do you see as your major challenge in becoming a culturally skilled counselor?

_____

_____

_____

## SUGGESTED ACTIVITY
## Personal Issues in Counseling and Psychotherapy

**Directions:** Fill in the blanks with the answers you think are appropriate for you. Of course, there are no "correct" answers. Try to give your immediate response to each question. Bring your answers to class for discussion.

1. List two major personal qualities, or strengths, that you think will be assets for you as a counselor.

_____

_____

_____

2. List two personal limitations, or areas that you need to examine, that might interfere with your work as a counselor.

_____

_____

_____

3. What are a few of your specific concerns or anxieties regarding your work as a beginning counselor?

_____

_____

_____

4. How would you respond if you were required to participate in personal psychotherapy as a basic part of your degree program?

_____

_____

_____

5. Can you think of specific instances in which you might give your clients advice?

_____

_____

_____

6. What might you do if one of your values sharply contrasted with your client's values?

_____

_____

_____

7. What one life experience do you believe has had the greatest influence on your ability as a therapist?

_____

_____

_____

8. How do you think your personal values will influence your ability to assist clients in clarifying their own values?

_____

_____

_____

9. What are your thoughts about the division of responsibility between your clients and you as a counselor?

_I think you must do this in order to succeed_

10. How might you best learn how to use techniques appropriately in your counseling practice?

_Research, observation_

11. How might you react if you suggested a technique and your client refused to participate?

_Think of a different option together_

12. If you were being interviewed for a counselor's position, how would you answer the question "How do you view your role as a counselor?"

_To teach and guide_

13. Knowing yourself, what factors in your life and your personality might contribute most to your own burnout or loss of spirit?

_Thinking too much about client outside of work_

14. What important steps would you be willing to take to prevent burnout?

_Make sure to leave work at the office_

15. How do you think you can best ensure that you will be able to keep yourself alive both as a person and as a professional?

_By learning to seperate + enjoy my own life outside of work_

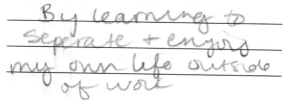

## A SMALL GROUP EXERCISE
### Personal Strategies for Preventing Burnout

Although you cannot always control stressful events, you do have a great deal of control over how you interpret and react to these events. In small groups, explore ways that you can best learn to manage stress in your life. What concrete steps can you take to prevent the negative impact of stress? Become attuned to the subtle signs of burnout rather than waiting for a full-blown condition of emotional and physical exhaustion to set in. Develop your own strategy for keeping yourself alive personally and professionally. In your discussion group, identify a few specific strategies that you would be willing to put into practice. Here are some suggestions for preventing burnout that you might explore in your group:

- Evaluate your goals, priorities, and expectations to see if they are realistic and if they are getting you what you want.
- Recognize that you can be an active agent in your life.
- Find other interests besides work, especially if your work is not meeting your most important needs.
- Think of ways to bring more variety into your work.

- Take the initiative to start new projects that have personal meaning.
- Learn to monitor the impact of stress, both on the job and at home.
- Attend to your health through adequate sleep, an exercise program, proper diet, meditation, and relaxation.
- Develop a few friendships that are characterized by a mutuality of giving and receiving.
- Learn how to ask for what you want, but don't expect always to get it.
- Learn how to be internally motivated and to work for self-rewards as opposed to looking to others to confirm your worth.
- Find meaning through play, travel, or new experiences.
- Avoid assuming burdens or responsibilities that are properly the responsibility of others.
- Learn your own limits, and learn to set limits with others.
- Learn to accept yourself with your imperfections, including being able to forgive yourself when you make a mistake or do not live up to your ideals.
- Form a support group with colleagues to share feelings of frustration and to find better ways of approaching the reality of difficult job situations.
- Cultivate some hobbies and make time for fun.
- Make time for your spiritual growth.
- Become more active in your professional organization.
- Seek counseling as an avenue of personal development.

This is not an exhaustive list, but it does provide some direction for thinking about ways to keep yourself alive. Which of the above suggestions most appeals to you? Are there any not on this list that you would add?

_____

_____

_____

_____

_____

_____

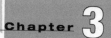

# Ethical Issues in Counseling Practice

 ## ETHICAL ISSUES AND PROBLEMS FOR EXAMINATION

These groups of questions correspond to the sections in Chapter 3 of the textbook. Make a brief outline of your position on each of these ethical issues.

1. *Introduction*

   a. What one ethical issue would you most want to explore and talk about in class?

   b. In what sense are ethical issues an integral part of counseling practice regardless of one's theoretical orientation?

2. *Putting clients' needs before your own*

   a. What are some of your personal needs that you think will help you become a more effective counselor?

   b. What are some of your personal needs that you think may hinder you in effectively counseling clients?

3. *Ethical decision making*

   a. In what way can you make the ethics codes work for you? How might the codes be a catalyst for your thinking about ethical dilemmas?

   b. If you were faced with an ethical dilemma, what specific steps would you take in making a decision?

4. *The right of informed consent*

   a. The ethics codes of most professional organizations require that clients be presented with enough data to make informed choices about entering the client–therapist relationship. What are some matters you would explore with your clients at the first and second counseling sessions?

   b. Assume that during an initial session with a client you determine that this individual would best be helped by a referral. If there were no referral source available, what would you do?

5. *Dimensions of confidentiality*

   a. What information would you give your clients about the nature and purpose of confidentiality? What would you say if a client asked you under what circumstances you would break confidentiality? How would you explain the limits of confidentiality to your clients during the initial session?

   b. Some states allow children and adolescents to participate in psychological counseling without parental knowledge and consent. What particular factors do you think might justify minors receiving treatment without parental consent? Why? What would you tell minors about confidentiality as it pertains to talking about them to their parents?

   c. Assume that you are counseling an elementary school child in a community clinic and that the child's parents show up one day and want to know what is going on. How will you cope with your responsibility to the parents without divulging certain confidences revealed to you by the child?

   d. Court decisions make it clear that therapists have a duty to warn and protect. What guidelines can you think of to help you assess a situation in which you would feel responsible to warn and protect?

6. *Ethical issues in a multicultural perspective*

   a. What ethical questions, if any, should be raised if you counsel someone who differs from you with respect to race? culture? sexual orientation? age? disability? gender? socioeconomic status?

   b. To what degree do you think counseling practice is culture-bound?

   c. What life experiences have you had that would either aid or hinder you in working with clients from diverse ethnic and cultural backgrounds?

   d. What are the challenges of addressing both individual and environmental factors in the practice of multicultural counseling?

7. *Ethical issues in the assessment and diagnostic process*

   a. What are the ethical issues involved in using a diagnostic category for a client?

   b. What ethical concerns might you have, if any, if you were expected to provide a DSM-IV-TR diagnosis for clients during the initial session?

   c. What are your thoughts about the values and limitations of diagnosis as a part of the assessment process?

8. *Dual relationships in counseling practice*

   a. Do you think dual relationships are an inevitable part of practicing in any setting? Explain.

   b. As you read the text, consider what specific dual or multiple relationships you consider to be the most problematic. How would you determine if a relationship was either inappropriate or unethical?

   c. If you were involved in a dual relationship with a client, what procedures could you follow to minimize the risk of harm?

   d. Can you think of some ways you would deal differently with *avoidable* dual relationships than with those that were unavoidable?

# SELF-INVENTORY OF ATTITUDES RELATING TO ETHICAL ISSUES

This inventory is designed to assess your attitudes and beliefs on specific ethical issues. Select the response that comes closest to your position, or write your own response in "e." Bring the completed inventory to class for discussion.

1. A therapist should terminate a therapeutic relationship when

   a. the client decides to terminate.
   b. the therapist judges that it is time to terminate.
   c. it is reasonably clear that the client is not benefiting from therapy.
   d. the client reaches an impasse.
   e. _____

2. Regarding confidentiality, my position is that

   a. it is never ethical to disclose anything a client tells me under any circumstances.
   b. it is ethical to break a confidence when the therapist deems that the client might do harm to him- or herself or to others.
   c. confidences can be shared with the parents of the client if the parents request information.
   d. it applies only to licensed therapists.
   e. _____

3. A sexual relationship between a client and a therapist is
   a. ethical if a client initiates it.
   b. ethical if the therapist decides it would be in the best interests of the client.
   c. ethical only when both the therapist and the client discuss the issue and agree to such a relationship.
   d. never ethical under any circumstances.
   e. _____

4. Regarding the issue of counseling friends, I think that
   a. it is acceptable to have a valued friend as a client.
   b. it should be done rarely and then only if it is clear that the friendship will not interfere with the therapeutic relationship.
   c. friendship and therapy should not be mixed.
   d. a friend could be accepted as a client only when the friend asks to be.
   e. _____

5. I would tend to refer a client to another professional if
   a. it were clear that the client was not benefiting in the relationship with me.
   b. I felt a strong sexual attraction to the person.
   c. the client continually stirred up painful feelings in me (reminded me of my mother, father, ex-spouse, and so on).
   d. I had a hard time caring for or being interested in the client.
   e. _____

6. Regarding the ethics of social and personal relationships with clients, it is my position that
   a. it is never wise to see or to get involved with clients on a social basis.
   b. it is an acceptable practice to strike up a social relationship once the therapy relationship has ended if both want to do so.
   c. with some clients a personal and social relationship might well enhance the therapeutic relationship by building trust.
   d. it is ethical to combine a social and therapeutic relationship if both parties agree.
   e. _____

7. One of the best ways that I can think of to help me determine on what occasions and under what circumstances I would break confidentiality with a client is to
   a. confer with a supervisor or a consultant.
   b. check out my perceptions with several colleagues.
   c. follow my own intuitions and trust my own judgment.
   d. discuss the matter with my client and solicit his or her opinion.
   e. _____

8. In terms of appreciating and understanding the value systems of clients who are culturally different from me,
   a. I see it as my responsibility to learn about their values and not impose mine on them.
   b. I would encourage them to accept the values of the dominant culture for survival purposes.
   c. I would attempt to modify my counseling procedures to fit their cultural values.
   d. it is imperative that I learn about the specific cultural values my clients hold.
   e. _____all above_____

9. To be effective in counseling clients from a different culture, a counselor must
   a. possess specific knowledge about the particular group he or she is counseling.
   b. be able to accurately "read" nonverbal messages.
   c. have had direct contact with this group.
   d. treat these clients no differently from clients from his or her own cultural background.
   e. _____

10. My definition of an ethical therapist is one who
    a. knows the right thing to do in each problem situation in counseling.
    b. follows all of the ethical codes of the profession.
    c. continually devotes time to self-examination on ethical issues.
    d. does not take advantage of the client.
    e. _____all above_____

## Some Suggestions for Using This Self-Inventory

- On completing this inventory, look over the items, and circle those you would like to bring to class and discuss with others. Limit yourself to a few issues that have stimulated your thinking the most.
- Look over the initial inventory that you completed in Chapter 1 of this manual. Compare the general tone of your responses in the two surveys.
- Work in pairs on certain questions. Compare your positions on each issue.
- Divide the class into small groups, each group taking one of the issues for discussion: confidentiality, mandatory counseling, therapist responsibility, the client–therapist relationship, therapist competence, therapist values and needs, and so on.
- Next, each group can report a consensus to the rest of the class. Some good material for debates can be generated when divergent viewpoints are established within or between groups.

# CASES INVOLVING ETHICAL DILEMMAS

Try your hand at dealing with these cases. Look for what you consider to be the core of the ethical dilemma in each case. Identify the issues, and clarify the position you would take in each situation. Working with these cases in class is an excellent way for you to expand your awareness of the ethical dimension of practice, and it will help you learn a process of ethical decision making. I suggest that you try role-playing these vignettes first. After you have had opportunities to be both the client and the counselor, discuss the issues involved in each situation.

## Dealing With Sexual Attractions

You have been treating client A for 6 weeks and find that your sexual attraction to him or her has been growing as the counseling relationship develops. It is becoming more and more difficult to focus on the therapy process because of your attraction. You feel, in turn, that A is flirtatious, although you have begun to doubt your own judgment and objectivity. You find yourself thinking about your client often, and you would like to extend the time you have together beyond the counseling sessions. You have had two sexual dreams involving the client. Although you are concerned about A's best interests, it is difficult for you to really listen, and you are aware of being preoccupied with being liked and accepted by A. At this point you are feeling some guilt and wondering if these feelings are "normal" in this situation.

1. Does this attraction present both a personal and a professional problem? If so, how?
2. Might you be inclined to discuss your attraction with your client? Give your rationale for either doing so or not doing so.
3. Would you discuss this situation with another professional, such as a colleague? your supervisor? your therapist?
4. Would you continue working with A, or would you refer him or her to another counselor? If you chose the first course, how would you deal with both your feelings toward A and A's feelings toward you? If you took the latter course, what reasons would you give to A for wanting to make this referral?

## Dealing With a Client's Initiative

Still considering the prior case, assume that before you had made a decision concerning the way you would proceed with A, he or she returned the next week and began the session by telling you:

There is something I really need to talk about. Lately I've been thinking a lot about you, and I'd really like to spend more time with you—outside of this office. You are very exciting to me, not just sexually but as a person, and I'd so much like to get to know more about you. By the way, it's important for me to know how you feel about me.

1. What are your feelings and thoughts as you listen to A?
2. What might you tell A about your feelings for him or her?
3. How would you deal with A's request to spend some time with you out of the office?
4. What do you see as the ethical issues involved in the way you might proceed?

## A Colleague Having an Affair With a Former Student

You have just found out that a psychologist who works in your student mental health clinic is having an affair with one of his former students. The affair began 10 months after the student completed therapy with him. The psychologist was teaching a counseling skills course on campus, and after the course ended, they began dating in earnest. There has been quite a lot of gossip and debate in the clinic about the relationship, but the psychologist refuses to discuss it. Your colleagues wonder if it violates professional ethics. There is also the question of whether it violates the ethics of the student–teacher relationship.

1. What are your thoughts about a psychologist who is an educator and on rare occasions dates a former student? Do you see any difference between a therapist–client relationship and an instructor–student relationship?
2. Given the fact that there is gossip, what might you say to your colleague? If your colleague refused to talk about the matter, what might you do?
3. What are your thoughts about the ethics of forming social or intimate relationships with *former* clients? Besides the amount of time that has elapsed since the end of therapy, what other factors need to be considered?
4. Assume that the psychologist in this situation approached you and *asked* for your reactions. For a start, what might you say? (This scenario would be a good one to role-play.)

## Racism Among Your Colleagues

What do you do when there is sexism or racism among your colleagues? You work in the Psychiatry Department of a major metropolitan hospital and have become quite disturbed at the element of bias that you see around you. You have heard several therapists refer to clients in derogatory terms. In particular, you fear that the attitudes of one White male therapist who is counseling several African American women may be affecting his professional judgment. From some comments that you have heard from this therapist, it sounds to you as if he has definite prejudices against minorities and women.

1. Would you be likely to confront this therapist? Why or why not?
2. What would you want to ask him or tell him?
3. What ethical issues are involved in this situation?

## Some Cases Pertaining to Confidentiality

After reading about the general guidelines for confidentiality in the textbook, reflect on your position if you were the counselor in each of these cases.

1. You have been seeing an adolescent girl in a community mental health clinic for 3 months. Lately she has complained of severe depression and says that life seems

hopeless. She is threatening suicide and even wants details from you concerning how she can successfully go through with it. Are you obliged to disclose this information to her guardians because she is under legal age? What will you tell your client? What consultation might you seek?

2. A client reveals to you that he has stolen some expensive laboratory equipment from the college where you are a counselor. A week later the dean calls you into her office to talk with you about this particular client. What do you tell the dean? And what do you not tell her?

3. You are working in a community agency that provides testing and counseling services for those suspected of being infected by HIV. The legal and ethical problem your staff is debating is the duty to protect others from HIV infection by a client. What input would you give your staff on this question: Must counselors violate confidentiality and perhaps take coercive action when a client known to be HIV-positive is believed to be sexually active or sharing needles?

4. In the course of a counseling session, a youth tells you that he is planning to do serious physical harm to a fellow student. What would you tell your client? How would you proceed?

5. Your client is a 15-year-old girl sent to you by her parents. One day the parents request a session to discuss their daughter's progress and to see what they can do to help. What information can you share with the parents, and what can you not disclose? What might you discuss with the girl before you see her parents? What will you do if she makes it clear that she does not want you to see her parents or tell them anything?

## SUGGESTED ACTIVITIES AND EXERCISES

Here are some activities that you can do on your own, in small groups in the classroom, in pairs, or by contacting professional counselors to sample their reactions to some of these ethical issues. Because there are more activities than you can probably realistically complete, select those topics that have the most meaning for you.

1. Assume that you are in a field placement as a counselor in a community agency. The administrators tell you that they do *not* want you to inform your clients that you are a student intern. They explain that your clients might feel that they were getting second-class service if they found out that you were in training. The administrators contend that your clients are paying for the services they receive (on a sliding scale based on their ability to pay) and that it would not be psychologically good to give them any information that might cause them to conclude that they were not getting the best help available. What would you say and do if you found yourself as an intern in this situation? Would it be ethical to follow this directive and not inform your clients that you were a trainee and that you were receiving supervision? Do you agree or disagree with the rationale of the administrators? Might you accept the internship assignment under the terms outlined if you could not find any other field placements?

2. How might you proceed if you knew of the unethical practice of a colleague? What kinds of unethical behavior of your colleagues, if any, do you think you would report?

3. Discuss some ways in which you can prepare clients for issues pertaining to confidentiality. How can you teach them about its purposes and the legal restrictions on it? Think particularly about counseling minors.

4. What experiences have you had with people from a different cultural background? Did you learn anything about your potential prejudices? What prejudices, if any, did you feel directed at you? You might bring your experiences to class. Also, I suggest that you interview other students or faculty members who identify themselves as ethnically or

culturally different from you. What might they teach you about differences that you as a counselor would need to take into consideration to work more effectively with them?

5. Assume that you are applying for a job or writing a résumé to be used in private practice. Write your own professional disclosure statement in a page or two. Consider writing the essence of your views about matters such as these: the nature and purpose of counseling; what clients might expect from the process; a division of responsibilities between your client and you; a summary of your theoretical position, including the main techniques you are likely to use; a statement of the kinds of clients and problems you are best qualified to work with; matters that might affect your relationship with your clients (such as legal restrictions, agency policy, and limits of confidentiality); and any other topics that you think could help clients decide if they wanted to consult with you. Another suggestion is to bring your disclosure statement to class and have fellow students review what you've written. They can then interview you, and you can get some practice in talking with "prospective clients." This exercise can help you clarify your own positions and give you valuable practice for job interviews, licensure exams, and interviews for graduate school admission.

6. Write an *informed consent document* that you might give to clients. This could be in the form of a contract that outlines your responsibilities to clients. It can be considered an extension of the professional disclosure statement that you wrote in the previous exercise. The point of this exercise is to give you an opportunity to develop your own version of an information sheet that you might provide for your clients.

# KNOW THE CODES OF ETHICS OF PROFESSIONAL ORGANIZATIONS

Each of the major mental health professional organizations has its own code of ethics, which can be obtained by contacting the particular organization. Some of the professional mental health organizations that have formulated codes are the American Counseling Association (ACA, 1995), the American Psychological Association (APA, 2003), the National Association of Social Workers (NASW, 1999), the National Organization for Human Service Education (NOHSE, 2000), and the American Association for Marriage and Family Therapy (AAMFT, 2001).

I strongly recommend that you obtain a copy of the ethics code of at least one mental health profession and familiarize yourself with the basic guidelines for ethical practice. Although ethics codes do not provide answers to ethical dilemmas you will encounter, they do offer general guidance. It is essential that you know the basic content of the codes of your profession.

All of the following codes of ethics and guidelines for practice are available in the booklet, *Codes of Ethics for the Helping Professions* (Brooks/Cole Thomson Learning, 2003), which is sold at a nominal price when packaged with the textbook, *Theory and Practice of Counseling and Psychotherapy.*

- ACA Code of Ethics and Standards of Practice
- ACA Ethical Standards for Internet On-Line Counseling
- Ethical Guidelines for Counseling Supervisors
- Code of Ethics of the American Mental Health Counselors Association
- Ethical Standards for School Counselors
- Association for Specialists in Group Work: Best Practice Guidelines
- ASGW Professional Standards for the Training of Group Workers
- ASGW Principles for Diversity-Competent Group Workers

- AAMFT Code of Ethics
- APA Ethical Principles of Psychologists and Code of Conduct
- Ethics of the International Association of Marriage and Family Counselors
- NASW Code of Ethics
- National Board for Certified Counselors, Inc. and Center for Credentialing and Education, Inc.
- Ethical Standards of Human Service Professionals, NOHSE
- Standards for the Ethical Practice of Web Counseling, National Board for Certified Counselors
- Ethical Standards for School Counselors, American School Counselor Association (ASCA)
- Rehabilitation Counseling Codes
- Codes of Canadian Counseling Association

# A GUIDE TO PROFESSIONAL ORGANIZATIONS

It is a good idea while a student to begin your identification with state, regional, and national professional associations. To assist you in learning about student memberships, some of the major national professional organizations are listed here along with their addresses.

### American Counseling Association (ACA)

Students qualify for a special annual membership rate of $80. Student memberships are available to both undergraduate and graduate students enrolled at least half-time or more at the college level.

ACA membership provides many benefits, including a subscription to the *Journal of Counseling and Development* and a monthly newspaper entitled *Counseling Today*, eligibility for professional liability insurance programs, legal defense services, and professional development through workshops and conventions. ACA puts out a resource catalog that provides information on the various aspects of the counseling profession, as well as giving detailed information about membership, journals, books, home-study programs, videotapes, audiotapes, and liability insurance. For further information, contact:

> American Counseling Association
> 5999 Stevenson Avenue
> Alexandria, VA 22304-3300
> Telephone: (703) 823-9800 or (800) 347-6647
> Fax: (703) 823-0252
> Web site: http://www.counseling.org

### American Psychological Association

The APA has a Student Affiliates category rather than student membership. Journals and subscriptions are extra. Each year in mid-August or late August the APA holds a national convention. For further information contact:

> American Psychological Association
> 750 First Street, NE
> Washington, DC 20002-4242
> Telephone: (202) 336-5500 or (800) 374-2721
> Fax: (202) 336-5568
> Web site: http://www.apa.org

## National Association of Social Workers (NASW)

NASW membership is open to all professional social workers and there is a student membership category. The NASW Press, which produces *Social Work* and the *NASW News* as membership benefits, is a major service in professional development. A number of pamphlets are available through NASW. For information, contact:

> National Association of Social Workers
> 750 First Street, NE, Suite 700
> Washington, DC 20002-4241
> Telephone: (202) 408-8600 or (800) 638-8799
> Fax: (202) 336-8311
> Web site: http://www.socialworkers.org

## American Association for Marriage and Family Therapy (AAMFT)

The AAMFT has a student membership category. Members receive the *Journal of Marital and Family Therapy,* which is published four times a year, and a subscription to six issues yearly of *Family Therapy News.* For membership applications and further information, contact:

> American Association for Marriage and Family Therapy
> 112 S. Alford Street
> Alexandria, VA 22314
> Telephone: (703) 838-9808
> Fax: (703) 838-9805
> Web site: http://www.aamft.org

## National Organization for Human Service Education (NOHSE)

NOHSE is made up of members from diverse disciplines: mental health, child care, social services, gerontology, recreation, corrections, and developmental disabilities. Membership is open to human service educators, students, fieldwork supervisors, and direct-care professionals. Student membership includes a subscription to the newsletter the *Link,* the yearly journal *Human Services Education,* and a discount price for the yearly conference (held in October). For further information, contact:

> Chrisanne Christensen
> Sul Ross State University
> Rio Grande College
> Rt. 3, Box 1200
> Eagle Pass, TX  78852
> Telephone: (830) 758-5112
> Fax: (830) 758-5001
> Web site: http://www.nohse.com

**PART** 2

# Theories and Techniques of Counseling

**4**  Psychoanalytic Therapy

**5**  Adlerian Therapy

**6**  Existential Therapy

**7**  Person-Centered Therapy

**8**  Gestalt Therapy

**9**  Behavior Therapy

**10**  Cognitive Behavior Therapy

**11**  Reality Therapy

**12**  Feminist Therapy

**13**  Postmodern Approaches

**14**  Family Systems Therapy

# Chapter 4

# Psychoanalytic Therapy

 PRECHAPTER SELF-INVENTORIES

**Directions:** The purpose of this self-inventory scale is to identify and clarify your attitudes and beliefs related to the key concepts of and issues raised by each therapeutic approach. Complete the self-inventory before you read the corresponding textbook chapter. Then, after reading the chapter and discussing it in class, take the self-inventory again to determine whether you have modified your position on any of the issues. Respond to each statement, giving the initial response that most clearly identifies how you really think or feel. Remember that the idea is for you to express your view, not to decide which is the "correct" answer. Each statement is a true assumption of the particular approach. Thus, you are rating your degree of agreement or disagreement with the assumptions that are a part of each theory.

Using the following code, write the number of the response that most closely reflects your viewpoint on the line at the left of each statement:

5 = I *strongly agree* with this statement.

4 = I *agree*, in most respects, with this statement.

3 = I am *undecided* in my opinion about this statement.

2 = I *disagree*, in most respects, with this statement.

1 = I *strongly disagree* with this statement.

Compare your responses with those of your classmates, and use the statements as points for discussion in class sessions.

_____ 1. Clients are ready to terminate therapy when they have clarified and accepted their current emotional problems, and also have understood the historical roots of their difficulties.

_____ 2. Our infantile conflicts may never be fully resolved even though many aspects of transference are worked through with a therapist.

_____ 3. We experience transference with many people, and our past is always a vital part of the person we are presently becoming.

_____ 4. The transference situation is considered valuable in therapy because its manifestations provide clients with the opportunity to reexperience a variety of feelings that would otherwise be inaccessible.

_____ 5. The key to understanding human behavior is understanding the unconscious.

_____ 6. Most psychological conflicts are not open to conscious control because their source has been repressed and remains unconscious.

_____ 7. The unconscious, even though it is out of awareness, has a great influence on behavior.

_____ 8. Development during the first 6 years of life is a crucial determinant of the adult personality.

_____ 9. Most personality and behavior problems have roots in a failure to resolve some phase of psychosexual development in early childhood.

_____ 10. One learns the basic sense of trust in one's world during the first year of life.

_____ 11. To progress toward healthy development, one must learn how to deal with feelings of rage, hostility, and anger during the second and third years of life.

_____ 12. It is normal for children around the age of 5 to have concerns about their sexuality, their sex roles, and their sexual feelings.

_____ 13. Insight, understanding, and working through earlier, repressed material are essential aspects of therapy.

_____ 14. Therapists should engage in relatively little self-revelation and should remain anonymous.

_____ 15. For therapy to be effective, clients must be willing to commit themselves to an intensive and long-term therapeutic process.

_____ 16. Therapy is not complete unless the client works through the transference process.

_____ 17. Analysis and interpretation are essential elements in the therapeutic process.

_____ 18. It is important that a client relive the past in therapy.

_____ 19. Effective therapy cannot occur unless the underlying causes of a client's problem are understood and treated.

_____ 20. The basic aim of therapy is to make the unconscious conscious.

## OVERVIEW OF PSYCHOANALYTIC THERAPY

### Key Figures and Major Focus

Original key figure: Sigmund Freud. Ego psychologist: Erik Erikson. Object relations: Margaret Mahler. Historically, psychoanalysis was the first system of psychotherapy. It is a personality theory, a philosophy of human nature, and a method of therapy.

### Philosophy and Basic Assumptions

Although the Freudian view of human nature is basically deterministic and focuses on irrational forces, biological and instinctual drives, and unconscious motivation, later developments in psychoanalysis stressed social and cultural factors. Contemporary psychoanalytic thinking emphasizes the development of the ego and the differentiation and individuation of the self.

### Key Concepts

Key notions include the division of the personality into the id, ego, and superego; the unconscious; anxiety; the functioning of ego-defense mechanisms; and a focus on the past for clues to present problems. Healthy personality development is based on successful resolution of both psychosexual and psychosocial issues at the appropriate stages. Psychopathology is the result of failing to meet some critical developmental task or becoming fixated at some early level of development. Freudian psychoanalysis is basically an id psychology, whereas the newer formulations of psychoanalytic therapy are based on an ego psychology. The contemporary trends stress psychosocial development throughout the life span.

## Therapeutic Goals

A primary goal is to make the unconscious conscious. Both psychoanalysis and psychoanalytically oriented therapy seek the growth of the ego through analysis of resistance and transference, allowing the ego to solve the unconscious conflicts. The restructuring of personality is the main goal, rather than solving immediate problems.

## Therapeutic Relationship

In classical psychoanalysis the anonymity of the therapist is stressed, so that clients can project feelings onto the therapist. With psychoanalytically oriented therapy the therapist tries to relate objectively with warm detachment but does not remain anonymous. Both transference and countertransference are central aspects in the relationship. The focus is on resistances that occur in the therapeutic process, on interpretation of these resistances, and on working through transference feelings. Through this process, clients explore the parallels between their past and present experience and gain new understanding that can be the basis for personality change.

## Techniques and Procedures

All techniques are designed to help the client gain insight and bring repressed material to the surface so that it can be dealt with in a conscious way. Major techniques include maintaining the analytic framework, free association, interpretation, dream analysis, analysis of resistance, and analysis of transference. These techniques are geared to increasing awareness, gaining intellectual insight, and beginning a working-through process that will lead to a reorganization of the personality.

## Applications

Good candidates for analytic therapy include professionals who wish to become therapists as well as people who have been helped by intensive therapy and want to go further. This therapy demands sacrifices of time, money, and personal commitment and is typically a long-term process. Psychoanalytic concepts can be applied to understanding the psychodynamics of behavior on many levels and in many areas such as the arts, religion, education, and human development.

## Contributions

Many other models have developed as reactions against psychoanalysis. The theory provides a comprehensive and detailed system of personality. It emphasizes the legitimate place of the unconscious as a determinant of behavior, highlights the profound effect of early childhood development, and provides procedures for tapping the unconscious. Several factors can be applied by practitioners with nonanalytic orientations, such as understanding how resistance is manifested, how early trauma can be worked through so that a client is not fixated, the manifestations of transference and countertransference in the therapy relationship, and the functioning of ego-defense mechanisms.

## Limitations

Psychoanalysis involves lengthy training for the therapist and a great amount of time and expense for clients. The approach stresses the role of insight but does not give due recognition to the importance of action methods. The model is based on the study of neurotics, not of healthy people. The orthodox Freudian approach, with its stress on instinctual forces, plays down social, cultural, and interpersonal factors. The techniques of this long-term approach are of limited applicability to crisis counseling, working with minorities, and social work.

## GLOSSARY OF KEY TERMS

**Blank screen** An anonymous stance assumed by classical psychoanalysts aimed at fostering transference.

**Borderline personality** A disorder characterized by instability, irritability, self-destructive acts, impulsivity, and extreme mood shifts. Such people lack a sense of their own identity and do not have a deep understanding of others.

**Brief psychodynamic therapy (BPT)** An adaptation of the principles of psychoanalytic theory and therapy aimed at treating selective disorders within a preestablished time limit.

**Collective unconscious** From a Jungian perspective, the deepest level of the psyche that contains an accumulation of inherited experiences.

**Countertransference** The therapist's unconscious emotional responses to a client that are likely to interfere with objectivity; unresolved conflicts of the therapist that are projected onto the client.

**Ego** The part of the personality that is the mediator between external reality and inner demands.

**Ego-defense mechanisms** Intrapsychic processes that operate unconsciously to protect the person from threatening and, therefore, anxiety-producing thoughts, feelings, and impulses.

**Ego psychology** The psychosocial approach of Erik Erikson; emphasizes the development of the ego or self at various stages of life.

**Fixation** The condition of being arrested, or "stuck," at one level of psychosexual development.

**Free association** A primary technique, consisting of spontaneous and uncensored verbalization by the client, which gives clues to the nature of the client's unconscious conflicts.

**Id** The part of personality, present at birth, that is blind, demanding, and insistent. Its function is to discharge tension and return to homeostasis.

**Identity crisis** A developmental challenge, occurring during adolescence, whereby the person seeks to establish a stable view of self and to define a place in life.

**Individuation** The harmonious integration of the conscious and unconscious aspects of personality.

**Libido** The instinctual drives of the id and the source of psychic energy.

**Narcissism** Extreme self-love, as opposed to love of others. A narcissistic personality is characterized by a grandiose and exaggerated sense of self-importance and an exploitive attitude toward others, which hides a poor self-concept.

**Object relatedness** Interpersonal relationships as they are represented intrapsychically.

**Object-relations theory** A newer version of psychoanalytic thinking, which focuses on predictable developmental sequences in which early experiences of self shift in relation to an expanding awareness of others. It holds that individuals go through phases of autism, normal symbiosis, and separation and individuation, culminating in a state of integration.

**Psychodynamics** The interplay of opposing forces and intrapsychic conflicts, providing a basis for understanding human motivation.

**Psychosexual stages** The Freudian chronological phases of development, beginning in infancy. Each is characterized by a primary way of gaining sensual and sexual gratification.

**Psychosocial stages** Erikson's turning points, from infancy through old age. Each presents psychological and social tasks that must be mastered if maturation is to proceed in a healthy fashion.

**Reaction formation** A defense against a threatening impulse, involving actively expressing the opposite impulse.

**Relational analysis** An analytic model based on the assumption that therapy is an interactive process between client and therapist. The interpersonal analyst assumes that countertransference is a source of information about the client's character and dynamics.

**Repression** The ego-defense mechanism whereby threatening or painful thoughts or feelings are excluded from awareness.

**Resistance**   The client's reluctance to bring to awareness threatening unconscious material that has been repressed.

**Shadow**   A Jungian archetype representing thoughts, feelings, and actions that we tend to disown by projecting them outward.

**Superego**   That aspect of personality that represents one's moral training. It strives for perfection, not pleasure.

**Transference**   The client's unconscious shifting to the therapist of feelings and fantasies, both positive and negative, that are displacements from reactions to significant others from the client's past.

**Unconscious**   That aspect of psychological functioning or of personality that houses experiences, wishes, impulses, and memories in an out-of-awareness state as a protection against anxiety.

**Working through**   A process of resolving basic conflicts that are manifested in the client's relationship with the therapist; achieved by the repetition of interpretations and by exploring forms of resistance.

## QUESTIONS FOR DISCUSSION AND EVALUATION

1. Psychoanalytic psychotherapy is not a creed handed down by Freud never to be changed; it is a dynamic, continually developing method of helping people solve psychological problems. As you think about this chapter, look for evidence to support this contention. What aspects of the Freudian revisionists and the contemporary psychoanalytic writers do you find of the most value to you personally?

2. The psychoanalytic approach underscores the importance of early psychosexual development. Do you see evidence that one's current problems are rooted in the significant events of one's first 6 years of life? When you apply this concept specifically to yourself, what connections between your childhood experiences and your present personality are you aware of? What additions has Erik Erikson made to this view of development?

3. Contrast Carl Jung's view of human nature with Freud's view, especially with respect to the influence of the past on the development of present personality structure. What are the implications for counseling practice of these two perspectives of human development?

4. In your work as a counselor, many psychoanalytic techniques such as free association, dream interpretation, probing the unconscious, and interpretation and analysis of resistance and transference may not be appropriate, or they may be beyond your level of training. What are some concepts of the psychoanalytic approach that can nevertheless provide you with a useful framework in deepening your understanding of human behavior? How do you see psychoanalytic views as being potentially related to your work as a counselor?

5. The analyst tends to maintain warm detachment, objectivity, and anonymity so as to foster transference. What are your reactions to the therapeutic value of the therapist's assuming such a role? How do you think a self-disclosing stance on the therapist's part would alter the course of psychotherapy?

6. Describe some psychoanalytic concepts that you think have validity and can be incorporated into a counseling approach even if you do not employ psychoanalytic techniques. Discuss how you see these concepts as useful.

7. This approach places considerable emphasis on therapists' awareness of their own needs and reactions toward clients (or awareness of countertransference). At this time, what kind of client behavior do you think you'd find most difficult? Are you aware of any of your vulnerabilities, unresolved personal concerns, or unmet needs that might interfere with your objectivity and effectiveness as a therapist? How might you work with your countertransference reactions?

8. The psychoanalytic view of anxiety is that it is largely the result of keeping unconscious conflicts buried and that ego defenses develop to help the person curb anxiety.

What implications does this view have for your work with people? Do you think defenses are necessary? What are the possible values of defense mechanisms? What do you think might happen if you were able to successfully strip away a client's defenses?

9. What is your evaluation of the psychoanalytic view of personality development? Consider the stages of early development, particularly with respect to how fully a person's basic needs were met at each stage. Do you think it is necessary or important to explore with clients areas of conflict and unmet needs of their early years? Do you believe people can resolve their adult problems that stem from childhood experiences without exploring past events? How much emphasis would you place on a person's past?

10. Can you apply any aspects of the psychoanalytic theory to your own personal growth? Does this approach help you deepen your self-understanding? If so, in what ways?

## SUGGESTED ACTIVITIES AND EXERCISES

1. Write a letter to Freud. Tell him what you think of his contribution to psychology and how his theory applies to your life (or how it does not apply). Bring your letter to class, and share it with the other members.

2. Reread the section in the text that discusses the importance of the first 6 years of life. Then do the following:
   a. Write down a few key questions about your own psychosexual and psychosocial development from birth through age 6 that you would like to have answered.
   b. Seek out your relatives, and ask them some of the questions.
   c. Gather up any reminders of your early years.
   d. If possible, visit the place or places where you lived.
   e. Attempt to answer your own questions briefly in written form.
   f. Construct a chart showing key influences on your development during those early years.
   g. If the class wishes, bring the charts to class, and discuss in small groups the effects of each member's developmental history on his or her present life.

3. Try this free-association exercise at home by yourself. Get a tape recorder and say aloud *whatever comes into your mind* for about 15 or 20 minutes. Then listen to the tape for pauses or hesitations, recurring themes, and key remarks. Then make a list of about 10 key words based on this tape. Now, make another tape, this time by free-associating with each of the key words. Listen to the second tape. What do you hear? Do you notice any patterns? You might want to bring into class a brief written statement describing what the free-associating experience was like for you.

## JERRY COREY'S WORK WITH RUTH FROM A PSYCHOANALYTIC PERSPECTIVE

### Some Background Data

Because this is the first presentation of the case of Ruth, and because you will be exposed to Ruth's case from each of the following theoretical approaches, a brief description of data from her intake form is provided here.

Age: 39
Sex: Female
Race: Caucasian

Marital Status: Married

Socioeconomic Status: Middle class

Appearance: Dresses meticulously, is overweight, fidgets constantly with her clothes, avoids eye contact, and speaks rapidly.

Living Situation: Recently graduated from college as an elementary-education major, lives with husband (John, 45) and her children (Rob, 19; Jennifer, 18; Susan, 17; and Adam, 16).

## Presenting Problem

Client reports general dissatisfaction. She says her life is rather uneventful and pre-dictable, and she feels some panic over reaching the age of 39, wondering where the years have gone. For 2 years she has been troubled with a range of psychosomatic complaints, including sleep disturbances, anxiety, dizziness, heart palpitations, and headaches. At times she has to push herself to leave the house. Client complains that she cries easily over trivial matters, often feels depressed, and has a weight problem.

## History of Presenting Problem

Client's major career was as a housewife and mother until her children became adoles-cents. She then entered college part time and obtained a bachelor's degree. She has re-cently begun work toward a credential in elementary education. Through her contacts with others at the university, she became aware of how she has limited herself, how she has fostered her family's dependence on her, and how frightened she is of branching out from her roles as mother and wife. Ruth completed a course in introduction to counsel-ing that encouraged her to look at the direction of her own life. As a part of the course, she participated in self-awareness groups, had a few individual counseling sessions, and wrote several papers dealing with the turning points in her own life. One of the require-ments was to write an extensive autobiography based on an application of the principles of the counseling course to her own personal development. This course and her experi-ences with fellow students in it acted as a catalyst in getting her to take an honest look at her life. Ruth is not clear at this point who she is, apart from being mother, wife, and stu-dent. She realizes that she does not have a good sense of what she wants for herself and that she typically lived up to what others in her life wanted for her. Ruth has decided to seek individual counseling to explore her concerns in several areas:

- A physician whom she consulted could find no organic or medical basis for her physi-cal symptoms and recommended personal therapy. In her words, her major symptoms are these: "I sometimes feel very panicky, especially at night when I'm trying to sleep. Sometimes I'll wake up and find it difficult to breathe, my heart will be pounding, and I'll break out in a cold sweat. I toss and turn trying to relax, and instead I feel tense and worry a lot about many little things. It's hard for me to turn off these thoughts. Then during the day I'm so tired I can hardly function, and I find that lately I cry very easily if even minor things go wrong."

- Ruth is aware that she has lived a very structured and disciplined life, that she has functioned largely by taking care of the home and the needs of her four children and her husband, and that to some degree she is no longer content with this. Yet she re-ports that she doesn't know what "more than this" is. Although she would like to get more involved professionally, the thought of doing so frightens her. She worries about her right to think and act selfishly, she fears not succeeding in the professional world, and most of all she worries about how becoming more professionally involved might threaten her family.

- Ruth's children range in age from 16 to 19, and all of them are now finding more of their satisfactions outside the family and the home and are spending increasing time with their friends. Ruth sees these changes and is concerned about "losing" them. She is having particular problems with her daughter Jennifer, and she is at a loss how to deal with Jennifer's rebellion. In general, Ruth feels very much unappreciated by her children.

- In thinking about her future, Ruth is not really sure who or what she wants to become. She would like to develop a sense of herself apart from the expectations of others. She finds herself wondering what she "should" want and what she "should" be doing. Ruth does not find her relationship with her husband, John, at all satisfactory. He appears to be resisting her attempts to make changes and prefers that she remain as she was. But she is anxious over the prospects of challenging this relationship, fearing that if she does she might end up alone.

- Lately, Ruth is experiencing more concern over aging and losing her "looks." All of these factors combined have provided the motivation for her to take the necessary steps to initiate individual therapy. Perhaps the greatest catalyst that triggered her to come for therapy is the increase of her physical symptoms and her anxiety.

### Psychosocial History

Client was the oldest of four children. Her father is a fundamentalist minister, and her mother, a housewife. She describes her father as distant, authoritarian, and rigid; her relationship with him was one of unquestioning, fearful adherence to his rules and standards. She remembers her mother as being critical, and she thought that she could never do enough to please her. At other times her mother was supportive. The family demonstrated little affection. In many ways Ruth took on the role of caring for her younger brother and sisters, largely in the hope of winning the approval of her parents. When she attempted to have any kind of fun, Ruth encountered her father's disapproval and outright scorn. To a large extent this pattern of taking care of others has extended throughout her life.

One critical incident took place when Ruth was 6 years old. She reported: "My father caught me 'playing doctor' with an 8-year-old boy. He lectured me and refused to speak to me for weeks. I felt extremely guilty and ashamed." It appears that Ruth carried feelings of guilt into her adolescence and that she repressed her own emerging sexuality.

In her social relationships Ruth had difficulty making and keeping friends. She felt socially isolated from her peers because they viewed her as "weird." Although she wanted the approval of others, she was not willing to compromise her morals for fear of consequences.

She was not allowed to date until she completed high school. At the age of 19 she married the first person that she dated. She used her mother as a role model by becoming a homemaker.

## Exploring Psychoanalytic Themes With Ruth

### Exploring Ruth's Transference

After Ruth has been in therapy for some time, she grows more disenchanted with me because she does not see me as giving enough. She complains that she is the one doing all the giving and that she is beginning to resent it. I encourage her to express more about the ways in which she sees me as ungiving. At this stage in her therapy she is experiencing some very basic feelings of wanting to be special and wanting proof of it, and these feelings can be usefully explored in her sessions.

Ruth is beginning to discover from the way she responds to me some connections between how she related to significant people in her life. She looks to me in some of the same ways that she looked to her father for approval and for love. I encourage her recollection of feelings associated with these past events so that she can work through barriers that are preventing her from functioning as a mature adult.

### Exploring Past Experiences

Ruth's father's response when he caught her in an act of sexual experimentation (at the age of 6) needs to be considered as we work with her present attitudes and feelings about sex. In the session on the video that deals with exploring how the past is related to present struggles, I demonstrate how I work with Ruth's feelings of guilt and shame over her sexual feelings. She internalized many of her father's strict views of sexuality. Because her father manifested a negative attitude toward her increased sexual awareness, she learned that her body and sexual pleasure were both "dirty" and that her curiosity about sexual matters was unacceptable. Her sexual feelings became anxiety provoking and were rigidly controlled. The denial of sexuality that was established at this age has been carried over into her adult life and gives rise to severe conflicts, guilt, remorse, and self-condemnation.

## You Continue Working With Ruth

1. How would you react to Ruth's feelings toward you of not sharing enough of yourself personally?

2. What are some ways you might work with Ruth's present sexual inhibitions in light of her disclosure that she still feels guilty and ashamed over her sexual curiosity when she was a young girl?

3. If you were to continue counseling Ruth, what direction would you likely follow in exploring the themes described in questions 1 and 2?

4. Refer to *Case Approach to Counseling and Psychotherapy* (Chapter 2) for an illustration of how a psychoanalytically oriented therapist (William Blau) works with Ruth's case. In this chapter, I also demonstrate my version of counseling Ruth from a psychoanalytically oriented perspective.

5. See the *CD-ROM for the Art of Integrative Counseling* (the sessions dealing with resistance, transference and countertransference, and understanding the past) and analyze my attempt to incorporate psychoanalytic concepts in my work with Ruth.

# QUIZ ON PSYCHOANALYTIC THERAPY:

## A Comprehension Check

Score _____%

**Note:** Please refer to Appendix 1 for the scoring key for these quizzes. Count 4 points for each error, and subtract the total from 100 to get your percentage score. I recommend that you review these comprehension checks for midterm and final examinations. I also suggest that you bring to class questions that you would like clarified. If you get a wrong answer that you believe is right, bring it up for discussion. My classes have had some lively discussions, which have helped students learn to defend their positions.

**True/false items:** Decide if the following statements are "more true" or "more false" as they apply to psychoanalytic therapy.

T  F   1. The psychosocial perspective is not at all compatible with the psychosexual view of development.

T  F   2. Children who do not experience the opportunity to differentiate self from others may later develop a narcissistic character disorder.

T  F   3. The contemporary trends in psychoanalytic theory are reflected in object-relations theory, the self-psychology model, and the relational model.

T  F   4. Brief psychodynamic therapists assume a neutral therapeutic stance as a way to promote transference.

T  F   5. Analytic therapy is oriented toward achieving insight.

T  F   6. Working through is achieved almost totally by catharsis, including getting out deeply buried emotions.

T  F   7. From the Freudian perspective, resistance is typically a conscious process, or a stubbornness on the client's part.

T  F   8. The approach of Erik Erikson is known as object-relations theory.

T  F   9. Object-relations theorists focus on symbiosis, separation, differentiation, and integration.

T  F   10. In object-relations theory there is an emphasis on early development as a decisive factor influencing later development.

**Multiple-choice items:** Select the *one best answer* of those alternatives given. Consider each question within the framework of psychoanalytic therapy.

_____ 11. Who of the following is *not* considered an object-relations theorist?

a. Heinz Kohut
b. Margaret Mahler
c. Otto Kernberg
d. Erik Erikson

_____ 12. Which of the following is *not* considered a contemporary psychoanalytic approach?

a. object-relations theory
b. self-psychology
c. relational psychoanalysis
d. classical psychoanalysis

_____ 13. Which of the following is *not* a characteristic of the newer psychoanalytic thinking?

a. Emphasis is on the origins, transformations, and organizational functions of the self.
b. The contrasting experiences of others is highlighted.
c. People are classified as compliant, aggressive, or detached types.
d. Focus is on the differentiations between and integration of the self and others.
e. Early development is seen as critical to understanding later development.

_____ 14. All of the following are concepts developed by Carl Jung except:

a. the shadow.
b. normal infantile autism.
c. animus and anima.
d. collective unconscious.
e. archetypes.

_____ 15. According to Erikson's psychosocial view, the struggle between industry and inferiority occurs during

a. adolescence.
b. old age.
c. school age.
d. infancy.
e. middle age.

_____ 16. Erikson's preschool-age phase corresponds to which Freudian stage?

a. oral
b. anal
c. phallic
d. latency
e. genital

_____ 17. Which term refers to the repetition of interpretations and the overcoming of resistance so that clients can resolve neurotic patterns?

a. working through
b. transference
c. countertransference
d. catharsis
e. acting out

_____ 18. Analysis of transference is central to psychoanalysis because it

a. keeps the therapist hidden and thus feeling secure.
b. allows clients to relive their past in therapy.
c. helps clients formulate specific plans to change behavior.
d. is considered the only way to get at unconscious material.
e. helps clients experience their emotions.

_____ 19. In brief psychodynamic therapy (BPT) the therapist:

    a. assumes a nondirective and even passive role.

    b. deals exclusively with a single presenting problem.

    c. assumes an active role in quickly formulating a therapeutic focus that goes beyond the surface of presenting problems.

    d. avoids treating any underlying issue.

_____ 20. The Electra complex and the Oedipus complex are associated with what psychosexual stage of development?

    a. oral stage

    b. anal stage

    c. phallic stage

    d. latency stage

    e. genital stage

_____ 21. Borderline and narcissistic disorders have been given attention by

    a. traditional psychoanalysis.

    b. Jungian therapy.

    c. object-relations theory.

    d. Erikson's developmental approach.

    e. none of the above

_____ 22. During psychoanalytic treatment, clients are typically asked

    a. to monitor their behavioral changes by keeping a journal that describes what they do at home and at work.

    b. to make major changes in their lifestyle.

    c. not to make radical changes in their lifestyle.

    d. to give up their friendships.

    e. none of the above.

_____ 23. Countertransference refers to

    a. the irrational reactions clients have toward their therapists.

    b. the irrational reactions therapists have toward their clients.

    c. the projections of the client.

    d. the client's need to be special in the therapist's eyes.

    e. all except (a).

_____ 24. "Maintaining the analytic framework" refers to

    a. the whole range of procedural factors in the treatment process.

    b. the analyst's relative anonymity.

    c. agreement on the payment of fees.

    d. the regularity and consistency of meetings.

    e. all of the above.

_____ 25. In psychoanalytic therapy (as opposed to classical analysis), which of the following procedures is *least* likely to be used?

    a. the client lying on the couch

    b. working with transference feelings

    c. relating present struggles with past events

    d. working with dreams

    e. interpretation of resistance

**Note:** Another suggestion for feedback and for review is to retake the prechapter self-inventory. All 20 items are true statements as applied to the particular therapy, so thinking about them is a good way to review.

# Chapter 5

# Adlerian Therapy

 PRECHAPTER SELF-INVENTORY

**Directions:** Refer to page 41 for general directions. Use the following code:

5 = I *strongly agree* with this statement.

4 = I *agree,* in most respects, with this statement.

3 = I am *undecided* in my opinion about this statement.

2 = I *disagree,* in most respects, with this statement.

1 = I *strongly disagree* with this statement.

_____ 1. The social determinants of personality development are more powerful than the sexual determinants.

_____ 2. Humans can be understood by looking at where they are going and what they are striving toward.

_____ 3. People have a need to overcome inferiority feelings and strive for success.

_____ 4. Although we are not determined by our past, we are significantly influenced by our perceptions and interpretations of these past events.

_____ 5. People are best understood by seeing through the "spectacles" by which they view themselves in relation to the world.

_____ 6. Culture influences all of us, but individuals' expression of their culture differs due to their perception, evaluation, and interpretation.

_____ 7. It is therapeutically useful to ask clients to recall their earliest memories.

_____ 8. Each person develops a unique lifestyle, which should be a focal point of examination in counseling.

_____ 9. Clients in counseling should not be viewed as being "sick" and needing to be "cured"; it is better to see them as being discouraged and in need of reeducation.

_____ 10. Knowing about clients' position in their family of origin is important as a reference point for therapy.

_____ 11. Typically, clients come to therapy with mistaken assumptions or faulty beliefs about life.

_____ 12. Because emotions are integrated with our cognitive behavioral processes, it is appropriate that the counseling process be aimed at the exploration of the client's thoughts, goals, and beliefs.

_____ 13. Although a good client–therapist relationship is essential for counseling to progress, this relationship alone will not bring about change.

_____ 14. One of a counselor's main tasks is to gather information about family relationships and then to summarize and interpret this material.

_____ 15. People tend to remember only those past events that are consistent with their current view of themselves.

_____ 16. Dreams are rehearsals for possible future courses of action.

_____ 17. Conscious factors should be given more attention than unconscious factors in the therapy process.

_____ 18. Although insight is a powerful adjunct to motivational change, it is not a prerequisite for change.

_____ 19. Insight can best be defined as translating self-understanding into constructive action.

_____ 20. At its best, counseling is a cooperative relationship geared toward helping clients identify and change their mistaken beliefs and goals.

## OVERVIEW OF ADLERIAN THERAPY

### Key Figures and Major Focus

Founder: Alfred Adler. Significant developer: Rudolf Dreikurs. Individual Psychology (a term Adler used to describe his emphasis on the uniqueness and unity of the individual) began in Europe in the early 1900s under Adler's leadership. Dreikurs was the main figure responsible for transplanting Adlerian principles to the United States, especially in applying these principles to education, child guidance, and group work.

### Philosophy and Basic Assumptions

More than any other theorist, Adler stresses social psychology and a positive view of human nature. He views human beings as influenced more by social than by biological forces. People are in control of their fate, not victims of it. Individuals create a distinctive lifestyle at an early age, rather than being merely shaped by childhood experiences. This lifestyle tends to remain relatively constant and defines their beliefs about life and ways of dealing with its tasks.

### Key Concepts

Consciousness, not the unconscious, is the center of personality. The Adlerian approach, based on a growth model, stresses the individual's positive capacities to live fully in society. It is characterized by seeing unity in the personality, understanding a person's world from a subjective vantage point, and stressing life goals that give direction to behavior. Humans are motivated by social interest, or a sense of belonging and having a significant place in society. Feelings of inferiority often serve as the wellspring of creativity, motivating people to strive for mastery, superiority, and perfection.

### Therapeutic Goals

Adlerians are mainly concerned with challenging clients' mistaken notions and faulty assumptions, which helps them develop on the useful side of life. Working cooperatively with clients, therapists try to provide encouragement so that clients can develop socially useful goals. Some specific goals include fostering social interest, helping clients overcome feelings of discouragement, changing faulty motivation, restructuring mistaken assumptions, and assisting clients to feel a sense of equality with others.

## Therapeutic Relationship

The client–therapist relationship is based on mutual respect, and both client and counselor are active. Clients are not viewed as passive recipients; rather, they are active parties in a relationship between equals. Through this collaborative partnership, clients recognize that they are responsible for their behavior. The focus is on examining the client's lifestyle, which is expressed in everything the client does. Therapists frequently interpret this lifestyle by demonstrating a connection between the past, the present, and the client's future strivings. Without initial trust and rapport, the difficult work of changing one's style of living is not likely to occur.

## Techniques and Procedures

Adlerians have developed a variety of techniques and therapeutic styles. A strength of Adlerian therapy is the variety of cognitive, behavioral, and experiential techniques that can be applied to a diverse range of clients in a variety of settings and formats. Therapists are not bound to follow a specific set of procedures; rather, they can tap their creativity by applying those techniques that they think are most appropriate for each client. Therapists are mainly concerned about the needs of their clients, rather than squeezing clients into one theoretical framework. Some of the specific techniques they often employ are attending, encouragement, confrontation, paradoxical intention, summarizing, interpretation of the family constellation and early recollections, suggestion, and homework assignments. Most of these procedures were originally developed by Adler.

## Applications

As a growth model, Adlerian theory is concerned with helping people reach their full potential. Its principles have been applied to a broad range of human problems and to alleviating social conditions that interfere with growth. The theory has been widely adopted in elementary education, consultation groups with teachers, child guidance work, parent education groups, parent–child counseling, individual therapy, and social work. Being grounded in the principles of social psychology, it is ideally suited for working with groups, couples, and families.

## Contributions

Adler founded one of the major humanistic approaches to psychology, and his ideas have been integrated into many other therapies. The model is a forerunner of most current approaches to counseling. Adlerian therapy has a psychoeducational focus, a present and future orientation, and is a brief or time-limited approach. Adler's influence has extended into the community mental health movement. The interpersonal emphasis is most appropriate for counseling culturally diverse populations. Adlerian theory addressed social equality issues and social embeddedness of humans long before muliculturalism assumed central importance in the counseling profession.

## Limitations

Some of the approach's basic concepts are vague and not precisely defined, which makes it difficult to validate them empirically. Critics contend that the approach oversimplifies complex human functioning and is based too heavily on a commonsense perspective.

# GLOSSARY OF KEY TERMS

**Basic mistakes** Faulty, self-defeating perceptions, attitudes, and beliefs, which may have been appropriate at one time but are no longer. These are myths that are influential in shaping personality. Examples include denying one's worth, an exaggerated need for security, and setting impossible goals.

**Community feeling** An individual's awareness of being part of the human community.

**Convictions** Conclusions based on life experiences and the interpretation of such experiences.

**Courage** The willingness to move forward in life even when fearful; the willingness to take appropriate risks.

**Early recollections** Childhood memories (before the age of 9) of one-time events. People retain these memories as capsule summaries of their present philosophy of life. From a series of early recollections, it is possible to understand mistaken notions, present attitudes, social interests, and possible future behavior.

**Encouragement** The process of increasing one's courage to face life tasks; used throughout therapy as a way to counter discouragement and to help people set realistic goals.

**Family constellation** The social and psychological structure of the family system; includes birth order, the individual's perception of self, sibling characteristics and ratings, and parental relationships. Each person forms his or her unique view of self, others, and life through the family constellation.

**Fictional finalism** An imagined central goal that gives direction to behavior and unity to the personality; an image of what people would be like if they were perfect and perfectly secure.

**Goal alignment** A congruence between the client's and the counselor's goals and the collaborative effort of two persons working equally toward specific, agreed-on goals.

**Guiding self-ideal** Another term for fictional finalism which represents an individual's image of a goal of perfection.

**Holism** Studying people as integrated beings with a focus on the ways in which they proceed through life; a reaction against separating personality into parts.

**Inferiority feelings** The early determining force in behavior; the source of human striving and the wellspring of creativity. Humans attempt to compensate for both imagined and real inferiorities, which helps them overcome handicaps.

**Insight** A special form of awareness that facilitates a meaningful understanding within the therapeutic relationship and acts as a foundation for change.

**Lifestyle** The core beliefs and assumptions through which the person organizes his or her reality and finds meaning in life events. (See style of life.)

**Life tasks** Universal problems in human life, including the tasks of friendship (community), work (a division of labor), and intimacy (love and marriage).

**Phenomenological approach** Focus on the way people perceive their world. For Adlerians, objective reality is less important than how people interpret reality and the meanings they attach to what they experience.

**Priorities** Characteristics that involve a dominant behavior pattern with supporting convictions that an individual uses to cope. Examples are superiority, control, comfort, and pleasing.

**The question** Used in an initial assessment to gain understanding of the purpose that symptoms or actions have in a person's life. The question is, "How would your life be different, and what would you do differently, if you did not have this symptom or problem?"

**Social interest** A sense of identification with humanity; a feeling of belonging; an interest in the common good.

**Striving for superiority** A strong inclination toward becoming competent, toward mastering our environment, and toward self-improvement. The striving for perfection (and superiority) is a movement toward enhancement of self.

**Style of life** An individual's way of thinking, feeling, and acting; a conceptual framework by which the world is perceived and by which people are able to cope with life tasks; the person's personality.

**Teleology** The study of goals and the goal-directedness of human behavior. Humans live by aims and purposes, not by being pushed by outside forces.

## QUESTIONS FOR REFLECTION AND DISCUSSION

1. Adlerians contend that first we think (and decide), then we feel, and then we act. Their emphasis is on cognition (thinking, beliefs, assumptions about life, attitudes). What are the strengths and limitations of this focus for a counselor?

2. Adlerians typically begin the counseling process with a lifestyle assessment, which focuses on the family constellation and early recollections. Within these areas, what information would you be most interested in gathering as you faced a new client?

3. When you think of yourself working with clients from diverse cultural and socioeconomic backgrounds, what aspects of Adlerian therapy do you think would be most useful? What techniques might you be inclined to use?

4. What are some major areas of contrast between Freud's and Adler's theories? Which perspective appeals to you more, and why? Do you see any basis for reconciling the differences and integrating Freudian and Adlerian concepts in therapeutic practice?

5. When you look at Adler's life experiences and the development of his theory, what do you conclude? To what degree do you think it is possible to separate the theory from the theorist?

6. Adler sees individuals as the actors, creators, and artists of their life. How does this description fit your own life experience?

7. The Adlerian notion of striving for superiority holds that we seek to change weakness into strength by excelling in a particular area as a compensation for perceived inferiority. What are some ways in which you strive for superiority? Does this process of compensation and striving work well for you?

8. Reread the descriptions of the oldest child, the second-born, the middle child, the youngest child, and the only child. What position did you occupy in your family? To what degree do you see your experiences as a child in your family as a factor shaping the person you are now?

9. In addition to focusing on the family constellation, Adlerians ask for a few early recollections. What is your earliest memory? What meaning does this recollection hold for you today?

10. Adlerians pay a lot of attention to "basic mistakes," or "private logic." In thinking about some of the conclusions you formed based on a series of life experiences, can you identify any mistaken assumptions you hold now or have held in the past? How do you think some of your basic mistakes affect the ways in which you think, feel, and act?

## PERSONAL APPLICATION: THE LIFESTYLE ASSESSMENT

The lifestyle assessment is typically done at the initial phase of therapy as a way to obtain information about the client's family constellation, early recollections, dreams, and strengths as a person. This information is then summarized and interpreted, especially in light of the client's faulty assumptions about life (or "basic mistakes"). From the results of this assessment procedure, counselors make tentative interpretations about the client's lifestyle.

Although there are a number of formats for the lifestyle questionnaire, counselors may develop their own variation by focusing on information deemed most valuable for exploration in therapy. What follows is an example of a lifestyle questionnaire that has been modified and adapted from various sources, but especially from Mosak and Shulman's *Life Style Inventory* (1988). To give you an experiential sense of the process of thinking and responding to this early life-history material, complete the following questionnaire as it applies to you. As much as possible, try to give your initial responses, without worrying about what you can and cannot remember or about any "correct" responses. I strongly encourage you to fill in the blanks and to make brief summaries after each section. Assume that you are interested in being a *client* in Adlerian therapy. Based on the outcomes of this questionnaire, what areas of your life would you most like to explore? How much help is this questionnaire in getting you focused on what you might want from a therapeutic relationship?

## Family Constellation: Birth Order and Sibling Description

1. List the siblings from oldest to youngest. Give a brief description of each (including yourself). What most stands out for each sibling?

   _____
   _____
   _____
   _____
   _____

2. Do a rating of each of the siblings, from the highest to the lowest, on each of the following personality dimensions. Include your own position in relationship to your siblings.

   *Most to Least*

   intelligent _____
   achievement-oriented _____
   hardworking _____
   pleasing _____
   assertive _____
   charming _____
   conforming _____
   methodical _____
   athletic _____
   rebellious _____
   spoiled _____
   critical of others _____
   bossy _____

   *Most to Least*

   feminine _____
   masculine _____
   easygoing _____
   daring _____
   responsible _____
   idealistic _____
   materialistic _____
   fun-loving _____
   demanding _____
   critical of self _____
   withdrawn _____
   sensitive _____

3. Which sibling is the most different from you, and how? _____
   _____
   _____

4. Which is most like you, and how? _____
   _____

5. Which played together? _____

6. Which fought each other? _____

7. Who took care of whom? _____

8. Were there any unusual achievements by the siblings? _____
   _____

9. Any accidents or sickness? _____

_____

10. What kind of child were you? _____

_____

_____

11. What was school like for you? _____

_____

12. What childhood fears did you have? _____

_____

13. What were your childhood ambitions? _____

_____

14. What was your role in your peer group? _____

_____

15. Were there any significant events in your physical and sexual development? _____

_____

_____

16. Any highlights in your social development? _____

_____

17. What were the most important values in your family? _____

_____

_____

18. What stands out the most for you about your family life? _____

_____

_____

## Family Constellation: Parental Figures and Relationships

1. Your father's current age. _____     Mother's age. _____

2. His occupation. _____     Her occupation. _____

3. What kind of person is he? _____     What kind of person is she? _____

_____     _____

_____

4. His ambitions for the children. _____     Her ambitions for the children. _____

_____     _____

_____

5. Your childhood view of your father. _____     Your childhood view of your mother. _____

_____     _____

_____     _____

_____

6. His favorite child, and why? _____    Her favorite child, and why? _____
_____    _____
_____    _____

7. Relationship to children. _____    Relationship to children. _____
_____    _____
_____    _____

8. Sibling most like father. In what ways?    Sibling most like mother. In what ways?
_____    _____
_____    _____
_____    _____

9. Describe your parents' relationship with each other. _____
_____
_____

10. In general, how did each of the siblings view and react to your parents? _____
_____
_____

11. In general, what was your parents' relationship to the children? _____
_____
_____

12. Besides your mother and father, were there any other significant adults in your life?
Who were they? How did they affect you? _____
_____
_____

## Early Recollections and Dreams

1. What is your earliest single and specific memory? _____
_____
_____

2. What are some other early recollections? Be as detailed as possible. _____
_____
_____
_____

3. What feelings are associated with any of these early memories? _____
_____

4. Can you recall any childhood dreams? _____
_____

5. Do you have any recurring dreams? _____

## Lifestyle Summary

1. Give a summary of your family constellation. (What stands out most about your role in your family? Are there any themes in your family history?) _____

   _I was always the one who_

   _took care of my father and_

   _my mom was ... to ..._

   _I ...                    ... or_

   _..._____

2. Summarize your early recollections. (Are there any themes running through your early memories? Do you see any meaning in your early recollections?) _____

   _...              ..._

   _family and ...  big_

   _...      ... life_

3. List your mistaken self-defeating perceptions. (What do you see as your "basic mistakes"?)

   _____

   _____

   _____

4. Summarize what you consider to be your strengths as a person. (What are your assets?)

   _____

   _and understanding person_

   _____

   _____

Now that you are finished with this lifestyle questionnaire:

- What did you learn from taking it and reviewing it?
- Assuming you will be a client in counseling, what theme(s) do you most want to address?
- Do you see connections between your past and the person you are today? What about any continuity from your past and present to your strivings toward the future?
- Do you see any patterns in your life? Are there any themes running through from childhood to the present?
- Consider bringing the results of your lifestyle summary to class. Form small groups and exchange with others what you learned from taking this self-assessment questionnaire.

# LIFESTYLE ASSESSMENT OF STAN
# FROM AN ADLERIAN PERSPECTIVE

To provide more background material on Stan's developmental history, I will complete with him the lifestyle questionnaire that you just took.* (Now would be a good time to review Stan's background as presented in the text.)

---

\* This assessment is an adaptation of Mosak and Shulman's *Life Style Inventory* (1988).

## Family Constellation: Birth Order and Sibling Description

1. List all the siblings from oldest to youngest, giving a brief description of each.

| *Judy +7* | *Frank +4* | *Stan 25* | *Karl –2* |
|---|---|---|---|
| attractive | athletic | immature | spoiled |
| brilliant | fun-loving | depressed a lot | devilish |
| out of my class | sociable | slow learner | demanding |
| highly capable | bright | a loner | overprotected |
| accomplished | masculine | scared | got his way |
| mature | well-liked | self-critical | argued with me |
| hard worker | respected | not too accomplished | liked by mother |
| responsible | made fun of me | the rejected child | daring |
| sensitive | didn't like me | one who tried hard | sensitive |

2. Rate the siblings on these traits, from most to least (*J* refers to Judy, *F* to Frank, *S* to Stan, and *K* to Karl).

| | | | | |
|---|---|---|---|---|
| intelligent | J F K S | feminine | J |
| achievement-oriented | F J K S | masculine | only F |
| hardworking | F J S K | easygoing | none of us |
| pleasing | J F K S | daring | K F J S |
| assertive | K F J S | responsible | J F S K |
| charming | K J F S | idealistic | J F S K |
| conforming | none | materialistic | K S F J |
| methodical | J F K S | fun-loving | F K J S |
| athletic | only F | demanding | K F S J |
| rebellious | S K F J | critical of self | S J F K |
| spoiled | only K | withdrawn | S J K F |
| critical of others | F K S J | sensitive | J K S F |
| bossy | K F S J | | |

3. Which sibling(s) is(are) the most different from you, and how? *Judy and Frank. They were both achievement-oriented, intelligent, respected by my parents, and liked by other kids. Whatever they did, they excelled in.*

4. Which sibling(s) is(are) most like you? *Really none. I always felt like the oddball in my family.*

5. Which played together? *Really nobody.*

6. Which fought each other? *Mainly my younger brother, Karl, and I.*

7. Who took care of whom? *Judy was responsible for taking care of me when I was a young kid.*

8. Any unusual achievements? *Judy won just about every award that was given out at school. Frank was at the top of his class and won athletic trophies.*

9. Any accidents or sickness? *I was hit by a car when I was 9 while I was riding my bicycle. My younger brother seemed sick a lot.*

10. What kind of child were you? *As a child I was lonely, felt hurt a lot, was withdrawn, felt as if I could never measure up to Frank and Judy, felt unwanted, and didn't feel the other kids wanted to play with me.*

11. What was school like for you? *For me, school was a real drag.*

12. What childhood fears did you have? *I was afraid of being picked on, afraid of being alone, and scared that I would fail at whatever I did.*

13. What were your childhood ambitions? *To build a race car and drive it!*

14. What was your role in your peer group? *The one who was chosen last.*

15. Any significant events in your physical and sexual development? *I was smaller than most other guys and didn't mature physically until late. I remember being scared of the sexual changes in my body — and confused!*

16. Any highlights in your social development? *I felt retarded. I always felt as if I was out of step, especially with girls.*

17. What were the most important values in your family? *To be honest, to work hard, and to get ahead.*

18. What stands out the most for you about your family life? *How I never really felt a part of the family, and how distant my older brother seemed to me.*

## Family Constellation: Parental Figures and Relationships

| Father | Mother |
|---|---|
| 1. Current age. *55* | Current age. *53* |
| 2. Occupation. *High school teacher* | Occupation. *Homemaker (part-time nurse)* |
| 3. Kind of person. *Devoted to his work, detached, distant at home, passive.* | Kind of person. *Bossy, dominant, very hard to please, capable, aggressive. Demands her way.* |
| 4. His ambitions for the children. *Strive and do well academically; never bring shame to the family.* | Her ambitions for the children. *To keep out of trouble, to succeed, to show respect for authority.* |
| 5. Your childhood view of him. *Hard worker, dominated by my mother, passive and quiet, distant from me.* | Your childhood view of her. *Rejecting of me, depressed a lot, responsible. Expected too much of me.* |
| 6. His favorite child. *Frank—he admired his academic and athletic accomplishments.* | Her favorite child. *Karl—she could see no wrong that the little brat could do.* |
| 7. Relationship to children. *He really liked Frank and Judy and did a lot with Frank. He ignored me and didn't have much to do with Karl.* | Relationship to children. *She seemed to like and have time for all the kids, except for me.* |
| 8. Sibling most like father. *Frank, in that he was smart and really loved school.* | Sibling most like mother. *Really none, except Judy might be most like her in that both are responsible and highly capable.* |

9. Describe your parents' relationship to each other. *Horrible! She berated him and ran over him, and he would never stand up to her. He escaped into his work. They were never really affectionate or close with each other.*

10. Siblings' view of parents. *Frank and Judy thought a good deal of both my mother and my father; Karl respected Mom but had trouble with Dad; I didn't have much use for either of my parents and didn't want much to do with them.*

11. Parents' relationship to the children. *Good for Frank and Judy, OK for mother and Karl, and rotten for me.*

12. Besides your parents, who was another significant adult in your life? *My uncle, who seemed to take an interest in me and liked me.*

## Early Recollections and Dreams

1. What is your earliest single and specific memory? *I was about 6. I went to school, and I was scared of the other kids and the teacher. When I came home, I cried and told my mother I didn't want to go back to school. She yelled at me and called me a baby.*

2. What are some other early recollections?

   a. *Age 6½: My family was visiting my grandparents. I was playing outside, and some neighborhood kid hit me for no reason. We got in a big fight, and my mother came out and scolded me for being such a rough kid. She wouldn't believe me when I told her he had started the fight.*

   b. *Age 8: I stuck some nails in the neighbor's tires, and he caught me in the act. He took me by the neck to my folks. They both yelled at me and punished me. My father didn't talk to me for weeks.*

   c. *Age 9: I was riding my bike to school, and all of a sudden a car hit me from the side. I remember lying there thinking I might die. I went to the hospital with a broken leg and concussion. Being in that hospital was lonely and scary.*

3. What feelings are associated with these early memories? *I often felt that I could do no right. I was scared most of the time, felt lonely and never really felt understood or cared for.*

4. Can you recall any childhood dreams? *I recall going to bed late at night and dreaming that the devil was at my window. It scared the hell out of me, and I remember burying myself under the covers to hide.*

5. Any recurring dreams? *I'm alone in the desert, dying of thirst. I see people with water, but nobody seems to notice me, and nobody comes over to give me any water.*

## Lifestyle Summary

1. Summary of Stan's family constellation: Stan was the third in a family of four children. Psychologically, he was a true middle child with two older children (one for each sex) in the family and a little brother who was the psychological youngest. The values of the family were achieving and doing well, yet he felt that he could never measure up to the standards of achievement of his older brother and sister. A central theme was that he felt excluded and unwanted. The attention was directed to his older siblings, and the only attention he could get was through negative means. He saw a cold war between his parents, and he learned to fear intimacy. Although he tried to make his parents feel proud of him, he was really never able to succeed. He kept to himself most of the time.

2. Summary of Stan's early recollections: "No matter what I do, I wind up being the fall guy and getting in trouble. Life is frightening, cruel, and punishing. I can't turn to either men or women for help or comfort: Women will be harsh and uncaring; men will withdraw from me for long periods."

3. Summary of Stan's basic mistakes: Stan's pattern and profile show a number of mistakes and self-defeating perceptions, some of which are:

   a. "Anything that can go wrong will go wrong, and I'll be blamed or punished for it."

   b. "Don't get close to people, especially women, because they will be harsh and uncaring."

    c. "If you can't do anything right, why try at all?"

    d. "Only perfect or near-perfect people make it in this world; I'm neither: I won't make it, I don't belong, and I'm not lovable."

    e. "If I don't let myself feel, I won't be hurt."

4. Summary of Stan's assets: Some of Stan's strengths that can be built on are:

    a. He has courage and is willing to look at his life.

    b. He is willing to question assumptions he has made that he did not question earlier.

    c. He realizes that he puts himself down a great deal, and he is determined to learn to accept and like himself.

    d. He has some clear goals—namely, to graduate and to work with kids as a counselor.

    e. He is motivated to work to feel equal to others, and he no longer wants to feel apologetic for his existence.

You proceed in working with Stan from an Adlerian perspective:

1. As you review Stan's lifestyle assessment, what stands out for you the most? What direction would you be inclined to pursue with him?

2. As you can see, Stan has made several "basic mistakes." How would you work with him on correcting some of these mistaken perceptions? How would you work with him on a cognitive level, as a way of changing his behavior and his feelings?

3. Stan comes to counseling as a discouraged person who feels victimized. Do you have any ideas on applying encouragement in your counseling with him? What might you do if he persisted in his vision of himself as a victim who is powerless to make changes now?

## JERRY COREY'S WORK WITH RUTH FROM AN ADLERIAN PERSPECTIVE

In the session dealing with termination (in the *CD-ROM for Integrative Counseling*) Ruth and I address her ambivalence about ending her therapy. The focus of this session is on specific changes she has made over the course of her therapy. In Adlerian terms, we are in the reorientation phase. In earlier sessions Ruth has made some new decisions and modified her goals. It was essential that she learn how to challenge her own thinking when she reverted to old patterns of being critical of herself. My encouragement was important in helping her discover her inner strength. Ruth has become more honest about what she is doing, and she is increasingly able to choose for herself instead of merely following the values she uncritically accepted as a child.

A most important ingredient of the final stages of Ruth's therapy is commitment. She is finally persuaded that if she hopes to change she will have to set specific tasks for herself and take concrete action now that formal therapy is ending. In this reorientation stage the central task is to encourage Ruth to translate her insights into acting in new and more effective ways. Ruth has acquired a new appreciation of herself, yet she realizes it will be essential for her to continue practicing new learnings. In this final session there is considerable attention on Ruth's looking to the future and establishing revised goals. Where does she want to go from here? What concrete plans can she put into action? What are some contracts that she can establish as a way to provide her with a useful direction?

### You Continue Working With Ruth

1. Refer to *Case Approach to Counseling and Psychotherapy* (Chapter 3) for an illustration of how Adlerian therapists (Jim Bitter and Bill Nicoll) conduct a comprehensive

lifestyle assessment with Ruth and engage her in exploring some of her life patterns. In this chapter, I also demonstrate my version of counseling Ruth from an Adlerian perspective.

2. See the *CD-ROM for Integrative Counseling* (the final session dealing with evaluation and termination) for a concrete illustration of assisting Ruth in the reorientation and action process.

3. Assume that you are counseling Ruth and that this is the termination phase of therapy. What are the major tasks you'd most want to accomplish?

4. During this reorientation phase of therapy, what kinds of encouragement would you be inclined to offer Ruth?

5. How would you work with Ruth in helping her identify a new set of goals that she can continue working on now that the counseling sessions are ending?

## JULIE: "It's My Father's Fault That I Can't Trust Men"

### Some Background Data

Julie is interested in exploring her relationships with men. She says that she cannot trust me because I am a man. She cannot trust men because her father was an alcoholic and was therefore untrustworthy. She recalls that he was never around when she needed him and that she would not have felt free to go to him with her problems in any case because he was loud and gruff. She tells me of the guilt she felt over her father's drinking because of her sense that in some way she was causing him to drink. Julie, who is now 35 and unmarried, is leery of men, convinced that they will somehow let her down if she gives them the chance. She has decided in advance that she will not be a fool again, that she will not let herself need or trust men.

Although Julie seems pretty clear about not wanting to risk trusting men, she realizes that this notion is self-defeating and would like to challenge her views. She wants to change the way she perceives and feels about men, but she seems to have an investment in her belief about their basic untrustworthiness. Julie is not very willing to look at her part in keeping this assumption about men alive. Rather, she would prefer to assign blame to her father. It was he who taught her this lesson, and now it is difficult for her to change, or so she reports.

### Jerry Corey's Way of Working With Julie From an Adlerian Perspective

Even if it is true that her father did treat her unkindly, my assessment is that it is a "basic mistake" for her to have generalized what she believes to be true of her father to all men. My hope is that our relationship, based on respect and cooperation, will be a catalyst for her in challenging her assumptions about men. At one point in her therapy, I ask Julie if she knows why she is so angry and upset with men. When she mentions her father, I say: "He's just one man. Do you know why you react in this way to most men—even today?"

As part of the assessment process, I am interested in exploring her early memories, especially those pertaining to her father and mother, the guiding lines for male and female relationships. We will also explore what it was like for her as a child in her family, what interpretation she gave to events, and what meaning she gave to herself, others, and the world. Some additional questions that I will pose are:

- What do you think you get from staying angry at your father and insisting that he is the cause of your fear of men?

- What do you imagine it would be like for you if you were to act as if men were trustworthy? What do you suppose really prevents you from doing that?
- What would happen or what would you be doing differently if you trusted men?
- If you could forgive your father, what do you imagine that would be like for you? for him? for your dealings with other men?
- If you keep the same attitudes until you die, how will that be for you?
- How would you like to be in 5 years?
- If you really want to change, what can you do to begin the process? What are you willing to do?

My relationship with Julie is the major vehicle with which to work in the sessions. A male counselor who emphasizes listening, mutual respect, honesty, partnership, and encouragement will give Julie a chance to examine her mistaken notions and try on new behaviors. A lifestyle assessment will help her see the broad pattern of her life and will reveal the convictions that are leading her to safeguard herself against all relationships with males.

Julie needs to take some action if she expects to change her views toward men. Thus, we work together to determine what she can do outside of the sessions. A major part of my work with Julie is directed at confronting her with the ways in which she is refusing to take responsibility for the things in herself that she does not like and at encouraging her to decide on some course of action to begin the process of modifying those things.

A very important phase of therapy is the reorientation stage, the action-oriented process of putting one's insights to work. As an Adlerian therapist, I am concerned that Julie do more than merely understand the dynamics of her behavior. My goal is to help Julie eventually see a wider range of alternatives. This reorientation phase of her therapy consists of Julie considering alternative attitudes, beliefs, goals, and behaviors. She is expected to make new decisions. I encourage her to "catch herself" in the process of repeating old patterns. When she meets a man and immediately assumes he cannot be trusted, for example, it helps if she is able to observe what she is doing. She can then ask herself if she wants to persist in clinging to old assumptions or if she is willing to let go of them and form impressions without bias.

This phase of counseling is a time for Julie to commit to the specific ways in which she would like to be different. Encouragement during the time that she is trying new behavior and working on new goals is most useful. This encouragement can take the form of having faith in her, of support, of recognizing the changes she makes, and of continuing to be psychologically available for her during our sessions.

## Follow-Up: You Continue as Julie's Therapist

1. What are some of your impressions and reactions to my work with Julie? Knowing what you know about these sessions and Julie, what might you most want to follow up with if you could see her for at least a couple of months?

2. How much do you imagine that your approach with Julie would be affected by your life experiences and views? How much would you want to share of yourself with her? In what ways do you think you could use yourself as a person in your work with her?

3. How might you deal with her apparent unwillingness to accept personal responsibility and her blaming of her father for her inability to trust men now?

4. What are some additional Adlerian techniques you might use with Julie?

5. Outline some of the steps in Adlerian counseling that you would expect to take for a series of sessions with Julie, showing why you are adopting that particular course of action.

# QUIZ ON ADLERIAN THERAPY

## A COMPREHENSION CHECK

Score _____%

**Note:** Please refer to Appendix 1 for the scoring key.

**True/false items:** Decide if the following statements are "more true" or "more false" as they apply to Adlerian therapy.

T   F   1. Adlerian therapy is well suited to a brief or time-limited approach.

T   F   2. Fictional finalism refers to the central goal that guides a person's behavior.

T   F   3. Striving for superiority is seen as a neurotic manifestation.

T   F   4. Adler maintains that our style of life is not set until middle age.

T   F   5. Adlerians operate in flexible ways from a theory that can be tailored to work with ethnically diverse clients.

T   F   6. Adlerians typically do not use the technique of interpretation. They believe clients can make their own interpretations without therapist interventions.

T   F   7. Adlerians place relatively little importance on the quality of the client–therapist relationship.

T   F   8. Analysis and assessment are a basic part of the counseling process.

T   F   9. Insight is best defined as understanding translated into action.

T   F   10. Adlerians believe childhood experiences in themselves are the decisive factor in shaping personality.

**Multiple-choice items:** Select the *one best answer* of those alternatives given. Consider each question within the framework of Adlerian therapy.

_____ 11. According to Adler, childhood experiences

    a. are not relevant to the practice of counseling.
    b. determine the adult personality.
    c. passively shape us.
    d. in themselves are not as crucial as our attitude toward these experiences.
    e. should provide the focus of therapy.

_____ 12. The Adlerian point of view toward the role of insight in therapy is best stated in this way:

    a. Insight is a prerequisite to any personality change.
    b. To be of value, insight must be translated into a constructive action program.
    c. People will not make changes until they know the precise causes of their personality problems.
    d. Emotional insight must precede intellectual insight.

    e. Cognitive understanding is absolutely essential before significant behavior changes can occur.

_____ 13. Which of the following statements is *not* true as it is applied to Adlerian therapy?

    a. Consciousness, not the unconscious, is the center of personality.
    b. The approach is grounded on the medical model.
    c. It is a phenomenological and humanistic orientation.
    d. Feelings of inferiority can be the wellspring of creativity.
    e. Early influences can predispose the child to a faulty lifestyle.

_____ 14. Which of the following comes closest to the therapeutic goal of Adlerians?

    a. re-authoring one's life story
    b. engaging in solution-talk instead of problem-talk
    c. experiencing feelings as intensely as possible

d. motivation modification
e. behavior modification

15. The lifestyle assessment includes information based on

a. the family constellation.
b. early recollections.
c. dreams.
d. mistaken, self-defeating perceptions.
e. all of the above.

16. Which is the correct sequence of human experiencing from an Adlerian perspective?

a. First we feel, then we think, then we act.
b. First we act, then we feel, then we think.
c. First we think, then we feel, then we act.
d. First we feel, then we act, then we think.
e. none of the above

17. Adlerians could best be described as using which techniques?

a. They use strictly cognitive techniques.
b. They use emotive and behavioral techniques to get people to think.
c. They are bound by a clear set of therapeutic techniques.
d. They fit a variety of techniques to the needs of each client.
e. They have an aversion to using techniques because they see the therapeutic relationship alone as the healing factor.

18. How would the Adlerian therapist view the personal problems of clients?

a. as the result of cultural conditioning
b. as the end result of a process of discouragement
c. as living with problem-saturated stories
d. as the product of our innate tendencies toward self-destruction
e. none of the above

19. What principle accounts for the consistency and directionality of an individual's psychological movement?

a. lifestyle
b. fictional goals
c. basic mistakes
d. social interest
e. phenomenology

20. Which term does *not* fit Adlerian therapy?

a. holistic
b. social
c. teleological
d. deterministic
e. phenomenological

21. Which of the following does Adler *not* stress?

a. the unity of personality
b. biological and instinctual drives
c. direction in which people are headed
d. unique style of life that is an expression of life goals
e. feelings of inferiority

22. The phenomenological orientation pays attention to the

a. events that occur at various stages of life.
b. manner in which biological and environmental forces limit us.
c. way in which people interact with each other.
d. internal dynamics that drive a person.
e. way in which individuals perceive their world.

23. The concept of fictional finalism refers to

a. an imagined central goal that guides a person's behavior.
b. the hopeless stance that leads to personal defeat.
c. the manner in which people express their need to belong.
d. the process of assessing one's style of life.
e. the interpretation that individuals give to life events.

_____ 24. Adlerians consider which factor(s) to be influential in an individual's life?

    a. psychological position in the family
    b. birth order
    c. interactions among siblings
    d. parent–child relationships
    e. all of the above

_____ 25. Adlerians value early recollections as an important clue to the understanding of

    a. one's sexual and aggressive instincts.
    b. the bonding process between mother and child.
    c. the individual's lifestyle.
    d. the unconscious dynamics that motivate behavior.
    e. the origin of psychological trauma in early childhood.

**Note:** As regular practice, after completing these quizzes, retake the prechapter self-inventory. Each of the items in the self-inventory is true as applied to a given theory. It is useful to see if any of your ratings have changed after your study of the chapter.

# Chapter 6

# Existential Therapy

 PRECHAPTER SELF-INVENTORY

**Directions:** Refer to page 41 for general directions. Use the following code:

5 = I *strongly agree* with this statement.

4 = I *agree*, in most respects, with this statement.

3 = I am *undecided* in my opinion about this statement.

2 = I *disagree*, in most respects, with this statement.

1 = I *strongly disagree* with this statement.

_____ 1. A therapist has the job of challenging clients with ways that they are living a restricted existence.

_____ 2. The therapist's main task is to attempt to understand the subjective world of clients to help them come to new awareness and options.

_____ 3. One of the therapist's tasks is to encourage clients to develop the courage to face life squarely—by taking a stance, by making a decision, and by taking action.

_____ 4. Psychotherapy should be viewed as an approach to human relationships rather than as a set of techniques.

_____ 5. We are not victims of circumstance, but we are what we choose to become.

_____ 6. Regardless of their past experiences, clients are challenged to take responsibility for how they are *now* choosing to be in their world.

_____ 7. Therapist authenticity and presence are crucial qualities in an effective therapeutic relationship.

_____ 8. The significance of our existence is never fixed once and for all; rather, we continue to re-create ourselves through our projects.

_____ 9. Responsibility, which is the crux of human existence, is based on the capacity for consciousness.

_____ 10. Freedom, self-determination, willingness, and decision making are qualities that form the very center of human existence.

_____ 11. The nature of freedom lies in the capacity to shape one's own personal development by choosing among alternatives.

_____ 12. Even though there are limits to freedom (such as environment and genetic endowment), humans have the capacity to choose.

_____ 13. The major themes of psychotherapy are freedom and responsibility, isolation, alienation, death and its implications for living, and the continual search for meaning.

_____ 14. By refusing to give easy solutions or answers, therapists confront clients with the reality that they alone must find their own answers.

_____ 15. The failure to establish relatedness to others results in a condition marked by alienation, estrangement, and isolation.

_____ 16. Because there is no preordained design for living, people are faced with the task of creating their own meaning and purpose.

_____ 17. Guilt and anxiety do not necessarily need to be cured, for they are part of the human condition.

_____ 18. Anxiety can be the result of the person's awareness of his or her aloneness, finiteness, and responsibility for choosing.

_____ 19. The reality of death gives significance to living.

_____ 20. Therapists can help clients become less of a stranger to themselves by selectively disclosing their own responses at appropriate times.

## OVERVIEW OF EXISTENTIAL THERAPY

### Key Figures and Major Focus

Key figures in existential philosophy, which strives to define the nature of human existence, are Søren Kierkegaard, Friedrich Nietzsche, Martin Heidegger, Jean-Paul Sartre, Martin Buber, Ludwig Binswanger, and Medard Boss. Four prominent developers of existential psychotherapy are Viktor Frankl, Rollo May, Irvin Yalom, and James Bugental—all of whom developed their existential approaches to psychotherapy from strong backgrounds in both existential and humanistic psychology. The approach focuses on central concerns of the person's existence, such as death, freedom, existential isolation, and meaninglessness.

### Philosophy and Basic Assumptions

Existential therapy reacts against the tendency to view therapy as a system of well-defined techniques; it affirms looking at those unique characteristics that make us human and building therapy on them. It emphasizes choice, freedom, responsibility, and self-determination. In essence, we are the author of our life. Thrust into a meaningless and absurd world, we are challenged to accept our aloneness and to create meaning in life. The awareness of our eventual nonbeing acts as a catalyst for finding meaning.

### Key Concepts

There are six key propositions of existential therapy: (1) We have the capacity for self-awareness. (2) Because we are basically free beings, we must accept the responsibility that accompanies our freedom. (3) We have a concern to preserve our uniqueness and identity; we come to know ourselves in relation to knowing and interacting with others. (4) The significance of our existence and the meaning of our life are never fixed once and for all; instead, we re-create ourselves through our projects. (5) Anxiety is part of the human condition. (6) Death is also a basic human condition, and awareness of it gives significance to living.

### Therapeutic Goals

Existential therapy provides an invitation to clients to recognize the ways in which they are not living fully authentic lives and to make choices that will lead to their becoming what they are capable of being. In existential therapy attention is given to clients' immediate, ongoing experience with the aim of helping them develop a greater presence in their quest for meaning and purpose. Some basic therapeutic goals are (1) to recognize factors that block freedom, (2) to challenge clients to recognize that they are doing something that they formerly thought was happening to them, and (3) to accept the freedom and responsibility that go along with action.

## Therapeutic Relationship

The client–therapist relationship is of paramount importance because the quality of the I/Thou encounter offers a context for change. Instead of prizing therapeutic objectivity and professional distance, existential therapists value being fully present, and they strive to create caring relationships with clients. Therapy is a collaborative relationship in which both client and therapist are involved in a journey of self-discovery.

## Techniques and Procedures

The approach places primary emphasis on understanding the client's current experience, not on using techniques. Existential therapists are free to adapt their interventions to their own personality and style, and they pay attention to what each client requires. Therapists are *not* bound by any prescribed procedures and can use techniques from other schools. Interventions are used in the service of broadening the ways in which clients live in their world. Techniques are tools to help clients become aware of their choices and their potential for action. Although existential practitioners may use techniques from other theoretical orientations, their interventions are guided by a philosophical framework about what it means to be human.

## Applications

The approach is especially appropriate for those seeking personal growth. It can be useful for clients who are experiencing a developmental crisis (career or marital failure, retirement, grief work, transition from one stage of life to another). Clients experience anxiety rising out of existential conflicts, such as making key choices, accepting freedom and the responsibility that goes with it, struggling to find meaning in life, and facing the anxiety of their eventual death. These existential realities provide a rich therapeutic context.

## Contributions

The essential humanity of the individual is highlighted. The person-to-person therapeutic relationship lessens the chances of dehumanizing therapy. The approach has something to offer counselors regardless of their theoretical orientation. It stresses self-determination, accepting the personal responsibility that accompanies freedom, and viewing oneself as the author of one's life. Further, it provides a perspective for understanding the value of anxiety and guilt, the role and meaning of death, and the creative aspects of being alone and choosing for oneself. A strength of the approach is that it enables clients to examine the degree to which their behavior is being influenced by social and cultural conditioning.

## Limitations

The approach lacks a systematic statement of principles and practices of therapy. Many existential writers use vague and global terms or abstract concepts that are difficult to grasp. The model has not been subjected to scientific research as a way of validating its procedures. It has limited applicability to lower-functioning clients, clients in extreme crisis who need direction, clients who are mostly concerned about meeting basic needs, and those who lack verbal skills.

# GLOSSARY OF KEY TERMS

**Existential analysis (dasein analyse)**   The emphasis of this therapy approach is on the subjective and spiritual dimensions of human existence.

**Existential anxiety**   An outcome of being confronted with the four givens of existence: death, freedom, existential isolation, and meaninglessness.

**Existential guilt**   The result of, or the consciousness of, evading the commitment to choosing for ourselves.

**Existential neurosis**   Feelings of despair and anxiety that result from inauthentic living, a failure to make choices, and avoidance of responsibility.

**Existential vacuum**   A condition of emptiness and hollowness that results from meaninglessness in life.

**Existentialism**   A philosophical movement stressing individual responsibility for creating one's ways of thinking, feeling, and behaving.

**Freedom**   An inescapable aspect of the human condition; we are the author of our life and therefore are responsible for our destiny and accountable for our actions.

**Logotherapy**   Developed by Frankl, this brand of existential therapy literally means "healing through reason." It focuses on challenging clients to search for meaning in life.

**Phenomenology**   A method of exploration that uses subjective human experiencing as its focus. The phenomenological approach is a part of the fabric of existentially oriented therapies, Adlerian therapy, person-centered therapy, Gestalt therapy, and reality therapy.

**Restricted existence**   A state of functioning with a limited degree of awareness of oneself and being vague about the nature of one's problems.

# QUESTIONS FOR REFLECTION AND DISCUSSION

1. What does personal freedom mean to you? Do you believe you are what you are now largely as a result of your choices, or do you believe you are the product of your circumstances?

2. As you reflect on some critical turning points in your life, what decisions appear to have been crucial to your present development?

3. Are you able to accept and exercise your own freedom and make significant decisions alone? Do you attempt to escape from freedom and responsibility? Are you inclined to give up some of your autonomy for the security of being taken care of by others?

4. Do you agree that each person is basically alone? What are the implications for counseling practice? In what ways might you have attempted to avoid your experience of aloneness?

5. What is your experience with anxiety? Does your anxiety result from the consideration that you must choose for yourself, the realization that you are alone, the fact that you will die, and the realization that you must create your own meaning and purpose in life? How have you dealt with anxiety in your own life?

6. To what extent do you believe that unless you take death seriously life has little meaning? What are the implications of this notion for the practice of therapy?

7. What specific things do you value most? What would your life be like without them? What gives your life meaning and a sense of purpose?

8. Have you experienced an "existential vacuum"? Is your life at times without substance, depth, and meaning? What is this experience of emptiness like for you, and how do you cope with it?

9. What are your reactions to the existential view of the importance of the client–therapist relationship? To what extent do you see yourself as being able to make the therapeutic journey with a client into unknown territory? To what degree are you open to challenging and changing your own life?

10. If you were working with a culturally diverse client population in a community agency, what existential concepts might you draw from, if any? What do you see as the major strengths and limitations of this approach as it is applied to multicultural counseling?

## SUGGESTED ACTIVITIES AND EXERCISES

### Ways of Being "Dead" but Still Existing

In counseling situations I find it useful to ask people to examine parts of themselves that they feel are "dead." In what ways are you dead? How do you prevent yourself from experiencing life? What would happen if you chose to live fully instead of settling for your half-life/half-death existence?

**Directions:** As you read these comments that express some ways in which clients may choose "death" over "life," reflect on these questions: "How fully alive do I feel? When do I feel most alive? least alive? What parts within me are 'dead' or 'dying'? What would it take for me to experience a new surge of vitality in these areas?" Then discuss in class, either in small groups or in dyads, the degree to which you feel fully alive. Also, share how the reality of death can give life a sense of meaning.

1. "I consistently choose to remain safe by avoiding any risks."
2. "I'll cut off all my feelings—that way I won't hurt. I've become a good computer, and I'll never experience pain."
3. "I'm dead, hollow, empty, with nothing inside. I can't find any real purpose for living. I just exist and wait for each day to pass."
4. "I live in isolation from people. I don't want to get close, so I just seal myself off from everyone."

Now list some possible ways in which parts of *you* are not fully "alive":

1. _____
2. _____
3. _____
4. _____

### Will We Really Change?

According to the existentialists, the best means of understanding individuals is watching their striving for the future. Because humans are always emerging and becoming, the future is the dominant mode of time for them. People can be understood as they project themselves forward.

One technique I have often used in group situations is to ask each person to fantasize his or her life as he or she would like it to be. I have asked questions such as "What future do you want for yourself? What do you want to be able to say about yourself in relation to the significant people in your life? What would you like to have inscribed on your tombstone? What are you doing now, or what can you do now to make your vision a reality?" A look into the future can be a stimulus for people to see choices they have made and the ways in which they can create and shape their own future. In some real ways they can be the architect of their future life.

**Directions:** Write down a brief response to each of these questions. Then discuss your answers in class, either in small groups or in dyads.

1. What do you think your future will be like if you stay very much as you are now? Complete the following statement: If I make no major changes, then I expect _____

_____

_____

2. List some things, situations, or people that you see as preventing your change or as making your change difficult. _____

_____

_____

_____

3. If you could make *one* significant change in your personality or behavior *now*, what would it be? _____

_____

4. What do you see that you can do *now* to make that one change? _____

_____

5. Write your own epitaph. _____

_____

## JERRY COREY'S WORK WITH RUTH FROM AN EXISTENTIAL PERSPECTIVE

Ruth states that her therapy is causing problems for her in her life. She even considered not coming to the session. She expresses her resistance about continuing with her therapy. I see it as important that she explore the meaning of her resistance. I am hopeful that she can share her doubts, and I encourage her to talk about her reservations and anxieties.

One of my aims is to show Ruth the connection between the choices she is making or failing to make and the anxiety she is experiencing. I do this by asking her to observe herself in various situations throughout the week. For instance, when does she put her own needs last and choose to be the giver to others? Through this self-observation process, Ruth gradually sees some specific ways in which her choices are directly contributing to her anxiety.

My goal in working with Ruth is not to eliminate her anxiety; rather, it is to help her understand what it means. Anxiety is a signal that all is not well, that a person is ready for some change in life. Ruth does learn that how she deals with her anxiety will have a lot to do with the type of new identity she creates.

Perhaps the critical aspect of Ruth's therapy is her recognition that she has a choice to make. She can continue to cling to the known and the familiar, even deciding to settle for what she has in life and quit therapy, or she can recognize that in life there are no guarantees. Ruth can learn to accept the uncertainty and anxiety in her life and still act, making choices and then living with the consequences.

### You Continue Working With Ruth

1. Refer to *Case Approach to Counseling and Psychotherapy* (Chapter 4) for an illustration of how an existential therapist (Donald Polkinghorne) intervenes with the purpose of

assisting Ruth in living more authentically. In this chapter I also demonstrate my style of counseling Ruth from an existential perspective.

2. See the *CD-ROM for Integrative Counseling* (the session with an emotive focus and the understanding resistance session) for a demonstration of exploring existential themes in Ruth's life.

3. Part of the work of the existential counselor is to help clients make critical choices. How would you work with Ruth if she expresses to you that she has little confidence in her capacity to make wise choices?

4. How might you deal with Ruth when she informs you that she is thinking about quitting therapy because of her anxiety that those in her family will be threatened by her changes?

## WALT: What Is There to Live For?

### Some Background Data

The question of meaning in life is especially critical to Walt, a 74-year-old retiree who has lived with his son and daughter-in-law in Wisconsin for 4 years, ever since his wife, Rose Ann, died. Walt lived in Honolulu from his birth until shortly after Rose Ann lost a long battle with cancer. The couple were married for 50 years. As a Pacific Islander he has experienced a great deal of loneliness and dislocation since he moved away from his home. Although he admits that the people in his new community near Green Bay are friendly, it has just not been the same for him. Not only has a huge gap been created in his life with the loss of Rose Ann, but he also must contend with feelings of being cut off from his roots in Hawaii.

During the last few months of Rose Ann's life, a number of people in the community helped Walt care for her at home. He says that he is surprised by how much he was able to do for her when she was so sick. However, he does feel guilty for having let her down in some ways. Shortly before she died, she wanted to talk with him about her impending death but he resisted this discussion. He felt that he could not handle the reality of her death, and he kept hoping that somehow she would be cured or would live several more years. Even though she has been dead for 4 years, Walt still suffers from guilt and regret over not having talked with her more. He feels that there were so many things left unsaid between the two of them, and now he ruminates over what he wishes he had done differently. He reports that he sleeps terribly, and when he is awake he simply cannot find enough things to keep him busy and to distract him from his endless rumination. He says that he misses all the friends they had for so many years in Honolulu and that he fears making new friends because "they'll all die anyway." He often wishes that he had died instead of Rose Ann, for she would have been better able to cope with his death than he has managed to cope with hers.

Before he was forced to retire, Walt taught in a high school. As a teacher he felt good because he had some measure of worth. For Walt retirement is next to death. He feels "put out to pasture," simply passing time without getting in people's way. His major problem is this lack of purpose in life. He is searching for something to take the place of his wife, his home, and his job, yet he sees little chance that he will find a substitute that will bring any meaning to his life. The losses are simply too great.

### Jerry Corey's Way of Working With Walt as an Existential Therapist

My goal in working with Walt is to provide adequate support for him at a very difficult time in his life. Walt needs an opportunity to talk about his regrets and how it feels to be depressed; he needs to feel that he is being heard and cared for. At the same time, I must challenge Walt to begin to create his own meaning, even though most of his support systems are gone. To accomplish this goal, I encourage Walt to talk, recounting things about his past that he regrets and wishes had been different. I urge him to talk about the losses he feels with Rose Ann gone, with his island community far away, and with his teaching career over. Early in his therapy Walt needs to talk freely and to be listened to, and he needs to express his feelings of guilt, regret, sorrow, and separation.

How do I proceed with Walt? I do not ignore his depression, for this is a symptom that carries a message. By beginning with his full recognition and acceptance of his hopelessness, I may be able to help him change. I am especially interested in how he derived meaning through his work. I want to know how teaching contributed to his feeling that he had something to offer people.

In some ways Walt is telling me that he is a *victim*—that his choices have mostly been taken from him, that there is little he can do to change the situation he finds himself in, and that he is for the most part doomed to live out a sterile future. He continually tells me that there is nothing that either of us can do to bring back his wife. He feels almost as hopeless when it comes to getting some kind of work, and he sees no way of being able to return to Hawaii to live out his remaining years. It is necessary for me to perceive Walt's world as he does, but I find it hard to accept his conclusions. I want to provide a supportive atmosphere so Walt can communicate to me what it is like for him to be in his world. At the same time, I want to challenge his passive stance toward life. Although he cannot change some of the events of his life, he can change how he continues to look at his life situation.

Because Walt continues to think about death and has suicidal fantasies, it is important for me to confront Walt with questions such as "What are you living for? What stops you from killing yourself?" I would not want to take lightly his mention of suicide. Walt is experiencing a good deal of depression, and it is critical to make an assessment of how likely he is to try to take his life. To make such an assessment, I want to find out how often Walt thinks about suicide and with what degree of detail. Is he preoccupied with suicidal impulses, or is such a fantasy rare? Does he have a detailed plan? Has he cut off social contacts? Has he made any prior attempts on his life? It is essential to carefully consider how seriously Walt is considering suicide before we take up other themes in his life. This may be his cry for help or a signal that in some way he wants me to offer him hope for a better existence. His prior hospitalization for his suicidal tendencies makes it even more imperative that we explore the degree of suicidal danger. I would arrange for a referral or hospitalization if Walt were acutely suicidal. Moreover, I'd let him know that I was legally obliged to take action if I determined that he was likely to take his life.

So much depends ultimately on Walt and what he is willing to choose and do for himself. I must not let myself be duped into thinking that I can create a will to live in him, that I can do his changing for him, or that I will have an answer for him. Where he ends up will largely be determined by *his* willingness to begin to move himself by taking the initial steps. The best I can offer is the inspiration to begin taking those steps. I hope that through our relationship he will see that he can move further than he previously allowed himself to imagine.

## Follow-Up: You Continue as Walt's Therapist

In what directions would you, as an existential therapist, move with Walt?

1. Walt brings out a number of key themes: his wife's death, his forced retirement, relocating from his home in Hawaii to live with his son's family in Wisconsin, his feeling of alienation from the sense of community he once knew, and his personal struggles. Which of these themes (or other ones) would you be most likely to encourage Walt to explore with you? Why?

2. If you are of a different age, gender, and ethnicity from Walt, do you think you'd be able to enter into his subjective world? How would you respond to him if he were to say: "I don't see how you can really understand what I'm going through. You're much younger than I am, you haven't lost your spouse, you don't really know about the culture I grew up in, and you've never felt as hopeless as I sometimes do."

3. The existential approach is based on the therapist seeing the world through the perspective of the client. In Walt's view he is a victim with little chance of changing his destiny. He feels that he is doomed to a meaningless existence, and he has resigned himself to simply marking time. What are the implications if you accept and respond to Walt from his vantage point? How might you help him open up to other possibilities for a different future?

4. How might you respond to Walt's talk about his suicidal fantasies? What would you feel (and probably do) if he told you he was going to kill himself because he saw no real hope for his future?

5. What would you see as your main function as Walt's therapist? Would you want mainly to support him? confront him? guide him into specific activities? teach him skills? be his friend?

## QUIZ ON EXISTENTIAL THERAPY

**A Comprehension Check**

Score _____%

**Note:**  Refer to Appendix 1 for the scoring key.

**True/false items:**  Decide if the following statements are "more true" or "more false" as they apply to existential therapy.

T (F)   1. Existential therapy is best considered as a system of highly developed techniques designed to foster authenticity.

(T) (F)   2. Existential therapists show wide latitude in the techniques they employ.

(T) F   3. According to Sartre, existential guilt is the consciousness of evading commitment to choose for ourselves.

(T) (F)   4. Existentialists maintain that our experience of aloneness is a result of our making inappropriate choices.

(T) F   5. Techniques are secondary in the therapeutic process, and a subjective understanding of the client is primary.

T (F)   6. To its credit, existential therapy derives its findings from empirical testing.

(T) F   7. Part of the human condition is that humans are both free and responsible.

T (F)   8. Anxiety is best considered as a neurotic manifestation; thus, the principal aim of therapy is to eliminate anxiety.

T (F)   9. Existential therapy is primarily classified as a cognitive approach.

(T) F   10. The existential approach is a reaction against *both* psychoanalysis and behaviorism.

**Multiple-choice items:**  Select the *one best answer* of those alternatives given. Consider each question within the framework of existential therapy.

_e_ 11. The basic goal(s) of existential therapy is (are)

    a. to expand self-awareness.

    b. to increase potentials for choice.

    c. to help clients accept the responsibility of choosing.

    d. to help clients experience authentic existence.

    e. all of the above.

_d_ 12. Which is *not* a key concept of existential therapy?

    a. It is based on a personal relationship between client and therapist.

    b. It stresses personal freedom in deciding one's fate.

    c. It places primary value on self-awareness.

    d. It is based on a well-defined set of techniques and procedures.

    e. None of the above is a key concept.

_b_ 13. The function of the existentially oriented counselor is to

    a. develop a specific treatment plan that can be objectively appraised.

    b. challenge the client's irrational beliefs.

    c. understand the client's subjective world.

    d. explore the client's past history in detail.

    e. assist the client in working through transference.

_b_ 14. According to the existential view, anxiety is a

    a. result of repressed sexuality.

    b. part of the human condition.

    c. neurotic symptom that needs to be cured.

    d. result of faulty learning.

_a_ 15. Existential therapy is best considered as

    a. an approach to understanding humans.

    b. a school of therapy.

    c. a system of techniques designed to create authentic humans.

    d. a strategy for uncovering game playing.

_d_ 16. Which might be considered the most crucial quality of a therapist in building an effective therapeutic relationship with a client?

    a. the therapist's knowledge of theory

    b. the therapist's skill in using techniques

    c. the therapist's ability to diagnose accurately

    d. the therapist's authenticity

_a_ 17. The central issue in therapy is

    a. freedom and responsibility.

    b. resistance.

    c. transference.

    d. examining irrational beliefs.

    e. none of the above.

_e_ 18. Guilt and anxiety are viewed as

    a. behaviors that are unrealistic.

    b. the result of traumatic situations in childhood.

    c. conditions that should be removed or cured.

    d. all of the above.

    e. none of the above.

_D_ 19. The existential emphasis is based on

    a. specific behaviors that can be assessed.

    b. a scientific orientation.

    c. a teaching–learning model that stresses the didactic aspects of therapy.

    d. the philosophical concern with what it means to be fully human.

    e. an analysis of our ego states.

_c_ 20. Existential therapy is basically

    a. a behavioral approach.

    b. a cognitive approach.

    c. an experiential approach.

    d. an action-oriented approach.

_____ 21. Existential therapy places emphasis on

   a. a systematic approach to changing behavior.
   b. the quality of the client–therapist relationship.
   c. teaching clients cognitive and behavioral coping skills.
   d. uncovering early childhood traumatic events.
   e. working through the transference relationship.

_____ 22. The central theme running through the works of Viktor Frankl is

   a. that freedom is a myth.
   b. the will to meaning.
   c. self-disclosure as the key to mental health.
   d. the notion of self-actualization.
   e. being thrown into the universe without purpose.

_____ 23. The existential therapist would probably agree that

   a. aloneness is a sign of detachment.
   b. aloneness is a condition that needs to be cured.
   c. ultimately we are alone.
   d. we are alone unless we have a religious faith.
   e. we are alone if we are not loved by others.

_____ 24. The concept of bad faith refers to

   a. not keeping up to date with paying one's therapist.
   b. leading an inauthentic existence.
   c. the failure to cooperate with the therapeutic venture.
   d. the experience of aloneness.
   e. the unwillingness to search for meaning in life.

_____ 25. Which of the following is a limitation of the existential approach in working with culturally diverse client populations?

   a. the focus on understanding and accepting the client
   b. the focus on finding meaning in one's life
   c. the focus on death as a catalyst to living fully
   d. the focus on one's own responsibility rather than on social conditions

# Chapter 7

# Person-Centered Therapy

 PRECHAPTER SELF-INVENTORY

**Directions:** Refer to page 41 for general directions. Use the following code:

5 = I *strongly agree* with this statement.

4 = I *agree*, in most respects, with this statement.

3 = I am *undecided* in my opinion about this statement.

2 = I *disagree*, in most respects, with this statement.

1 = I *strongly disagree* with this statement.

_____ 1. Therapists provide a supportive structure in which clients' self-healing capacities are activated, yet clients are the primary agents of change.

_____ 2. People have the capacity for understanding their problems and the resources for resolving them.

_____ 3. The basic goal of therapy is to create a psychological climate of safety in which clients will not feel threatened and will thus be able to drop their pretenses and defenses.

_____ 4. The therapist's function is rooted not primarily in techniques but in his or her ways of being and attitudes.

_____ 5. Effective therapists use themselves as instruments of change.

_____ 6. The client uses the therapeutic relationship to build new ways of relating to others in the outside world.

_____ 7. The client can make progress in therapy without the therapist's interpretations, diagnoses, evaluations, and directives.

_____ 8. The relationship between the therapist and the client is the crux of progress in therapy.

_____ 9. The therapist's genuineness, accurate empathy, and unconditional positive regard are essential qualities of effective therapy.

_____ 10. It is the therapist's attitudes and belief in the inner resources of the client that create the therapeutic climate for growth.

_____ 11. Forming a diagnosis and developing a case history are not important prerequisites for therapy.

_____ 12. It is important that the therapist avoid being judgmental about a client's feelings.

_____ 13. The therapist's presence is far more powerful than techniques he or she uses to bring about change.

_____ 14. It is important that the therapist, while experiencing empathy with clients, retain his or her own separateness and not get lost in the client's world.

_____ 15. Therapist congruence, or genuineness, is one of the most important conditions for establishing a therapeutic relationship.

_____ 16. It is best that therapists avoid giving advice.

_____ 17. Skills can be taught, but an effective therapist must be grounded, centered, present, focused, patient, and accepting.

_____ 18. Communicating a deep sense of understanding should always precede problem-solving interventions.

_____ 19. The primary responsibility for the direction of therapy rests not with the therapist but with the client.

_____ 20. Exploring transference is neither essential nor significant in the therapeutic process.

# OVERVIEW OF PERSON-CENTERED THERAPY

## Key Figure and Major Focus

Founder: Carl Rogers. A branch of humanistic psychology that stresses a phenomenological approach, person-centered therapy was originally developed in the 1940s as a reaction against psychoanalytic therapy. Based on a subjective view of human experience, it emphasizes the client's resources for becoming self-aware and for resolving blocks to personal growth. It puts the client, not the therapist, at the center of therapy. Rogers did not present his approach as being fixed and completed; rather, he expected the theory and practice to evolve over time.

## Philosophy and Basic Assumptions

The approach is grounded on a positive view of humanity that sees the person as innately striving toward becoming fully functioning. The basic assumption is that it is the therapist's attitudes and belief in the inner resources of the client that create the therapeutic climate for growth. By participating in the therapeutic relationship, clients' self-healing capacities are activated and they become empowered. Clients actualize their potential for growth, wholeness, spontaneity, and inner-directedness. It is not the therapist who primarily brings about change, but the client.

## Key Concepts

A key concept is that clients have the resourcefulness for positive movement. The client has the capacity for resolving life's problems effectively without interpretation and direction from an expert therapist. This approach emphasizes fully experiencing the present moment, learning to accept oneself, and deciding on ways to change. It views mental health as a congruence between what one wants to become and what one actually is.

## Therapeutic Goals

A major goal is to provide a climate of safety and trust in the therapeutic setting so that the client, by using the therapeutic relationship for self-exploration, can become aware of blocks to growth. The client tends to move toward more openness, greater self-trust, more willingness to evolve as opposed to being a fixed product, and more living by internal standards as opposed to taking external cues for what he or she should become. The aim of therapy is not merely to solve problems but to assist in the growth process, which will enable clients to better cope with present and future problems.

## Therapeutic Relationship

Rogers emphasizes the attitudes and personal characteristics of the therapist and the quality of the client–therapist relationship as the prime determinants of the outcomes of therapy. The qualities of the therapist that determine the relationship include genuineness, nonpossessive warmth, accurate empathy, unconditional acceptance of and respect for the client, permissiveness, caring, and the communication of those attitudes to the client. Research has revealed that effective therapy is based on the relationship of the therapist and client in combination with the inner and external resources of the client. The client is able to translate his or her learning in therapy to outside relationships with others.

## Techniques and Procedures

Because the approach stresses the client–therapist relationship, it specifies few techniques. Techniques are secondary to the therapist's attitudes. The approach minimizes directive techniques, interpretation, questioning, probing, diagnosis, and collecting history. It maximizes active listening and hearing, reflection of feelings, and clarification. The full participation of the therapist as a person in the therapeutic relationship is currently being emphasized.

## Applications

The approach has wide applicability to many person-to-person situations. It is a useful model for individual therapy, group counseling, student-centered teaching and learning, parent–child relations, and human relations training labs. The approach has been effectively applied with a wide range of client problems including anxiety disorders, alcoholism, psychosomatic problems, agoraphobia, interpersonal difficulties, depression, cancer, and personality disorders. It is especially well suited for the initial phases of crisis intervention work. Its principles have been applied to administration and management and to working with systems and institutions.

## Contributions

One of the first therapies to break from traditional psychoanalysis, person-centered therapy stresses the active role and responsibility of the client. It is a positive and optimistic view and calls attention to the need to account for a person's inner and subjective experiences. It makes the therapeutic process relationship-centered rather than technique-centered. It focuses on the crucial role of the therapist's attitudes. The model has generated a great deal of clinical research into both the process and the outcomes of therapy, which in turn has led to refining the tentative hypotheses. This approach has been applied to bringing people from diverse cultures together. Empathy, being present, and respecting the values of clients are essential attitudes and skills in counseling culturally diverse clients. Thus, the concepts of this approach have value in working within a multicultural context.

## Limitations

A possible danger is the therapist who, by merely reflecting content, brings little of his or her personhood into the therapeutic relationship. The core conditions are centered more in the therapist's attitudes and values rather than being reflected in skills. Without a person-centered attitude or way of being, mere application of skills are not likely to be effective. The approach has limited use with nonverbal clients. As an ahistorical approach, it tends to discount the significance of the past. Some of the main limitations are due not to the theory itself but to some counselors' misunderstanding of the basic concepts and to their dogmatic practical applications.

## GLOSSARY OF KEY TERMS

**Accurate empathic understanding**   The act of perceiving the internal frame of reference of another, of grasping the person's subjective world, without losing one's own identity.

**Congruence**   The state in which self-experiences are accurately symbolized in the self-concept. As applied to the therapist, congruence is a matching of one's inner experiencing with external expressions.

**Humanistic psychology**   A movement, often referred to as the "third force," that emphasizes freedom, choice, values, growth, self-actualization, becoming, spontaneity, creativity, play, humor, peak experiences, and psychological health.

**Self-actualizing tendency**   A growth force within us; an actualizing tendency leading to the full development of one's potential; the basis on which people can be trusted to identify and resolve their own problems in a therapeutic relationship.

**Therapeutic conditions**   The necessary and sufficient characteristics of the therapeutic relationship for client change to occur. These core conditions include therapist congruence (or genuineness), unconditional positive regard (acceptance and respect), and accurate empathic understanding.

**Unconditional positive regard**   The nonjudgmental expression of a fundamental respect for the person as a human; acceptance of a person's right to his or her feelings.

## QUESTIONS FOR REFLECTION AND DISCUSSION

1. Do you believe most clients have the capacity to understand and resolve their own problems without directive intervention by the therapist? Why or why not?

2. The person-centered view of human nature is grounded on the assumption that people have the tendency to develop in a positive and constructive manner *if* a climate of respect and trust is established. To what degree do you accept this premise?

3. A person-centered approach stresses listening to the deeper meanings of the client's behavior and allowing the client to provide the direction for the session. Are there any circumstances under which you might want to interpret the meaning of your client's behavior? Can you think of any situations in which you might actively intervene by making suggestions or leading your client?

4. In counseling clients who have a different cultural background from yours, what potential advantages or disadvantages can you see in adopting a person-centered perspective?

5. Regardless of which approach guides your practice, the core therapeutic conditions and the type of relationship emphasized in the person-centered approach seem to serve as the foundation for counseling. What are the basic concepts of this theory that you might consider incorporating into your personal style of counseling?

6. What would you do if you did not feel accepting of a certain person? Do you see any conflict between genuineness and acceptance?

7. How congruent, or real, can you be if you withhold your own values, feelings, and attitudes from your client? If you feel like making suggestions but refrain from doing so, are you being inauthentic?

8. What factors might interfere with your being genuine with a client? What about your need for the client's approval? Is there a danger that you might avoid a confrontation because you wanted to be liked?

9. What within you might make accurate empathic understanding difficult for you? Do you have broad life experiences that will help you identify with your client's struggles?

## PRACTICAL APPLICATION: Reflecting Clients' Feelings

**Directions:** The person-centered approach to counseling emphasizes understanding clients from an internal frame of reference. To do that, the therapist must be able to discriminate clients' feelings, hear accurately what messages they are sending, and reflect the deeper meanings that they are attempting to communicate. A common mistake that counselors make is to give a superficial reflection by merely repeating almost the same words the client used. The following exercises are designed to help you learn to grasp the more subtle messages of clients and to reflect feelings as well as content. Of course important nonverbal cues such as tone of voice and facial expressions are not captured in this exercise. Such nonverbal aspects would be most useful in understanding a client's message. First, write down a few key words or phrases that describe what the client is *experiencing*. Second, write down what your response would be if you were to *reflect* to the client what you heard.

**Example:** Woman, 42, tells you: "So often I feel that I'm alone, that nobody cares about me. My husband doesn't seem to notice me, my kids only demand from me, and I just dread getting up in the morning."

a. What is this person experiencing? *Ignored. Unappreciated. Taken advantage of. Unloved. A sense of futility.*

b. Respond by reflecting what you heard. *I sense a lot of loneliness and desperation, a feeling of "What's the use of going on this way?"*

1. Boy, 17, tells you: "I can't stand this school anymore. It doesn't mean anything. I'm bored and frustrated, and I hate school. I feel like dropping out today, but that's stupid because I'm graduating in 2 months."

a. What is this person experiencing? _____

_____

b. Respond by reflecting what you heard. _____

_____

_____

2. Girl, 14, tells you: "I feel like running away from home. My stepfather always criticizes me, and he puts me on restriction for things he claims I do that I don't do. My mother doesn't ever listen to me and always sides with him. They don't trust me at all."

a. What is this person experiencing? _____

_____

b. Respond by reflecting what you heard. _____

_____

_____

3. A fifth-grader tells you: "None of the other kids like me. They always pick on me and tease me. I try real hard to make friends, but everyone hates me."

a. What is this person experiencing? _____

_____

b. Respond by reflecting what you heard. _____

_____

_____

4. Woman teacher, 33, tells you: "I have really noticed a tremendous difference since I've been coming here for counseling. I'm a lot more open with my kids, and they are really noticing a change in me and like it, too! I am even able to talk to my principal without feeling like a scared little kid!"

   a. What is this person experiencing? _____

   _____

   b. Respond by reflecting what you heard. _____

   _____

5. Man, 45, tells you: "I'm so preoccupied since my wife left me that I can't think of anything but her. I keep going over in my head what I could and should have done so she would have stayed. It pisses me off that I can't get her out of my mind and go about my living!"

   a. What is this person experiencing? _____

   _____

   b. Respond by reflecting what you heard. _____

   _____

   _____

6. Man, 27, tells you: "Here I am, still in college and not a damn thing to show for my life. My wife is supporting me, and I know she resents me for not getting out and getting a job before this. But, you know, now I know what I want, and before I was just in school because my parents wanted me to be there."

   a. What is this person experiencing? _____

   _____

   b. Respond by reflecting what you heard. _____

   _____

   _____

 ## JERRY COREY'S WORK WITH RUTH FROM A PERSON-CENTERED PERSPECTIVE

Ruth lets me know how difficult it is for her to talk personally to me, and she tells me that it's especially uncomfortable for her to talk with me because I'm a man. I feel encouraged because she is willing to talk to me about her reservations and brings some of her feelings toward me out in the open.

RUTH: I've become aware that I'm careful about what I say around you. It's important that I feel understood, and sometimes I wonder if you can really understand the struggles I'm having as a woman.

JERRY: Perhaps you could tell me more about your doubts about my ability to understand you as a woman.

RUTH: It's not what you've said so far, but I'm fearful that I have to be careful around you. I'm not sure how you might judge me or react to me.

JERRY: I'd like the chance to relate to you as a person, so I hope you'll let me know when you feel judged or not understood by me.

RUTH: It's not easy for me to talk about myself to any man; all of this is so new to me.

Ruth continues by letting me know that she sometimes feels vulnerable when she talks about herself. She fears that if she shares some of her deepest struggles she will feel exposed. Furthermore, she wonders whether I will be able to really understand her and help her if she does share her feelings. Looking at herself and being the focus of attention is new for her, and she is still wondering about the process.

It is important that we pursue what might get in the way of Ruth's trust in me, for trust is the very foundation of the therapeutic relationship. As long as Ruth is willing to talk about what she is thinking and feeling while we are together in the sessions, we have a direction to follow. Staying with the immediacy of the relationship will inevitably open up other channels of fruitful exploration.

## You Continue Working With Ruth

1. Refer to *Case Approach to Counseling and Psychotherapy* (Chapter 5) for a demonstration of how a person-centered therapist (David Cain) assumes the role of helping Ruth learn how to learn. In this chapter I also demonstrate my style of applying person-centered concepts in counseling Ruth.

2. See the *CD-ROM for Integrative Counseling* (the session on the therapeutic relationship) for a demonstration of exploring person-centered themes in Ruth's life.

3. How would you respond to Ruth if she were to express her doubts about your capacity to understand her situation?

4. What steps can you think of taking to build a relationship with Ruth based on trust? How might you address Ruth's fears of feeling exposed and vulnerable as she shares parts of her life with you?

5. How comfortable would you feel without relying on techniques but dealing mainly with the immediacy between you and Ruth and following her leads for further exploration?

## DON: FEELING PRESSURE TO PROVE HIMSELF

### Some Background Data

Don, a major in the U.S. Air Force, comes to see me on a referral from a military doctor. He is of Latino background, is married, and has two daughters and two sons. As a member of a minority group, he feels under tremendous pressure to prove himself as an exceptional leader. He has encountered many obstacles in his attempt to rise through the military ranks. He is doing everything possible to get a promotion to lieutenant colonel, and ultimately he would like to be at least a "bird" colonel.

Don consulted with his physician because of continuing chest pains. Even though he is only in his mid-30s, he has had two mild heart attacks. These resulted in his being hospitalized and having to take a leave of absence. He is about 30 pounds overweight, has high blood pressure, has a high cholesterol level, smokes cigarettes, suffers at times from angina, and develops severe headaches that are chronic under stressful situations. His physician insisted that if he wanted to live he would have to learn to relax and deal with stress more constructively. Because his doctor was convinced that Don needed psychological as well as medical treatment, he was referred to me.

### Jerry Corey's Way of Working With Don From a Person-Centered Perspective

At our first meeting Don fills me in on his medical problems. He also talks of his feelings about being sent to see a psychologist and of how he hopes to benefit from our contact. He lets me know how unusual it is for him to ask for help with his personal life. He cannot remember a time that he felt a need to talk about personal matters. As he puts it, "If there is a job to be done, you get to it and do it." Our dialogue proceeds.

DON: Well, Doctor, it's really hard for me to admit that I have to ask for outside help. I mean, no offense or anything, but I don't need a shrink.

JERRY: I'd like to hear how it feels for you to be here now. Could you tell me in what ways seeing me is hard for you?

DON: Sure. I thought I'd never die, until I had my first heart attack, and then I realized that I might kick over long before my time. It's hard enough for me to admit that my body can't take it. Now to be told that I have mental problems that I also have to learn to deal with—that's too much.

JERRY: It seems easier to do something about your physical problems than to do something about your feelings.

DON: The physician I've been seeing says there's not much more he can do for me, besides give me the medication. I know my job has stress. I can handle my own responsibilities, but being expected to make sure that the other men under me follow through almost does me in. I worry constantly about whether they'll pull their end.

JERRY: As you talk, I hear how unsupported you feel, as well as how difficult it is for you to carry the weight for the rest of your men. You have all this burden on your shoulders.

DON: If I don't keep a close watch on the entire operation, everything is liable to go to pot. I can't live with myself knowing that I haven't done all that was expected of me—and then some.

JERRY: As I look at you, I see the weariness in your face. You look *very* tired and extremely tense. Sitting with you here I can feel your tension. It seems that you don't see any way out of assuming all this responsibility.

DON: I don't see any answer. I do feel exhausted and very tight. That's just the way I am— and that's the way it has always been. But I don't know how to change that.

JERRY: You say that it has always been that way. Could you say more?

DON [*a long pause and then a sigh*]: I just keep asking myself what's wrong with me that I can't take this stress more in stride. I *should* be able to get the job done without my body giving out on me. This is a hard one for me to take!

JERRY: Your body is speaking a loud message, and yet you're not willing to listen to what it's telling you. I sense how hard it is for you to accept that you can't manage everything in life by yourself.

DON: You're hearing me! I don't like being superman *all* of the time.

## Some Observations on Our Session

During this first session, I'm interested in seeing the world through Don's eyes. I want to understand what it's like for him to feel driven to prove himself, to be consistently strong, to meet all his obligations (and then some), to take on the responsibilities of everyone, and to keep moving ahead even if it kills him. At the same time I want him to know I have some understanding of how his life is. But I want to do more than merely reflect what I hear him saying.

I do want to get Don to begin to look at the obvious signs his body is sending him. I hope he can allow himself to tune in to his own tiredness and his own pain at always having to be strong. Without pushing my values on him and encouraging him to assume goals that are mine, I hope he can pay attention to what he is experiencing and the price he is paying for living in certain ways.

I do not think that Don will change merely from my telling him that he *should* be different—that he should allow himself to be "weak," should delegate responsibilities, or should slow down and take it easy. He has heard this from his physician, and he *knows* (intellectually) that this is what he should do; yet he *feels* (emotionally) that he has to stay together at all costs. My assumption is that he will be more open to change if I encourage him to share openly with me what it feels like for him to live the way he does. I hope that he will begin to question how hard he is on himself and that he may eventually challenge himself on the necessity of maintaining such standards.

In getting Don to take this look at himself, I will share what is being evoked in me, especially my tenseness and tiredness as I try to be with him. If I am myself with him, he is more likely to be himself with me. He may be willing to reveal whatever he is attempting to cover up by a show of strength. I do not need to give him answers, even though on some level he would like to know "the way" to cope with stress. If I can stay with him and encourage him to express whatever he is feeling, this expression will provide the needed direction for us to move in future sessions. He is giving plenty of clues to pursue, if I will listen and follow them. I do not need to rely on techniques to get him to open up or techniques to resolve his problems. The best I can offer Don is the relationship that we develop, regardless of how brief it may be. If I am able to accept him in a nonjudgmental way, I see a good chance that he will begin to listen to himself (including his body) and that he will grow toward self-acceptance, which can be the beginning of real change for him.

## Follow-Up: You Continue as Don's Therapist

1. How do you see Don? What are the major themes of his life that need to be focused on and explored more fully? How do you personally respond to him?

2. Assume that I were to refer Don to you for continued therapy (in the person-centered style). How do you imagine it would be for you to work with him? How might a person such as Don relate to you?

3. Assuming that you will be seeing Don for at least six more sessions, what specific issues do you most want to explore? How might you go about doing this with him?

4. Coming from a Latino cultural background, Don has certain notions of what it means to be a man. His self-concept and his masculine definition of self include being strong at all times, being able to handle his responsibilities, not showing signs of weakness, and being able to keep up with the other men he knows. Would you expect to have any difficulty in respecting his cultural differences and at the same time challenging him to examine his beliefs? What other cultural variables would you want to consider in your counseling with him?

5. This session with Don was characterized by my listening and responding to him rather than by my active intervention with therapeutic procedures and techniques. Do you think you would feel comfortable staying in such a role in your work with Don? Why or why not? Are there other techniques you might want to introduce?

## QUIZ ON PERSON-CENTERED THERAPY

### A Comprehension Check

Score _____%

**Note:** Refer to Appendix 1 for the scoring key.

**True/false items:** Decide if the following statements are "more true" or "more false" as they apply to person-centered therapy.

T (F) 1. Person-centered therapy is best described as a completed and fixed "school," or model, of therapy.

T (F) 2. Diagnosis of clients is seen as an important beginning point for therapy.

(T) F 3. A major contribution of this approach has been the willingness of Rogers to state his formulations as testable hypotheses and submit them to research.

T (F) 4. Accurate empathic understanding implies an objective understanding of a client and some form of diagnosis.

T (F) 5. Directive procedures are called for when clients feel that they are "stuck" in therapy.

(T) (F) 6. Free association is a basic part of this therapy.

(T) F 7. This approach holds that the direction of therapy is the primary responsibility of the client, not the therapist.

T (F) 8. A limitation of this approach is that it is a long-term process.

T (F) 9. Transference is seen as the core of this therapy.

(T) F 10. Interpretations by the therapist typically tend to interfere with client growth, according to Rogers.

**Multiple-choice items:** Select the *one best answer* of those alternatives given. Consider each question within the framework of person-centered therapy.

_e_ 11. The founder of person-centered therapy is

a. Rollo May.
b. Frederick Perls.
c. Abraham Maslow.
d. B. F. Skinner.
e. none of the above.

_b_ 12. Person-centered therapy is a form of

a. psychoanalysis.
b. humanistic therapy.
c. behavioral therapy.
d. cognitive-oriented therapy.
e. both (c) and (d).

_e_ 13. Which of the following is (are) considered important in person-centered therapy?

a. accurate diagnosis
b. accurate therapist interpretation
c. analysis of the transference relationship
d. all of the above
e. none of the above

_a_ 14. Congruence refers to the therapist's

a. genuineness.
b. empathy for clients.
c. positive regard.
d. respect for clients.
e. judgmental attitude.

_e_ 15. In person-centered therapy, transference is

a. a necessary, but not sufficient, condition of therapy.
b. a core part of the therapeutic process.
c. a neurotic distortion.
d. a result of ineptness on the therapist's part.
e. not an essential or significant factor in the therapy process.

_d_ 16. Unconditional positive regard implies

a. the therapist's acceptance of the client's right to all his or her feelings.
b. the therapist's acceptance of the client as a person of worth.
c. acceptance of all the client's past behavior.
d. both (a) and (b).

_d_ 17. Accurate empathic understanding refers to the therapist's ability to

a. accurately diagnose the client's central problem.
b. objectively understand the dynamics of a client.
c. like and care for the client.
d. sense the inner world of the client's subjective experience.

_____d_____ 18. Which technique(s) is (are) most often used in the person-centered approach?

    a. questioning and probing
    b. analysis of resistance
    c. free association
    d. active listening and reflection
    e. interpretation

_____d_____ 19. Which statement is most true of person-centered theory?

    a. Therapists should be judgmental at times.
    b. Therapists should direct the session when clients are silent.
    c. The skill a therapist possesses is more important than his or her attitude toward a client.
    d. The techniques a therapist uses are less important than are his or her attitudes.
    e. Both (a) and (b) are true.

_____e_____ 20. Which of the following is a contribution of the person-centered viewpoint?

    a. It calls attention to the need to account for a person's inner experience.
    b. It relies on research to validate the concepts and practices of the approach.
    c. It provides the therapist with a variety of therapeutic techniques.
    d. It focuses on an objective view of behavior.
    e. Both (a) and (b) are contributions.

_____d_____ 21. One strength of the person-centered approach is that

    a. it offers a wide range of cognitive techniques to change behavior.
    b. it teaches clients ways to explore the meaning of dreams.
    c. it emphasizes reliving one's early childhood memories.
    d. therapists have the latitude to develop their own counseling style.
    e. clients are given a concrete plan to follow.

_____b_____ 22. A limitation of the person-centered approach is a

    a. lack of research conducted on key concepts.
    b. tendency for practitioners to give support without challenging clients sufficiently.
    c. lack of attention to the therapeutic relationship.
    d. failure to allow clients to choose for themselves.

_____e_____ 23. Rogers made a contribution to

    a. developing the humanistic movement in psychotherapy.
    b. pioneering research in the process and outcomes of therapy.
    c. fostering world peace.
    d. pioneering the encounter-group movement.
    e. all of the above.

_____e_____ 24. As a result of experiencing person-centered therapy, it is hypothesized, the client will move toward

    a. self-trust.
    b. an internal source of evaluation.
    c. being more open to experience.
    d. a willingness to continue growing.
    e. all of the above.

_____b_____ 25. Unconditional positive regard refers to

    a. feeling a sense of liking for clients.
    b. accepting clients as worthy persons.
    c. approving of clients' behavior.
    d. agreeing with clients' values.
    e. accepting clients if they meet the therapist's expectations.

Chapter **8**

# Gestalt
# Therapy

## PRECHAPTER SELF-INVENTORY

**Directions:** Refer to page 41 for general directions. Use the following code:

5 = I *strongly agree* with this statement.

4 = I *agree*, in most respects, with this statement.

3 = I am *undecided* in my opinion about this statement.

2 = I *disagree*, in most respects, with this statement.

1 = I *strongly disagree* with this statement.

_____ 1. Growth occurs out of genuine contact between therapist and client more than from the therapist's interpretations or methods.

_____ 2. Therapy aims at awareness, contact with the environment, and integration.

_____ 3. The here-and-now focus of therapy is more important than a focus on the past or on the future.

_____ 4. It is more fruitful for the therapist to ask "what" and "how" questions than to ask "why" questions.

_____ 5. Rather than merely talking about feelings and experiences in therapy, it is more productive for clients to relive and reexperience those feelings as though they were happening now.

_____ 6. One's past is important to the degree that it is related to significant themes in one's present functioning.

_____ 7. A major therapeutic function is to devise experiments designed to increase clients' self-awareness of what they are doing and how they are doing it.

_____ 8. A primary aim of therapy is to expand a person's capacity for self-awareness, which is seen as curative in itself.

_____ 9. Awareness includes insight, self-acceptance, knowledge of the environment, responsibility for choices, and the ability to make contact with others.

_____ 10. Unfinished business from the past usually manifests itself in present problems in functioning effectively.

_____ 11. We change when we become aware of *what we are* as opposed to trying to become *what we are not*.

_____ 12. Focusing on the past can be a way to avoid coming to terms with the present.

_____ 13. Effective contact means interacting with nature and with other people without losing one's sense of individuality.

_____ 14. Therapy best focuses on the client's feelings, present awareness, body messages, and blocks to awareness.

_____ 15. The therapist's main function is to assist the client in gaining awareness of the "what" and "how" of experiencing in the here-and-now.

_____ 16. The therapist should avoid diagnosing, interpreting, and explaining at length the client's behavior.

_____ 17. In therapy it is extremely important to pay attention to the client's body language and other nonverbal cues.

_____ 18. As therapy progresses, the client can be expected to assume increasing responsibility for his or her own thoughts, feelings, and behavior.

_____ 19. It is important that therapists actively share their own present perceptions and experiences as they encounter clients in the here-and-now.

_____ 20. The most effective experiments grow out of genuine interaction between client and therapist and generally help clients gain increased awareness of fragmented and disowned aspects of themselves.

## OVERVIEW OF GESTALT THERAPY

### Key Figures and Major Focus

Founders: Frederick ("Fritz") Perls and Laura Perls. Other key figures: the late Miriam Polster and Erving Polster. The approach is an experiential therapy that stresses here-and-now awareness and integration of the fragmented parts of the personality. It focuses on the "what" and "how" of behavior and on the role of unfinished business from the past in preventing effective functioning in the present.

### Philosophy and Basic Assumptions

Gestalt therapy is an existential–phenomenological approach based on the premise that individuals must be understood in the context of their ongoing relationship with the environment. The approach is designed to help people experience the present moment more fully and gain awareness of what they are doing. The approach is _experiential_ in that clients come to grips with what they are thinking, feeling, and doing as they interact with the therapist. Growth occurs through the I/Thou relationship rather than through the therapist's techniques or interpretations. This dialogic approach creates the ground for contact and experiments that are spontaneous and organic to the moment-to-moment experience of the therapeutic engagement. Clients are assumed to have the capacity to do their own seeing, feeling, sensing, and interpreting. Client autonomy is fostered, and clients are expected to be active in therapy.

### Key Concepts

Key concepts are the here-and-now, direct (as opposed to talked-about) experiencing, awareness, bringing unfinished business from the past into the present, and dealing with impasses. Other concepts include energy and blocks to energy, contact and resistances to contact, and body work and nonverbal cues. Five major channels of resistance are challenged in Gestalt therapy: introjection, projection, retroflection, confluence, and deflection. Some basic principles of Gestalt therapy are holism, field theory, the figure-formation process, and organismic self-regulation.

### Therapeutic Goals

The goal is attaining awareness and greater choice. Awareness includes knowing the environment and knowing oneself, accepting oneself, and being able to make contact. Clients are helped to note their own awareness process so that they can be responsible and can selectively and discriminatingly make choices. Awareness emerges within the context of the I/Thou relationship between client and therapist. With awareness the client is able to recognize denied aspects of the self and proceed toward reintegration of all its parts.

## Therapeutic Relationship

This approach stresses the I/Thou relationship. The focus is not on the techniques employed by the therapist but on who the therapist is as a person and what the therapist is doing. Contemporary Gestalt therapy stresses factors such as presence, authentic dialogue, gentleness, more direct self-expression by the therapist, decreased use of stereotypic exercises, and a greater trust in the client's experiencing. The counselor assists clients in experiencing all feelings more fully and lets them make their own interpretations. The therapist does not interpret for clients but focuses on the "what" and "how" of their behavior. Clients identify their own unfinished business from the past that is interfering with their present functioning by reexperiencing past situations as though they were happening at the present moment.

## Techniques and Procedures

Although the therapist functions as a guide and a catalyst, presents experiments, and shares observations, the basic work of therapy is done by the client. Technical expertise is important, but the therapeutic engagement is paramount. Therapists do not force change on clients; rather, they create experiments within a context of the I/Thou dialogue in a here-and-now framework. These experiments are the cornerstone of experiential learning. Although the therapist suggests the experiments, this is a collaborative process with full participation by the client. Gestalt experiments take many forms: setting up a dialogue between a client and a significant person in his or her life; assuming the identity of a key figure through role playing; reliving a painful event; exaggerating a gesture, posture, or some nonverbal mannerism; or carrying on a dialogue between two conflicting aspects within an individual. Clients often engage in role playing. By playing out all the various parts and polarities alone, clients gain greater awareness of the conflicts within themselves. For effective application of Gestalt procedures, it is essential that clients be prepared for such experiments. Client resistance is fertile material for exploration. It is essential that therapists respect the client's resistance and not force participation in any experiment.

## Applications

The approach is well suited to group work, but it can also be used for individual counseling. It is applicable to elementary and secondary classrooms. In deciding the appropriateness of employing Gestalt techniques, questions of "when," "with whom," and "in what situation" should be raised. The techniques are most effectively applied to overly socialized, restrained, and constricted individuals, and they can be useful in working with couples and families. These techniques are less applicable for more severely disturbed individuals. The methods are powerful catalysts for opening up feelings and getting clients into contact with their present-centered experience.

## Contributions

By encouraging direct contact and the expression of feelings, the approach deemphasizes abstract intellectualization of one's problems. Intense experiencing can occur quickly, so therapy can be relatively brief. The approach recognizes the value of working with the past as it is important to the here-and-now. Its focus is on recognition of one's own projections and the refusal to accept helplessness and emphasizes doing and experiencing as opposed to merely talking about problems in a detached way. Gestalt therapy gives attention to nonverbal and body messages. It provides a perspective on growth and enhancement, not merely a treatment of disorders. The method of working with dreams is a creative pathway to increased awareness of key existential messages in life.

## Limitations

In the hands of an ineffective therapist Gestalt procedures can become a series of mechanical exercises behind which the therapist as a person can remain hidden. The theoretical grounds of Gestalt therapy leave something to be desired. Moreover, there is a potential for the therapist to manipulate the client with these powerful methods. Training and supervision in Gestalt therapy are essential, as well as self-knowledge and introspection on the therapist's part.

## GLOSSARY OF KEY TERMS

**Awareness**   The process of attending to and observing one's own sensing, thinking, feelings, and actions; paying attention to the flowing nature of one's present-centered experience.

**Confluence**   A disturbance in which the sense of the boundary between self and environment is lost.

**Confrontation**   An invitation for the client to become aware of discrepancies between verbal and nonverbal expressions, between feelings and actions, or between thoughts and feelings.

**Contact**   The process of interacting with nature and with other people without losing one's sense of individuality. Contact is made by seeing, hearing, smelling, touching, and moving.

**Deflection**   A way of avoiding contact and awareness by being vague and indirect.

**Dichotomy**   A split by which a person experiences or sees opposing forces; a polarity (weak/strong, dependent/independent).

**Experiments**   Procedures aimed at encouraging spontaneity and inventiveness by bringing the possibilities for action directly into the therapy session. Experiments are designed to enhance here-and-now awareness. They are activities clients try out as a way of testing new ways of thinking, feeling, and behaving.

**Field theory**   Paying attention to and exploring what is occurring at the boundary between the person and the environment.

**Holism**   Attending to a client's thoughts, feelings, behaviors, body, and dreams.

**Impasse**   The stuck point in a situation in which individuals believe they are unable to support themselves and thus seek external support.

**Introjection**   The uncritical acceptance of others' beliefs and standards without assimilating them into one's own personality.

**Projection**   The process by which we disown certain aspects of ourselves by ascribing them to the environment; the opposite of introjection.

**Retroflection**   The act of turning back onto ourselves something we would like to do (or have done) to someone else.

**Unfinished business**   Unexpressed feelings (such as resentment, guilt, anger, grief) dating back to childhood that now interfere with effective psychological functioning; needless emotional debris that clutters present-centered awareness.

## QUESTIONS FOR REFLECTION AND DISCUSSION

1. What are the values and limitations of the Gestalt focus on the here-and-now? Do you think this approach adequately deals with one's past and one's future? Explain.

2. Gestalt therapy discourages "why" questions and focuses instead on the "what" and "how" of experiencing. What are your reactions to this emphasis? Do you agree or disagree that "why" questions generally lead to heady ruminations?

3. Gestalt therapy tends to focus on what people are *feeling* moment to moment. Does this emphasis preclude thinking about one's experiencing? Explain.

4. Gestalt therapists are often confrontational in their work. Although this confrontation can be done in a gentle way with care, respect, and sensitivity for clients, there are also some dangers. In your view what risks are inherent in using confrontation?

5. How comfortable do you think you would be using some of the experiments described in this chapter? Do you think it is important that *you* experience these experiments first *as a client* before you attempt to use them with others? How might you prepare your clients so that they would be more likely to benefit from Gestalt experiments?

6. In Gestalt therapy the past is dealt with by asking the client to bring it into the present and to confront significant people as though they were present. The emphasis is on having clients embody some conflict *now*, as opposed to merely talking about an issue. What are your reactions to such an approach?

7. How can unfinished business from the past affect current functioning? Can you think of any unfinished business in your life that has a significant influence on you today? How might Gestalt methods work for you in these areas?

8. Assume that you work with a wide variety of ethnic minority clients in a community agency. Given the challenges of meeting the needs of this diverse population, what promise do you see in employing certain Gestalt techniques? What are potential pitfalls when using Gestalt experiments with culturally diverse clients?

9. Gestalt therapy and person-centered therapy share some philosophical views regarding human nature. But Gestalt therapy relies on active experimentation initiated by the therapist, whereas person-centered therapy deemphasizes techniques and therapist direction. Do you see any basis for integrating Gestalt approaches with some person-centered concepts? Why or why not?

10. What are the implications of Gestalt therapy for your own personal growth? How can you use some of the techniques, experiments, and concepts as a way of furthering self-understanding and promoting personality change in yourself?

## ISSUES AND QUESTIONS FOR PERSONAL APPLICATION

1. When a person talks about a problem in the past, he or she is asked to reenact the drama as though it were occurring *now* by "being there" in fantasy and reliving the experience psychologically. Following are two brief examples, one of a client talking about a problem with his father and the other of the client talking directly (in fantasy) to his father.

> *Example 1:* When I was a kid, my father was never around. I wanted him to give me some approval and recognize that I existed. Instead, he was always doing other things. I know I was scared of him and hated him a bit for not being more of a father, but I just kept on feeling rejected by him. I guess that's why I have such a hell of a time showing affection to my own kids—I never really got any love from him. Do you suppose that's why I can't get *really* close to my own kids now?

Assume that you are a Gestalt therapist. Instead of answering the client's last question, you ask him to *talk directly* to his father—that is, to be 16 years old again and to say in fantasy what he was not able to say then to his father. Ask him to relive his feelings of rejection as though they were happening now and to tell his father what he is experiencing.

> *Example 2:* You know, Dad, I hurt so much because all I really want is for you just to say that I mean something to you. I keep trying to please you, and

no matter how hard I try, you never notice me. Damn it, I don't think there's anything I could ever do to make you care for me. I get so scared of you, because I'm afraid you'll beat me up if I let you know what I'm feeling. If I only knew what it would take to please you!

Do you see any qualitative difference between the two examples? Do you think the latter could lead the client to experience his feelings of rejection more fully than by merely talking about the rejection in an intellectual way? Now select a problem or concern that *you* have, and do two things: (1) deliberately talk about your problem, and (2) attempt, through fantasy, to put the problem into the here-and-now. What differences do you notice between the two approaches?

2. Unfinished business generally involves unexpressed feelings such as resentment, rage, hatred, pain, anxiety, grief, guilt, rejection, and so on. Because those feelings are not expressed, they are carried into the present in ways that interfere with effective contact with oneself and with others. Identify some aspect of unfinished business in your life now. How do you think it might affect you in your work as a counselor? Do you see any potential conflicts in working with your clients' unfinished business if you have the same problem?

3. According to Perls, it is imperative to express resentments, because unexpressed resentment is converted into guilt. Try this experiment: Make a spontaneous list of all your conscious guilt feelings. Then, change the word *guilt* to *resentment* and see if it is appropriate. For example, you might say, "I feel *guilty* because I don't make enough money to support my wife and kids in elegant style." Now, change the word *guilty* to *resentful*. Do this for every item on your list of things that you feel guilty about.

4. Gestalt therapists speak about "catastrophic expectations" that lead us to feel stuck. We imagine some terrible thing will happen if _____. List some threatening feelings or catastrophic fantasies that keep you from taking certain risks. What are some of your unreasonable fears? What risks do you avoid taking because of those expectations? How might you attempt to help a client deal with his or her catastrophic expectations?

## SUGGESTED ACTIVITIES AND EXERCISES

**Directions:** Some Gestalt techniques lend themselves to being experienced in a classroom setting. Before you do the following exercises, review the description of the Gestalt exercises in the textbook. Experiment with the use of the techniques by applying them to yourself in the classroom setting. The example provided for the first exercise will help you get into focus.

### The Internal Dialogue Exercise

A person is engaged in a struggle between wanting to remain married and longing for the freedom of not being committed to anyone. The person is asked to sit in the center of the room, where two pillows are placed, and he carries on a dialogue between the two conflicting parts: the "committed side" and the "uncommitted side."

COMMITTED: It feels great to feel special and to feel loved by a woman, and I like being married to my wife most of the time.

UNCOMMMITTED: Sure, but some of the time marriage is a drag. It gets old and stale living with just one woman. Think of all the fun I'm missing by limiting myself.

COMMITTED: But think of all the possible risks of getting rejected. Besides I *do* like what I have now. It could get awfully lonely trying to meet new people.

UNCOMMITTED: And it could also be very exciting. Now I'm not free, so even though I'm not lonely, I'm not excited.

COMMITTED: But it's not worth the price of putting my marriage in danger in the hope of finding more excitement.

UNCOMMITTED: Is my marriage worth that much if I won't challenge it? Think of all the things I could do as a single person!

Now consider some type of polarity, or inner conflict, that you are struggling with, and carry on a dialogue between both parts. For example, your conflicts might be between your need to be loved and your need to tell yourself that you don't need anything from anybody, between your need to be tender and gentle and your need for aggression or toughness, or between your fighting side and your side that wants to give up.

## The Reversal Technique

This exercise is sometimes useful when a person has attempted to deny or disown a side of his or her personality. For example, one who plays the role of "tough guy" may be covering up a gentle side. Or one who is always excessively nice may be trying to deny or disown negative feelings toward others. Select one of your traits, and then assume the opposite characteristic as fully as possible. What is the experience like for you? What value or limitations, or both, do you see in this technique?

## The Rehearsal Exercise

Much of our thinking is rehearsing. It is almost as though we rehearse, in fantasy, performances we think we are expected to play. In this exercise select some situation where you might typically be rehearsing all kinds of pros and cons. Then "rehearse" out loud. Act out all the things that you might experience inwardly. Try to get the feel of the exercise. For example, you might consider such situations as volunteering for something, asking a person for a date, applying for a job, or facing someone you are afraid of.

## The Exaggeration Exercise

This exercise is designed to call attention to body language and nonverbal cues. For this exercise, *exaggerate* some movement—a mannerism or a gesture—repeatedly. For example, if you habitually smile (even when you feel hurt or angry), exaggerate this smile. Really get into it, smiling as broadly as you can before each group member. Another example is to exaggerate a frown if you habitually tend to frown. Go around to each person and intensify your frowning. Other examples of behavior that are used for the exaggeration technique are pointing a finger at people, crossing arms tightly, nervous tapping of feet, clenching of fists, and shaking of hands. What do you experience as you exaggerate certain of your behaviors? What therapeutic value do you see in this technique? What limitations?

## JERRY COREY'S WORK WITH RUTH FROM A GESTALT THERAPY PERSPECTIVE

In dealing with Ruth's past I ask her to enact certain critical events that come to her awareness. In one of our sessions Ruth recalls an early experience with sexual experimentation in which she was discovered by her father. I ask her not merely to report what happened but also to bring her father into the room now and talk to him about the feelings she is experiencing. She goes back to a past event and relives it—the time at 6 years old when she was reprimanded by her father in the bedroom. She begins by saying how scared she was then and how she did not know what to say to him after he had caught her in sexual play. I encourage her to stay with her scared feelings and to tell her father all the things that she was feeling then but did not say. Ruth says some of the following in the enactment: "I feel so ashamed that I let you down. It's hard for me to look at you. I feel guilty for what I did, and I don't know what to say to you. I am so afraid that you will never love me now for what I've done."

With the use of this Gestalt intervention, Ruth is reexperiencing some of the feelings she actually felt at the time her father found her with a neighbor boy. Ruth is no longer merely reporting an event; as she symbolically talks to her father, she is living this vivid life situation. Some possibilities for further work are:

- Ruth can stay with whatever surfaces in her awareness and continue her dialogue with her father.
- Ruth can "become her father," saying some of the things she suspects he thought and felt then.
- Ruth might alternate in a dialogue, allowing herself to be the child and tell her father what it was like for her to be found out and then becoming the father and telling Ruth what he thinks of her.
- Ruth could assume the role of the ideal father. Through symbolically becoming her father she could say what she wished he would have said then.
- Ruth can talk to her father in a role play and address the ways she is presently affected by his response to her sexual curiosity.

## You Continue Working With Ruth

1. Refer to *Case Approach to Counseling and Psychotherapy* (Chapter 6) for a Gestalt therapists' perspective (Jon Frew) on Ruth's case. In this chapter I also illustrate my Gestalt orientation in working with Ruth.
2. See the *CD-ROM for Integrative Counseling* (the session on exploring the past) for a demonstration creating Gestalt experiments with Ruth.
3. From a Gestalt framework, what interventions would you make in helping Ruth deal with her feelings of shame and guilt?
4. What kind of role-playing possibilities would be useful in exploring the impact of this early event?
5. What value do you see in dealing with a past event by asking Ruth to bring her work into the here-and-now?

 ## CHRISTINA: A Student Works With Her Feelings Toward Her Supervisor and Her Father

### Some Background Data

Christina is a former student in my group counseling class. She says that she was constantly uncomfortable in the class, that the group class and I threatened her, and that she would like to deal with some of the feelings she sat on during that entire semester. She has taken the initiative to ask for an individual counseling session to work on these feelings and on her relationship with me.

### Jerry Corey's Way of Working With Christina From a Gestalt Therapy Perspective

JERRY: What would you like to get from this session, Christina?

CHRISTINA: I just get so down on myself for the way I let other people make me feel unimportant. I really became aware of this in your class. So I want to work on the feelings I had toward you then.

JERRY: Feelings you *had*? If you still have any of those feelings now, I'd like to hear more about them.

CHRISTINA: Oh, I suppose I still have those feelings, or at least it wouldn't be too difficult to get them back again. I just don't like the way you make me feel, Jerry.

JERRY: I still don't know what *those feelings* are, but I do know you're making me responsible for them—I make you feel? I don't like being put in that position.

CHRISTINA: Well, you *do* make me feel inadequate when I'm around you. I'm afraid to approach you because you seem so busy, and I think you'll just brush me off. I don't want to give you the chance *not* to listen to me. I'm afraid you won't have time to hear my feelings, so that's why I stayed away from you that semester I had your class.

Without getting defensive, I want to let Christina know that I would like to be allowed to decide whether I have the time or the willingness to listen to her. I do not like being written off in advance or being told *who* I am and *how* I am without being given the chance to speak for myself. I let her know this directly, because I think my honest reactions toward what she is saying will be a vital component to building the kind of relationship between us that is needed to deal effectively with her feelings. Further, I call her on her unwillingness to accept responsibility for her own feelings, as expressed in her statements of "You make me feel . . ."

JERRY: If you're willing, I'd like to try an experiment. Would you just rattle off all the ways that you can think of that you feel around me, and after listing each of them, I'd like you to add *"and you make me feel that way!"* OK?

CHRISTINA: Sure, now I get my chance. This could be fun! Are you ready for this? When I'm around you, I feel so small and so inadequate—and you make me feel this way! When I'm around you, I feel judged. I feel that whatever I do isn't what you expect, and that whatever I do it won't be enough to please you—and you make me feel that way! [*She seems more excited and is getting into the exercise with her voice and her postures and gestures.*] I have to read all those damn books for the course. And then I feel I'll never be able to write papers that are clear enough for you, and I'll feel stupid and inferior. And it's *your* fault that I feel this way—you *make* me feel this way! You're always rushing around doing so many things that I can't catch you long enough to get you to listen to me. Then I feel unimportant—and *you* make me feel this way.

I want Christina to say out loud many of the things that I imagine she has said silently to herself. As she lists all the ways she feels around me, as well as restating over and over that I make her feel those ways, I listen and encourage her to continue. I want her to become aware of her resentments and *experience her feelings*, not just talk abstractly about them. I see this awareness as essential before any change can occur. While she is doing this, I pay attention to *how* she is delivering her message. Her body provides excellent leads to follow up on. I listen for changes in the tone and pitch of her voice. I notice any discrepancies between her words and her facial expressions. I pay attention to her pointed finger or to her clenched fist. I notice her tapping foot. I also notice her blushing, her moist eyes, and any changes in her posture. I frequently check in with her on what she is feeling right now. This determines the direction we take next.

JERRY: What are you experiencing now?

CHRISTINA: I'm afraid you're judging me.

JERRY: What do you imagine I'm saying about you?

CHRISTINA: You're thinking I'm really immature and stupid. I'm feeling small again. And I'm also feeling vulnerable . . . weak . . . helpless . . . but mostly as if you're up there and I'm down here looking up at you. And I don't like feeling little and making you that important.

JERRY: What would your "littleness" say to me now?

CHRISTINA: I'm feeling hopeless. As if I'll never be able to touch you or really reach you. [*a long pause follows*]

JERRY: What are you experiencing now?

CHRISTINA: I'm thinking about my father.

JERRY: What about your father? Let me be him, and you talk to me.

CHRISTINA: I'll never be able to touch you or really reach you. I feel so dumb with you. [*another long pause*]

JERRY: And what else do you want to say to your father right now?

CHRISTINA: I'd love to really be able to talk to you.

JERRY: You're talking to him right now. He's listening. Tell him more.

CHRISTINA: I've always been scared of you. I'd so much like to spend time with you and tell you about my pains and joys. I like that you're listening to me now. It feels so good.

JERRY: It feels good . . . What is *it*?

CHRISTINA [*smilingly*]: I feel good. [*another pause*]

JERRY: What do you want to do next?

CHRISTINA: I'd like to give you a hug, Dad. [*She gives Dad a hug, sits down.*]

JERRY: You look different now than earlier.

CHRISTINA: I feel more at peace with myself.

JERRY: Anything else you'd like to say?

CHRISTINA: To my Dad or to you?

JERRY: To either or both of us?

CHRISTINA: You know, Jerry, right now you don't seem so much *up there* as you did. I think I could actually talk to you now and feel straight across with you—in fact, I'm feeling that way now. It feels good to me not to give you all that power, and the more I talk, the less scared I feel. Right now I'm feeling a real strength. I think you can see me for what I am, and I *am* worth something! I *am* important! And looking at you now, I feel that you're with me and that you're *not* judging me and putting me down. I'm feeling good saying all this.

JERRY: Sitting across from you and looking at your face now and hearing you, I'm feeling good too. I don't like being put in unreachable places and then told how distant I am. I feel good sensing a quiet power in you, and I really like the way you are with me.

I continue by telling her some of the observations I had of her work and sharing what I was feeling at different points in our dialogue. I also tell her how I experience her very differently when she is soft, yet direct and powerful, instead of whining and giving me critical glances. I again offer her support and recognize the difficulty of her work.

## Commentary on the Session

Gestalt techniques are powerful ways to help bring feelings out and into focus. There is a vitality to Christina's work as she lets herself assume the identities of various objects. She can begin to reclaim disowned sides of herself and to integrate parts within herself. She is doing far more than reporting in an abstract fashion details from the past. She is bringing this unfinished business from her past into the present and dealing with whatever feelings arise in her.

Although I value Gestalt techniques as a way to take Christina further into whatever she is experiencing, I want to stress that these techniques cannot be used as a substitute for an honest exchange and dialogue between us. I can use myself and my own feelings to enhance the work of the session. Even though I will be departing from "pure" Gestalt, I want to integrate some cognitive work by asking Christina to put into words the meaning of what she has experienced and encourage her to talk about any associations between her work in our session and other aspects of her life. She may continue to talk about her awareness of how she puts all authority figures up high and what this is like for her. Blending this cognitive work with her affective work often results in longer-lasting learning.

### Follow-Up: You Continue as Christina's Therapist

Assume that Christina and I decide that it is best that she continue her counseling with another therapist, one with a Gestalt orientation. I refer her to you.

1. Overall, what are your general impressions of Christina? Does she evoke any reactions in you? Knowing what you know of yourself and of Christina, how do you imagine she will respond to you?

2. How comfortable would you be using Gestalt interventions similar to the ones I demonstrated in my work with Christina? Are there other Gestalt experiments you would like to try in your sessions with her?

3. I put a lot of emphasis on helping Christina pay attention to whatever she was feeling or experiencing at the moment. Why do you think I did this? What value, if any, do you see in this?

4. Does my work with Christina bring to the foreground any of your own unfinished business? How might your own conflicts affect your work with her?

5. Where would you go from here with her? How?

## QUIZ ON GESTALT THERAPY

### A Comprehension Check

Score _____ %

**Note:** Refer to Appendix 1 for the scoring key.

**True/false items:** Decide if the following statements are "more true" or "more false" as they apply to Gestalt therapy.

T  F    1. Resistance refers to defenses we develop that prevent us from experiencing the present in a full and real way.

T  F    2. Blocked energy can be considered a form of resistance.

T  F    3. The basic goal of Gestalt therapy is adjustment to society.

T  F    4. Recent trends in Gestalt practice include more emphasis on confrontation, more anonymity of the therapist, and increased reliance on techniques.

T  F    5. Dreams contain existential messages, and each piece of dream work leads to assimilation of disowned aspects of the self.

T  F    6. In Gestalt therapy, therapeutic skill and knowledge of techniques are *the* crucial ingredients in successful therapy.

T  F    7. One of the functions of the therapist is to pay attention to the client's body language.

T  F    8. Gestalt techniques are primarily aimed at teaching clients to think rationally.

T  F    9. A major function of the therapist is to make interpretations of clients' behavior so that they can begin to think of their patterns.

T  F    10. Perls contends that the most frequent source of unfinished business is resentment.

**Multiple-choice items:** Select the *one best answer* of those alternatives given. Consider each question within the framework of Gestalt therapy.

_____E_____ 11. The founder of Gestalt therapy is
   a. Carl Rogers.
   b. Sidney Jourard.
   c. Albert Ellis.
   d. William Glasser.
   e. none of the above.

_____E_____ 12. Which is *not* true of Gestalt therapy?
   a. The focus is on the "what" and "how" of behavior.
   b. The focus is on the here-and-now.
   c. The focus is on integrating fragmented parts of the personality.
   d. The focus is on unfinished business from the past.
   e. The focus is on the "why" of behavior.

_____B_____ 13. Which of the following is *not* a key concept of Gestalt therapy?
   a. acceptance of personal responsibility
   b. intellectual understanding of one's problems
   c. awareness
   d. unfinished business
   e. dealing with the impasse

_____A_____ 14. According to the Gestalt view, awareness
   a. is by itself therapeutic.
   b. is a necessary, but not sufficient, condition for change.
   c. without specific behavioral change is useless.
   d. consists of understanding the causes of one's problems.

_____A_____ 15. The basic goal of Gestalt therapy is to help clients
   a. move from environmental support to self-support.
   b. recognize which ego state they are functioning in.
   c. uncover unconscious motivations.
   d. work through the transference relationship with the therapist.
   e. challenge their philosophy of life.

_____B_____ 16. The impasse is the point in therapy at which clients
   a. avoid experiencing threatening feelings.
   b. experience a sense of "being stuck."
   c. imagine that something terrible will happen.
   d. do all of the above.
   e. do none of the above.

_____B_____ 17. Gestalt therapy can *best* be characterized as
   a. an insight therapy.
   b. an experiential therapy.
   c. an action-oriented therapy.
   d. all of the above.
   e. none of the above.

_____E_____ 18. Gestalt therapy encourages clients to
   a. experience feelings intensely.
   b. stay in the here-and-now.
   c. work through the impasse.
   d. pay attention to their own nonverbal messages.
   e. do all of the above.

_____C_____ 19. The focus of Gestalt therapy is on
   a. the relationship between client and counselor.
   b. free associating to the client's dreams.
   c. recognizing one's own projections and refusing to accept helplessness.
   d. understanding why we feel as we do.
   e. all of the above.

_____D_____ 20. A contribution of this therapeutic approach is that it
   a. sheds light on transference.
   b. is primarily a cognitive perspective.
   c. stresses talking about problems.
   d. deals with the past in a lively manner.

_____ 21. The process of distraction, which makes it difficult to maintain sustained contact, is

a. introjection.
b. projection.
c. retroflection.
d. confluence.
e. deflection.

_____ 22. The process of turning back to ourselves what we would like to do to someone else is

a. introjection.
b. projection.
c. retroflection.
d. confluence.
e. deflection.

_____ 23. The tendency to uncritically accept others' beliefs without assimilating or internalizing them is

a. introjection.
b. projection.
c. retroflection.
d. confluence.
e. deflection.

_____ 24. The process of blurring awareness of the boundary between self and environment is

a. introjection.
b. projection.
c. retroflection.
d. confluence.
e. deflection.

_____ 25. What is a limitation (or limitations) of Gestalt therapy as it is applied to working with culturally diverse populations?

a. Clients who have been culturally conditioned to be emotionally reserved may not see value in experiential techniques.
b. Clients may be "put off" by a focus on catharsis.
c. Clients may be looking for specific advice on solving practical problems.
d. Clients may believe showing one's vulnerability is being weak.
e. All of the above are limitations.

# Chapter 9

# Behavior Therapy

 PRECHAPTER SELF-INVENTORY

**Directions:** Refer to page 41 for general directions. Use the following code:

5 = I *strongly agree* with this statement.
4 = I *agree*, in most respects, with this statement.
3 = I am *undecided* in my opinion about this statement.
2 = I *disagree*, in most respects, with this statement.
1 = I *strongly disagree* with this statement.

_____ 1. It is important to state treatment goals in concrete and objective terms to make replication of interventions possible.

_____ 2. It is essential that the client be fully informed about the therapy process and have a major part in setting treatment goals.

_____ 3. In therapy the client controls *what* behavior is to be changed, and the therapist controls *how* behavior is changed.

_____ 4. A client's problems are influenced primarily by present conditions.

_____ 5. Understanding the origins of personal problems (insight) is not essential for producing behavior change.

_____ 6. Therapists do well to identify their values and explain how such values might influence their evaluation of the client's goals.

_____ 7. Past history should be the focus of therapy only to the degree to which such factors are actively and directly contributing to a client's current difficulties.

_____ 8. Therapy best focuses primarily on overt and specific behavior rather than on a client's feelings about a situation.

_____ 9. Any program of behavioral change should begin with a comprehensive assessment of the individual.

_____ 10. A good working relationship between the client and the therapist is a necessary but not sufficient condition for behavior change to occur.

_____ 11. Clients are both the producer and the product of their environment.

_____ 12. The therapist should provide positive reinforcement for clients so that learning can be enhanced.

_____ 13. Some proper roles of the therapist include serving as teacher, consultant, facilitator, coach, model, director, and problem solver.

_____ 14. The therapist's interest, attention, and approval are powerful reinforcers of client behavior.

_____ 15. It is important that clients be actively involved in the assessment, planning, treatment, and evaluation of a therapy program.

_____ 16. Specific techniques of therapy or a behavioral-management program must be tailored to the requirements and needs of each individual client.

_____ 17. Therapeutic procedures should be aimed at behavior change.

_____ 18. Evidence-based treatments increase the chances that clients are getting the best therapy possible.

_____ 19. Because real-life problems must be solved with new behaviors outside therapy, the process is not complete unless actions follow verbalizations.

_____ 20. It is essential that the outcomes of therapy be evaluated to assess the degree of success or failure of treatment.

## OVERVIEW OF BEHAVIOR THERAPY

### Key Figures and Major Focus

Key figures: B. F. Skinner, Joseph Wolpe, Arnold Lazarus, and Albert Bandura. Historically, the behavioral trend developed in the 1950s and early 1960s as a radical departure from the psychoanalytic perspective. Four major phases in the development of behavior therapy are (1) classical conditioning, (2) operant conditioning, (3) social learning theory, and (4) cognitive behavior therapy.

### Philosophy and Basic Assumptions

Behavior is the product of learning. We are both the product and the producer of our environment. No set of unifying assumptions about behavior can incorporate all the existing procedures in the behavioral field. Due to the diversity of views and strategies, it is more accurate to think of *behavioral therapies* rather than a unified approach. Contemporary behavior therapy encompasses a variety of conceptualizations, research methods, and treatment procedures to explain and change behavior. These central characteristics unite the field of behavior therapy: a focus on observable behavior, current determinants of behavior, learning experiences to promote change, and rigorous assessment and evaluation.

### Key Concepts

The approach emphasizes current behavior as opposed to historical antecedents, precise treatment goals, diverse therapeutic strategies tailored to these goals, and objective evaluation of therapeutic outcomes. Therapy focuses on behavior change in the present and on action programs. Concepts and procedures are stated explicitly, tested empirically, and revised continually. Specific behaviors are measured before and after an intervention to determine whether behavior changed as a result of a procedure.

### Therapeutic Goals

A hallmark of behavior therapy is the identification of specific goals at the outset of the therapeutic process. The general goals are to increase personal choice and to create new conditions for learning. An aim is to eliminate maladaptive behaviors and learn more effective behavior patterns. Generally, client and therapist collaboratively specify treatment goals in concrete, measurable, and objective terms.

## Therapeutic Relationship

Clients make progress primarily because of the specific behavioral techniques used, but a good working relationship is an essential precondition for effective therapy. The skilled therapist can conceptualize problems behaviorally and make use of the therapeutic relationship in bringing about change. The therapist's role is primarily to explore alternative courses of action and their possible consequences. Part of the therapist's job is to teach concrete skills through the provision of instructions, modeling, and performance feedback. Therapists tend to be active and directive and to function as consultants and problem solvers. Clients must also be actively involved in the therapeutic process from beginning to end, and they are expected to cooperate in carrying out therapeutic activities, both in the sessions and outside of therapy.

## Techniques and Procedures

Behavioral treatment interventions are individually tailored to specific problems experienced by different clients. Any technique that can be demonstrated to change behavior may be incorporated in a treatment plan. A strength of the approach lies in the many and varied techniques aimed at producing behavior change, a few of which are relaxation methods, systematic desensitization, in vivo desensitization, flooding, eye movement desensitization reprocessing, assertion training, self-management programs, and multimodal therapy.

## Applications

The approach has wide applicability to a range of clients desiring specific behavioral changes. A few problem areas for which behavior therapy appears to be effective include phobic disorders, depression, anxiety disorders, sexual disorders, substance abuse, eating disorders, pain management, hypertension, children's disorders, and the prevention and treatment of cardiovascular disease. Going beyond the usual areas of clinical practice, behavioral approaches are deeply enmeshed in geriatrics, pediatrics, stress management, self-management, sports psychology, rehabilitation, behavioral medicine, business and management, gerontology, and education, to mention only a few.

## Contributions

Behavior therapy is a short-term approach that has wide applicability. It emphasizes research into and assessment of the techniques used, thus providing accountability. Specific problems are identified and attacked, and clients are kept informed about the therapeutic process and about what gains are being made. The approach has demonstrated effectiveness in many areas of human functioning. The concepts and procedures are easily grasped. The therapist is an explicit reinforcer, consultant, model, teacher, and expert in behavioral change. The approach has undergone tremendous development and expansion over the past two decades, and the literature continues to expand at a phenomenal rate. Behavioral approaches can be appropriately integrated into counseling with culturally diverse client populations, particularly because of their emphasis on teaching clients about the therapeutic process and the structure that is provided by the model. There is an attempt to develop culture-specific procedures and to obtain the client's adherence and cooperation.

## Limitations

The success of the approach is in proportion to the ability to control environmental variables. In institutional settings (schools, psychiatric hospitals, mental health outpatient clinics) the danger exists of imposing conforming behavior. Therapists can manipulate clients toward ends they have not chosen. A basic criticism leveled at this approach is that it does not address broader human problems—such as meaning, the search for values, and identity issues—but focuses instead on very specific and narrow behavioral problems.

# GLOSSARY OF KEY TERMS

**Applied behavior analysis**    Another term for behavior modification; this approach seeks to understand the causes of behavior and address these causes by changing antecedents and consequences.

**Assertion training**    A set of techniques that involves behavioral rehearsal, coaching, and learning more effective social skills; specific skills training procedures used to teach people ways to express both positive and negative feelings openly and directly.

**BASIC I.D.**    The conceptual framework of multimodal therapy, based on the premise that human personality can be understood by assessing seven major areas of functioning: behavior, affective responses, sensations, images, cognitions, interpersonal relationships, and drugs/biological functions.

**Behavior modification**    A therapeutic approach that deals with analyzing and modifying human behavior.

**Behavior rehearsal**    A technique consisting of trying out in therapy new behaviors (performing target behaviors) that are to be used in everyday situations.

**Classical conditioning**    Also known as Pavlovian conditioning and respondent conditioning. A form of learning in which a neutral stimulus is repeatedly paired with a stimulus that naturally elicits a particular response. The result is that eventually the neutral stimulus alone elicits the response.

**Cognitive behavioral coping skills therapy**    Procedures aimed at teaching clients specific skills to deal effectively with problematic situations.

**Cognitive processes**    Internal events such as thoughts, beliefs, perceptions, and self-statements.

**Consequences**    Events that take place as a result of a specific behavior being performed.

**Contingency contracting**    Written agreement between a client and another person that specifies the relationship between performing target behaviors and their consequences.

**Dialectical behavior therapy**    A blend of behavioral and psychoanalytic techniques that was primarily designed to treat borderline personality disorders.

**Exposure therapy**    Treatment for anxiety and fear responses that exposes clients to situations or events that create the unwanted emotional responses.

**Extinction**    When a previously reinforced behavior is no longer followed by the reinforcing consequences, the result is a decrease in the frequency of a behavior in the future.

**Evidence-based treatments**    Interventions that have empirical evidence to support their use.

**Eye movement desensitization reprocessing (EMDR)**    An exposure-based therapy that involves imaginal flooding, cognitive restructuring, and the use of rhythmic eye movements and other bilateral stimulation to treat traumatic stress disorders and fearful memories of clients.

**Flooding**    Prolonged and intensive in vivo or imaginal exposure to highly anxiety-evoking stimuli without the opportunity to avoid or escape from them.

**Functional assessment**    The process of generating information on the events preceding and following the behavior in an attempt to determine which antecedents and consequences are associated with the occurrence of the behavior.

**In vivo desensitization**    Brief and graduated exposure to an actual fear situation or event.

**Modeling**    Learning through observation and imitation.

**Multimodal therapy**    A model endorsing technical eclecticism; uses procedures drawn from various sources without necessarily subscribing to the theories behind these techniques; developed by Arnold Lazarus.

**Negative reinforcement** The termination or withdrawal of an unpleasant stimulus as a result of performing some desired behavior.

**Operant conditioning** A type of learning in which behaviors are influenced mainly by the consequences that follow them.

**Positive reinforcement** A form of conditioning whereby the individual receives something desirable as a consequence of his or her behavior; a reward that increases the probability of its recurrence.

**Positive reinforcer** An event whose presentation increases the probability of a response that it follows.

**Punishment** The process in which a behavior is followed by a consequence that results in a decrease in the future probability of a behavior.

**Reinforcement** A specified event that strengthens the tendency for a response to be repeated. It involves some kind of reward or the removal of an aversive stimulus following a response.

**Self-efficacy** An individual's belief or expectation that he or she can master a situation and bring about desired change.

**Self-management** A collection of cognitive behavioral strategies based on the idea that change can be brought about by teaching people to use coping skills in problematic situations such as anxiety, depression, and pain.

**Self-monitoring** The process of observing one's own behavior patterns as well as one's interactions in various social situations.

**Skills training** A treatment package used to teach clients skills that include modeling, behavior rehearsal, and reinforcement.

**Social learning theory** A perspective holding that behavior is best understood by taking into consideration the social conditions under which learning occurs; developed primarily by Albert Bandura.

**Systematic desensitization** A procedure based on the principles of classical conditioning in which the client is taught to relax while imagining a graded series of progressively anxiety-arousing situations. Eventually, the client reaches a point at which the anxiety-producing stimulus no longer brings about the anxious response.

**Technical eclecticism** Using a variety of techniques in a way suited to the individual needs of a client (see multimodal therapy).

## QUESTIONS FOR REFLECTION AND DISCUSSION

1. Advocates of the psychoanalytic approach, which emphasizes identifying and resolving the underlying causes of behavioral problems, challenge behavior therapists by predicting that other symptoms will be substituted for the ones treated unless the underlying causes are also treated. Where do you stand with respect to this challenge?

2. In some ways it may seem that the behavioral approach and the existential approach are diametrically opposed. Yet some writers contend that combining behavioristic methods with humanistic values leads to a synthesis of the best attributes of both approaches. What do you think?

3. An increasing emphasis in current behavior therapy is on teaching clients self-control procedures and self-management skills. The assumption is that learning coping skills can increase the range of self-directed behavior. What are the possibilities of behavior therapy, as you see them, for enhancing a client's choosing, planning, and self-direction?

4. Considering the counseling of culturally diverse client populations, what are some of the merits of the behavioral approach? What specific aspects of behavior therapy, both concepts and techniques, would you want to apply in your work in a multicultural setting?

5. Which behavioral techniques would you be most inclined to use in your general practice? Why? Explain what problems and clients would be best suited for the techniques you have selected.

6. What ethical issues are involved in the use of behavior therapy techniques? List the techniques, as well as the issues, that you see as being central.

7. Some criticize behavior therapy for working too well; that is, they are concerned that conditioning techniques will be too effective and will be used to manipulate the client. What are your reactions to using behavioral strategies for social control?

8. What is your view of this approach's stress on empirical research to validate therapy results? As a practitioner, how might you attempt to assess the process and the outcomes of therapy?

9. How can the concepts and techniques of the other therapy systems that you have studied be integrated with a behavioral framework? Can you think of ways to develop an eclectic style as a counselor while staying within the behavioral spirit?

10. The text deals with five common criticisms and misconceptions regarding behavior therapy. What are your criticisms, if any, of behavior therapy?

## ISSUES FOR PERSONAL APPLICATION

### Designing a Self-Management Program

As you know from reading the textbook, there is an increased use of self-management strategies. These include self-monitoring, self-reward, self-contracting, and stimulus control. Select some behavior you might like to change (stopping excessive eating, drinking, or smoking; teaching yourself relaxation skills in the face of tense situations you must encounter; developing a regular program of physical exercising or meditating; and so forth). Show how you would specifically design, implement, and evaluate your self-change program. Ideally, you will consider actually trying out such a program for some behavior changes you want to make in your everyday life.

- What specific behavior do you want to change?
- What specific actions will help you reach this goal?
- What self-monitoring devices can you use to keep a record of your progress?
- What reinforcements (self-rewards) can you use as a way of carrying out your plans?
- How well is your plan for change working? What revisions are necessary for your plan to work more effectively?

## PRACTICAL APPLICATIONS

### Translating Broad Goals Into Specific Goals

**Directions:** An area of major concern in behavior therapy is the formulation of concrete and *specific* goals for counseling. Clients often approach the first counseling session with vague, generalized, abstract goals. A task for the therapist is to help the client formulate clear, concrete goals. The following exercises are designed to give you practice in that task. For each general statement in items 4–7 write a concrete goal, as illustrated in the three examples:

1. Broad goal: *I would like to be happier. I suppose I want to become self-actualized.*

   Specific goal: *I want to learn to know what I want and to have the courage to get it. I want to feel that I am doing what I really want to be doing.*

2. Broad goal: *I'd like to work on improving my relationship with people.*

   Specific goal: *I want to be able to ask those I'm close to for what I want and need. So often I keep my desires unknown, and thus I feel cheated with those people.*

3. Broad goal: *I suppose I need to work on my communication with my wife.*

   Specific goal: *I need to learn how to tell my wife what I'm thinking and feeling and not bury all this and expect her to guess if I'm pleased or not.*

4. Broad goal: *I want to know why I play all these stupid games with myself in my head.*
   Specific goal: _____
   _____
   _____

5. Broad goal: *I need to get in touch with my values and my philosophy of life.*
   Specific goal: _____
   _____
   _____

6. Broad goal: *It's awfully hard for me to be an autonomous and assertive individual.*
   Specific goal: _____
   _____
   _____

7. Broad goal: *I have all sorts of fears and worries, and just about everything gets me uptight.*
   Specific goal: _____
   _____
   _____

## Learning How to Be Concrete

One way to help clients become more specific in clarifying broad goals is to do it for yourself. Make a list of specific behaviors you would like to change in your own life. For example, your list might look like this:

1. I want to say no when I really mean no, instead of saying yes and feeling resentful.
2. I would like to spend less time studying and more time playing tennis and skiing.
3. I want to respond to my kids without shouting.
4. I want to lessen my fears about taking examinations.

List concrete goals in terms of specific *behavioral changes* you want for yourself:

1. _____
2. _____
3. _____
4. _____
5. _____
6. _____

 # SUGGESTED ACTIVITIES AND EXERCISES

1. Here is an exercise that you can do by yourself. For a period of at least a week, engage in relaxation training for approximately 20 to 30 minutes daily. The purpose of the exercise is to teach you to become more aware of the distinction between tension states and relaxation states. A further objective is to provide you with self-control procedures designed to reduce unnecessary anxiety and tension and to induce bodily relaxation. Self-relaxation is best learned in a quiet setting and in a prone position. The strategy for achieving muscular relaxation is the repeated tensing and relaxing of various muscular groups. Begin by tensing a specific set of muscles for several seconds and then relaxing those muscles for several seconds. In using this procedure, you should cover all

the major muscular groups by using about two tension/release cycles per muscular group. For the purpose of deepening your relaxation, auxiliary techniques such as concentrating on your breathing and imagining yourself in peaceful and personally relaxing situations can eventually be added to the self-relaxation procedure. You may want to make a tape of the sequence to listen to as you follow the instructions.

a. *Hands and arms.* Begin by sitting back or lying down in a relaxed position with your arms at your sides. Take several deep breaths to become relaxed, and hold each breath for at least 5 seconds. Keep your eyes closed during the exercise. Now hold out your dominant arm, and make a fist with the dominant hand. Clench your fist tightly, and feel the tension in the forearm and the hand. Now let go. Now feel the relaxation, and feel the difference from before. After 15 to 20 seconds repeat the procedure, this time concentrating on the differences between relaxation and tension. Repeat the process with the nondominant arm.

b. *Biceps.* Flex your dominant bicep, and notice the tension. Then, relax, tense, and relax again. Notice the warm feelings of relaxation.

c. *Fists.* Next, do the same for the dominant fist. Hold the fist tightly, relax, and study the differences. Then repeat the tension/relaxation procedure, making sure to take your time.

d. *Biceps.* Flex the nondominant bicep. Be aware of the tension, and then release. Repeat the tension/relaxation pattern. Take several deep breaths, hold them, and notice the relaxation in your arms.

e. *Fists.* Next, do the same for the nondominant fist. Hold the fist tightly, relax, and study the differences. Then repeat the tension/relaxation procedure, making sure to take your time.

f. *Upper face.* Tense up the muscles of your forehead by raising your eyebrows as high as possible. Hold this for 5 seconds and feel the tension building up. Relax and notice the difference. Then repeat this procedure.

g. *Eyes.* Now close your eyes tightly. Feel the tension around your eyes. Now relax those muscles, noting the difference between the tension and the relaxation. Repeat this process.

h. *Tongue and jaws.* Next clench your jaws by biting your teeth together. Pull the corners of your mouth back, and make an exaggerated smile. Release and let go, noticing the difference.

i. *Pressing the lips together.* Now press your lips together tightly, and notice the tension. Now relax the muscles around your mouth. Repeat.

j. *Breathing.* Take a few deep breaths and notice how relaxed your arms, head, and mouth feel. Enjoy these feelings of relaxation.

k. *Neck.* Try to touch your chin to your chest, and at the same time apply counterpressure to keep it from touching. Release, note the difference, and then repeat. Pull your head back, and try to touch your back, but push back the opposite way with the opposing muscles. Notice the tension, release, and relax. Then repeat this procedure.

l. *Chest and shoulders.* Next pull back your shoulders until the blades almost touch, and then relax. Repeat. Then try to touch your shoulders by pushing them forward as far as you can. Then release, and feel the difference. Repeat. Now shrug your shoulders, and try to touch them to your ears. Hold, release, and repeat.

m. *Breathing.* Take a deep breath, hold it for 7 seconds, and then exhale quickly. Do this again. Note the feelings of relaxation.

n. *Stomach muscles.* Tighten up your stomach muscles; make your stomach tight and hard like a knot. Relax those muscles. Repeat.

o. *Buttocks.* Now tighten your buttocks by pulling them together. Hold. Release. Repeat.

p. *Thighs.* Tense your thighs. Release the muscles quickly, and then repeat. Study the difference between the tension in the thighs and the relaxation you feel now.

q. *Toes.* Point your toes toward your head, and note the tension. Relax. Repeat. Then point your feet outward, and notice the tension. Release quickly and repeat. Point your feet inward and hold, and then relax. Repeat.

After each of the above muscle groups has been tensed and relaxed twice, the therapist typically concludes the relaxation training with a summary and review. This review consists of listing each muscle group and asking the client to let go of any tension. This is done for each of the above muscle groups, with the suggestion of becoming completely relaxed. The client is asked to notice the good feelings of relaxation, warmth, and calmness over the entire body.

2. Review the section in Chapter 9 of the textbook describing *systematic desensitization.* Select some anxiety-provoking experience for you, and then set up a systematic desensitization program to lessen your anxiety or fear. Follow your program privately as an out-of-class assignment. Class members may bring their results into class a week later to describe and share their experiences with the procedure. Following are a few guidelines for setting up a program for yourself:

a. Begin by using the relaxation procedure described in the previous exercise.

b. Decide what specific behavior or situations evoke anxiety reactions for you. For example, speaking in front of others may be anxiety-producing for you.

c. Construct a hierarchy, which should be arranged from the worst situation you can imagine to a situation that evokes the least anxiety. For example, the greatest anxiety for you might result from the thought of delivering a lecture to hundreds of people in an auditorium. The least anxiety-provoking situation might be talking with a fellow student you know well.

d. Apply the relaxation procedures you have learned; keep your eyes closed, and begin by imagining yourself in the least anxiety-arousing situation on your hierarchy. Then, while imagining a peaceful and pleasant scene, allow yourself also to imagine yourself in the next most anxiety-arousing situation. At the moment you experience anxiety as you imagine the more threatening situation, switch off that scene, put yourself back into the pleasant scene, and relax again.

e. The idea is to move progressively up the hierarchy until you can imagine the scene that produces the greatest degree of anxiety and still be able to induce relaxation again. This procedure ends when you can remain in a relaxed state even while you are imagining a particular scene that formerly was the most disturbing to you.

3. Assume that your client expresses a desire to lose 20 pounds and then keep his weight down. Using learning principles and behavioral techniques, show the specific steps for *weight control* that you might take with your client. As guidelines you might consider the following questions:

a. Has the client consulted a physician about his weight problem? If he has not, would you undertake a therapy program without having him first visit a physician?

b. What is his motivation for losing weight? What specific reinforcements might help him stick with his weight reduction program?

c. What kind of self-observation and charting behavior would you suggest? Would you ask him to keep a record of when he eats, what he eats, and so on?

d. How would you deal with him if he went on eating binges and failed to follow through with his program? What might you say or do?

e. What are the specific learning concepts involved in the weight control program?

Now assume that your client is a chain smoker and expresses a real interest in quitting. Having tried before, she stopped smoking but resumed the practice when she felt pressure in her daily life. With that information develop a program of *smoking control* designed to eliminate her smoking behavior by using the principles of learning theory. Describe the steps you would take in designing specific procedures of the program.

4. *Multimodal therapy* begins with a comprehensive assessment of the various modalities of human functioning. For practice in thinking about assessment within this framework, consider the case of Stan, and attempt an initial assessment of him on the dimensions outlined here:

a. *Behavior.* How active is Stan? What are some of his main strengths? What specific behaviors keep him from getting what he says he wants?

b. *Affect.* How emotional does Stan seem? What are some problematic emotions for him?

c. *Sensation.* How aware of his senses is Stan? Does he appear to be making full use of all his senses?

d. *Imagery.* How would you describe Stan's self-image? How does he describe himself now? How does he see himself?

e. *Cognition.* What are some of the main "shoulds," "oughts," and "musts" that appear to be in Stan's life now? How do they get in the way of effective living for him? How do his thoughts affect the way he feels and acts?

f. *Interpersonal relationships.* How much of a social being is Stan? How capable does he appear to be of handling intimate relationships? What does he expect from others in his life?

g. *Drugs/biology.* What do you know about Stan's health? Does he have any concerns about his health? Does he use any drugs?

Based on this initial assessment of Stan, what kind of treatment program would you outline for him as a behavior therapist?

## JERRY COREY'S WORK WITH RUTH FROM A BEHAVIORAL PERSPECTIVE

Functioning with a behavioral orientation I pay considerable attention to assessment and establishing goals as a basis for the direction of therapy. After assessing Ruth's strengths and weaknesses, I clarify with her the behaviors she wants to increase or decrease in frequency. She will set specific goals pertaining to problem areas in her life. Before treatment we establish baseline data for those behaviors that she wants to change. The baseline period is a point of reference against which her changes can be compared during and after treatment. By establishing such baseline data, we will be able to determine therapeutic progress. There is continual assessment throughout therapy to determine the degree to which her goals are being effectively met.

I view Ruth's problems as related to faulty learning. Much of our therapy will involve correcting faulty cognitions, acquiring social and interpersonal skills, and learning techniques of self-management so that she can become her own therapist. Based on my initial assessment of Ruth and on another session in which she and I discuss the matter of setting concrete and objective goals, we establish the following goals to guide the therapeutic process:

- Ruth does not like her physical appearance and wants to lose weight.
- It is important for Ruth to learn to stick to an exercise program.
- Ruth has difficulty getting along with one of her daughters and wants to improve the relationship.

- Ruth would like to improve her relationship with her husband.
- Ruth would like to be more assertive when the situation calls for assertive behavior.
- Ruth wants to learn and practice methods of relaxation and ways to more effectively cope with stress.

From a behavioral perspective I am interested in getting Ruth to be very specific and concrete in identifying her own goals. I suggest that she begin writing in a journal to keep track of how she is doing in meeting her goals. It is essential that Ruth gives considerable thought to what she wants to explore in the counseling sessions. Ruth is clearly the person who decides what she wants to explore and the areas she is most interested in changing.

Ruth will be able to make progress toward her self-defined goals because she is willing to become actively involved in challenging her assumptions and in carrying out behavioral exercises, both in the sessions and in her daily life. For instance, Ruth decided that she wanted to enroll in a fitness class as a part of her exercise program. However, the class was full and Ruth had an opportunity to practice her assertive behavior skills and was able to add the class. Earlier it would not have even occurred to Ruth to seek out the instructor and ask to be admitted to a class that is already full. Ruth is learning the importance of making specific plans aimed at translating what she is learning in the therapy sessions to various segments in her daily life. Although my job is to help Ruth learn how to change, she is the one who actually chooses to apply these skills, thus making change possible.

## You Continue Working With Ruth

1. In what ways could you incorporate ongoing assessment as a part of Ruth's therapy?
2. What are some ideas you have for working with Ruth on the specific target goals listed in this selection?
3. How would you help Ruth apply what she is learning in therapy sessions to challenges she meets in daily life?
4. What techniques might you use from the other therapeutic approaches in helping Ruth reach the goals she has set for herself in therapy with you?
5. Refer to *Case Approach to Counseling and Psychotherapy* (Chapter 7) for examples of two different behavior therapists' perspectives (Arnold Lazarus and Barbara Brownell D'Angelo) on Ruth's case. In this chapter, I also show my style of applying behavior therapy concepts in working with Ruth. What similarities and differences do you see between the styles of Lazarus and D'Angelo?
6. See the *CD-ROM for Integrative Counseling* (the sessions on therapeutic goals and working toward decisions and behavior change) for a demonstration of utilizing behavioral techniques in addressing concerns identified by Ruth. How would you assist Ruth in formulating specific, personal goals?

## SALLY: HOPING TO CURE A SOCIAL PHOBIA

### Some Background Data

Sally is 27 years old, single, Asian American. She supervises employees at a large office of the Internal Revenue Service. She has come to a community mental health center on the recommendation of a close friend. Sally has mixed feelings about seeking professional help, for this is not something that she ever saw herself doing. In her culture she would first attempt to work out her own problems by personal reflection. If she is unable to resolve her problems by herself, then she is likely to talk about personal concerns with family members, with a minister, or perhaps with a very close friend.

Sally's major presenting problem could be labeled a *social phobia*. She has a persistent and exaggerated fear of being exposed to scrutiny by others in social situations. She fears that she may act in ways that will be humiliating or embarrassing, so she tends to avoid social gatherings.

Sally's fears and difficulties in coping with the demands of everyday living are becoming so pressing that she feels she must defy her cultural injunctions and seek professional help. When she told her parents that she wanted to go to counseling, they were offended and took it personally. They tried to persuade her to see the minister instead. She respectfully, but with some guilt, declined to follow their advice.

## Jerry Corey's Way of Working With Sally From a Behavioral Perspective

I view the therapeutic relationship as a collaborative one. I am not an all-knowing expert who makes decisions for a passive client. Instead, from our first until our final session, Sally and I will work together toward goals that we have agreed will guide our sessions—if, in fact, she decides to enter counseling with me.

### Dealing With Sally's Immediate Feelings and Thoughts

Some of the things I know about Sally are important to attend to during the first session. I am aware that she comes to the office with some reluctance and only after the goading of a close friend. As a place to begin, I ask her how it was for her to call and make the appointment and what it was like for her as she walked into the waiting room. Building trust with her involves talking about her reservations about seeking counseling, about talking to a "stranger," and about the difficulties she had to overcome simply to be in the office now. Some questions that I ask are: "What would you most hope to get from this session or from the next several sessions? What is going on in your life now that prompted you to take the action of coming here today? What expectations did you have in mind after you talked to your friend?"

After we have had chance to talk for a time, I invite her to let me know how she feels about our exchange so far. This is especially important because I know she has difficulty encountering men and because she said she could never see herself talking personally to a "stranger." In several ways I could be a stranger. She is a 27-year-old, Asian American administrator, and I am a 67-year-old, White, male psychologist of Italian background. The fact that we differ in age, cultural background, and gender could influence a counseling relationship. I want to create a climate where Sally will be able to talk about her level of comfort in working with me, despite these differences.

### Goal Setting and Deciding on a Course of Action

Sally and I work at narrowing down her goals. Like many other clients she is approaching her therapy with global and fuzzy aims. It is my task to help her formulate clear and concrete goals, so that she and I will know what we are working toward and will have a basis for determining how well the therapy is working. When I ask her what she wants from therapy, for example, she replies: "I want to learn to communicate better. I want to be able to state my opinions without being afraid. I don't do very well in social situations. I'd like to get over feeling scared all the time."

Although her goals are general, they do relate to becoming more effective in social situations. I can facilitate her moving from global to specific goals by asking her: "Whom in your life do you have trouble talking to? Are there any particular people with whom you find it difficult to say what you'd like to say? What are some situations in which you have problems being assertive? In what social situations don't you do well? How would you like to change in these situations? Tell me about a few specific fears you experience? When you are frightened, what do you tell yourself? And what do you do at these times? What would you like to do differently? If you were not fearful in social situations, how do you think your life would be different?" My line of questioning is aimed at helping Sally translate fuzzy goals into clear statements pertaining to what she is thinking, feeling, and doing (and ways that she would like to think, feel, and behave differently).

Eventually, Sally and I draw up a contract that is geared to helping her develop a course of action to attain these goals. She will work on *identifying* and *lessening* (or, ideally, removing) her unrealistic fears. She will identify specific manifestations of unassertive behaviors on her part, which include her difficulty in expressing her opinions, in making contacts with people, in turning down others when that is what she wants to do, and in making her wants and needs clearly known to others. She will experiment with new behaviors, both in the therapy sessions and in daily life. Practicing these behaviors will lead to *increasing* her repertoire of social skills, especially her *assertive behavior*.

Because it will take some time for Sally to learn and practice the skills related to her stated goals, we discuss a realistic time frame for therapy. She decides to commit herself to a series of six one-hour individual counseling sessions. This kind of structuring will encourage Sally to evaluate her progress after each session and will serve to keep her focused.

## Sally Learns Systematic Desensitization

Sally initiates a discussion about dealing with her fears relating to men. She tends to avoid men, mainly because she is frightened of them. She is both put off by them and attracted to them, and she has the dual fear of being rejected by them and being accepted. Sally wonders what she would do if a man desired an intimate relationship with her.

Sally says that she would like to be free enough to go to parties, to accept dates, and to initiate social contacts with selected men. It is clear to her that initiating these contacts is particularly difficult because of her socialization, which has taught her that "proper" women do not behave in this manner.

We then proceed with systematic desensitization procedures, which start with a behavioral analysis of situations that evoke anxiety in her. We construct a hierarchy of her anxieties by ranking them in order, beginning with the situation that evokes the least anxiety and ending with the worst situation she can imagine. I then teach Sally some basic relaxation procedures, which she practices until she is completely relaxed in the session. I ask her to select a peaceful scene where she would like to be. She picks a lake in the forest. We proceed with the relaxation exercise until Sally is fully relaxed, has her eyes closed, and has the peaceful scene in her mind.

I describe a series of scenes to Sally and ask her to imagine herself in each of them. I present a neutral scene first. If she remains relaxed, I ask her to imagine the *least* anxiety-arousing scene she set up in her hierarchy (seeing a man whom she found pleasant on the far side of a room). I move progressively up the hierarchy until she signals by raising her index finger that she is experiencing anxiety, at which time I ask her to switch off that scene and become very relaxed and imagine herself at her lake. We continue until we progress to the *most* anxiety-arousing scene in her hierarchy (imagining an intimate relationship with a man who wants to continue the relationship).

In our therapy sessions we continue the desensitization procedure until Sally is able to imagine this "worst" scene without experiencing anxiety. Basically, this procedure consists of combining an incompatible stimulus and response. We pair the relaxation exercises and imagining a pleasant scene with scenes that evoke anxiety. Gradually the anxiety-provoking stimuli lose their potency. Now that we have successfully desensitized her of her fears of relating to a man she perceives as attractive on an imaginary level, I hope Sally is ready to try new behaviors in the world.

## Sally Goes on a Date

As a behaviorally oriented therapist, I believe in the value of homework assignments. These are not activities I pick out as good for Sally. Rather, *she* decides on some new behaviors she would like to experiment with outside of our sessions. Then Sally applies what she has learned in therapy to a social situation in the hope of acquiring new social skills and overcoming her inhibitions and negative self-talk. She tells me that she has decided to ask Julio, whom she met through her friend, to the upcoming office Christmas party.

Before she actually carries out this assignment, we examine what she is telling herself before inviting him. She recognizes that she is setting herself up for failure by telling herself that he probably will not want to go and that if he does accept it is only because he feels sorry for her. So we do some additional cognitive work that will lead to positive expectancies on her part. Before she asks Julio to the party, she practices her relaxation exercises and calms herself so that anxiety will not interfere with what she wants to do.

When Sally returns to her session the next week, she reports that all went well. She is feeling an increasing sense of confidence and is willing to tackle new social situations that are more difficult.

## A Commentary

Sally's therapy began with assessment, and at our last session we assess the degree to which she has met her goals. We also review what she has learned in these sessions as well as what she has done in various situations at school, at work, and at home. Our focus now is on consolidating what she has learned and helping her translate it into future real-life situations. I suggest that she continue by reading self-help books, doing her daily relaxation exercises, giving herself behavioral assignments, monitoring and assessing her behaviors, and keeping a behavioral log in her journal. Finally, she agrees to join a 10-week assertion training group designed to help students improve their social skills. In this way she is able to continue what we have begun in these sessions.

## Follow-Up: You Continue as Sally's Therapist

After my six individual sessions with Sally, she enters the 10-week assertion training group. Assume that she has now finished this group and consults you for further counseling.

1. What are your reactions to the very structured approach I used with Sally? To what degree would you be comfortable using such an approach, and how effective do you think you would be?

2. What cultural variables might you be alert to in this case? Some of the clues provided initially are these: Sally is reluctant to talk about her personal problems to people outside of her family; she has mixed feelings about admitting that she needs professional help; she has a desire to follow the traditions and expectations of her family; and she is struggling with a cultural injunction that says women should not be too direct and too assertive. How might you work with any of these themes?

3. What advantages, if any, would there be if Sally saw a female therapist? What factors would determine whether it might be best that she see an Asian American therapist?

4. If you are of a different gender and have a different ethnic background from Sally, how might this be for you as a counselor? Given what you know of her case, would you anticipate any difficulties in establishing rapport with Sally?

 QUIZ ON BEHAVIOR THERAPY

### A Comprehension Check

Score _____%

**Note:** Refer to Appendix 1 for the scoring key.

**True/false items:** Decide if the following statements are "more true" or "more false" as they apply to behavior therapy.

T (F) 1. Operant conditioning was mainly developed by B. F. Skinner.

T F 2. Behavior therapists look to current environmental events that maintain problem behaviors and help clients produce behavior change by changing environmental events.

(T) F 3. The emphasis of contemporary behavior therapy is on evidence-based treatments.

T F 4. There is no unifying set of assumptions about behavior that can incorporate all the existing procedures in the behavioral field.

T F 5. The newest trend in the development of behavior therapy is the focus on cognitive factors that are related to behavior.

T (F) 6. Typically, the goals of the therapeutic process are determined by the therapist.

(T) F 7. Behavior therapists tend to be active and directive, and they function as consultants and problem solvers.

T (F) 8. Multimodal therapy consists of a series of techniques that are used with all clients in much the same way.

T F 9. There is a growing trend toward integrating cognitive and behavioral methods to help clients manage their own problems.

T F 10. A program of behavioral change should begin with a comprehensive assessment of the client.

**Multiple-choice items:** Select the *one best answer* of those alternatives given. Consider each question within the framework of behavior therapy.

_____ 11. Behavior therapy is grounded on
  a. the psychodynamic aspects of a person.
  b. the principles of learning.
  c. a philosophical view of the human condition.
  d. the events of the first 5 years of life.

_____ 12. Behavior therapy is based on
  a. applying the experimental method to the therapeutic process.
  b. a systematic set of concepts.
  c. a well-developed theory of personality.
  d. the principle of self-actualization.
  e. both (b) and (c).

_____ 13. In behavior therapy it is generally agreed that
  a. the therapist should decide the treatment goals.
  b. the client should decide the treatment goals.
  c. goals of therapy are the same for all clients.
  d. goals are not necessary.

_____ 14. Which is not true as it is applied to behavior therapy?
  a. Insight is necessary for behavior change to occur.
  b. Therapy should focus on behavior change and not attitude change.
  c. Therapy is not complete unless actions follow verbalizations.
  d. A good working relationship between client and therapist is necessary for behavior change to occur.

_____ 15. According to most behavior therapists, a good working relationship between client and therapist is
  a. a necessary and sufficient condition for behavior change to occur.
  b. a necessary, but not sufficient, condition for behavior change to occur.
  c. neither a necessary nor a sufficient condition for behavior change to occur.

_____ 16. Applied behavior analysis makes use of
  a. classical conditioning techniques.

b. operant conditioning techniques.

c. cognitive behavioral techniques.

d. all of the above.

e. none of the above.

_____ 17. Which of the following is not a key concept of behavior therapy?

a. Behavior is learned through reinforcement.

b. Present behavior is stressed more than past behavior.

c. Emphasis is on evidence-based treatment procedures.

d. Emphasis is on action and experimenting with new behaviors.

e. Emphasis is on the role of insight in treatment.

_____ 18. Dialectical behavior therapy

a. has no empirical support for its validity.

b. is a promising blend of behavioral and psychoanalytic techniques.

c. is a long-term therapy for treating depression.

d. is a form of operant conditioning.

e. is a form of classical conditioning.

_____ 19. Which is not true of dialectical behavior therapy (DBT)?

a. The approach was formulated for treating borderline personality disorders.

b. DBT emphasizes the importance of the client–therapist relationship.

c. DBT incorporates mindfulness training and Zen practices.

d. DBT is a blend of Adlerian concepts and behavioral techniques.

e. DBT relies on empirical data to support its effectiveness.

_____ 20. An exposure-based procedure that involves imaginal flooding, cognitive restructuring, and the induction of rapid, rhythmic eye movements aimed at treatment of traumatic experiences is called

a. flooding.

b. in vivo desensitization.

c. systematic desensitization.

d. relaxation training.

e. eye movement desensitization reprocessing.

_____ 21. Prolonged/intense exposure—either in real life or in imagination—to highly anxiety-evoking stimuli is called

a. self-management training.

b. in vivo desensitization.

c. systematic desensitization.

d. flooding.

e. eye movement desensitization reprocessing.

_____ 22. A limitation of behavior therapy is its

a. lack of research to evaluate the effectiveness of techniques.

b. deemphasis on the role of feelings in therapy.

c. lack of clear concepts on which to base practice.

d. lack of attention paid to a good client–therapist relationship.

e. overemphasis on early childhood experiences.

_____ 23. Contemporary behavior therapy places emphasis on

a. the interplay between the individual and the environment.

b. helping clients acquire insight into the causes of their problems.

c. a phenomenological approach to understanding the person.

d. encouraging clients to reexperience unfinished business with significant others by role-playing with them in the present.

e. working through the transference relationship with the therapist.

_____ 24. Which is *not* true as it applies to multimodal therapy?

a. Therapeutic flexibility and versatility are valued highly.

b. Therapists adjust their procedures to effectively achieve the client's goals in therapy.

c. Great care is taken to fit the client to a predetermined type of treatment.

d. The approach encourages technical eclecticism.

e. The therapist makes a comprehensive assessment of the client's level of functioning at the outset of therapy.

_____ 25. Which of the following is *not* considered one of the basic characteristics of contemporary behavior therapy?

a. Experimentally derived principles of learning are systematically applied to help people change their maladaptive behaviors.

b. Emphasis is on using evidence-based treatment interventions.

c. The focus is on assessing overt and covert behavior directly, identifying the problem, and evaluating change.

d. The therapy is an experiential and insight-oriented approach.

e. There is an attempt to develop culture-specific procedures and obtain clients' adherence and cooperation in a treatment program.

# Cognitive Behavior Therapy

 PRECHAPTER SELF-INVENTORY

**Directions:** Refer to page 41 for general directions. Use the following code:

5 = I *strongly agree* with this statement.

4 = I *agree,* in most respects, with this statement.

3 = I am *undecided* in my opinion about this statement.

2 = I *disagree,* in most respects, with this statement.

1 = I *strongly disagree* with this statement.

**Note:** Items 1–8 refer to Ellis's rational emotive behavior therapy.

_____ 1. Humans are born with the potential for both rational thinking and irrational thinking.

_____ 2. Even though it is desirable to be loved and accepted, it is not necessary.

_____ 3. We tend to accept irrational ideas, with which we unthinkingly keep re-indoctrinating ourselves.

_____ 4. Because they continue to accept and perpetuate irrational beliefs, human beings are largely responsible for creating their own emotional disturbances.

_____ 5. The main goal of therapy should be to reduce clients' self-defeating outlook and help them acquire a more rational philosophy of life.

_____ 6. Central functions of the therapist should include challenging clients' illogical ideas and teaching them how to think and evaluate in a rational way.

_____ 7. It is appropriate for a therapist to persuade, to be highly directive, to attack faulty thinking, and to serve as a counterpropagandist.

_____ 8. A warm or deep personal relationship between client and therapist is neither a necessary nor a sufficient condition for psychotherapy.

**Note:** Items 9–14 refer to Beck's cognitive therapy.

_____ 9. The therapist's role is to help clients look for evidence that either supports or refutes their hypotheses and views.

_____ 10. To understand the nature of emotional disturbances, it is essential to focus on the cognitive content of an individual's reactions to the upsetting event.

_____ 11. The internal dialogue of clients is critical in understanding behavior.

_____ 12. Thinking plays a major role in depression.

_____ 13. The most direct route to changing dysfunctional emotions and behaviors is to modify inaccurate and faulty thinking.

_____ 14. Therapy should consist of a process of co-investigation, or collaborative empiricism, as a way to uncover and examine faulty interpretations.

**Note:** Items 15–20 refer to Meichenbaum's cognitive behavior modification.

_____ 15. As a basic prerequisite to behavior change, clients need to notice how they think, feel, and behave and the impact they have on others.

_____ 16. Therapy involves helping clients become aware of their self-talk.

_____ 17. Much of the therapy process consists of teaching clients more effective coping skills in the sessions.

_____ 18. In stress-management training it is essential to teach clients how they contribute to their stress.

_____ 19. If clients hope to change, it is imperative that they practice new self-statements and apply their new skills in real-life situations.

_____ 20. It is important to provide a simple conceptual framework to clients outlining how they can interpret and react to stress differently.

# OVERVIEW: Rational Emotive Behavior Therapy and Cognitive Therapy

## Key Figures and Major Focus

Founder: Albert Ellis is the founder of rational emotive behavior therapy (REBT) and is the grandfather of the other cognitive behavioral approaches. Aaron Beck is the key spokesperson for cognitive therapy (CT). A highly didactic, cognitive, behavior-oriented approach, REBT stresses the role of action and practice in combating irrational, self-indoctrinated ideas. It focuses on the role of thinking and belief systems as the roots of personal problems. Beck's CT shares with REBT the active, directive, time-limited, present-centered, structured approach used to treat various disorders such as depression, anxiety, and phobias. It is an insight-focused therapy that emphasizes recognizing and changing negative thoughts and maladaptive beliefs.

## Philosophy and Basic Assumptions

REBT assumes that individuals are born with the potential for rational thinking but tend to fall victim to the uncritical acceptance of irrational beliefs. The assumption is that thinking, evaluating, analyzing, questioning, doing, practicing, and redeciding are at the base of behavior change. REBT is a didactic and directive model. Therapy is a process of reeducation. The cognitive behavioral approaches are based on the assumption that a reorganization of one's self-statements will result in a corresponding reorganization of one's behavior.

Like REBT, cognitive therapy rests on the premise that cognitions are the major determinants of how we feel and act. CT assumes that the internal dialogue of clients plays a major role in their behavior. The ways in which individuals monitor and instruct themselves and interpret events shed light on the dynamics of disorders such as depression and anxiety.

## Key Concepts

REBT holds that although emotional disturbance is rooted in childhood, people keep telling themselves irrational and illogical sentences. The approach is based on the A-B-C theory of personality: A = actual event; B = belief system; C = consequence. Emotional problems are the result of one's beliefs, which need to be challenged. The scientific method of logical and rational thought is applied to irrational beliefs.

According to CT, psychological problems stem from commonplace processes such as faulty thinking, making incorrect inferences on the basis of inadequate or incorrect information, and failing to distinguish between fantasy and reality. Cognitive therapy consists of changing dysfunctional emotions and behaviors by modifying inaccurate and dysfunctional thinking. The techniques are designed to identify and test the client's misconceptions and faulty assumptions.

## Therapeutic Goals

The goal of REBT is to eliminate a self-defeating outlook on life and acquire a more rational and tolerant philosophy. Clients are taught that the events of life themselves do not disturb us; rather, our interpretation of events is what is critical. Clients are taught how to identify and uproot their "shoulds," "musts," and "oughts." Further, they are taught how to substitute preferences for demands.

The goal of cognitive therapy is to change the way clients think by using their automatic thoughts to reach the core schemata and begin to introduce the idea of schema restructuring. Changes in beliefs and thought processes tend to result in changes in the way people feel and how they behave. Clients in CT are encouraged to gather and weigh the evidence in support of their beliefs. Through the collaborative therapeutic effort, they learn to discriminate between their own thoughts and the events that occur in reality.

## Therapeutic Relationship

In REBT, a warm relationship between the client and the therapist is not essential. However, the client needs to feel unconditional positive regard from the therapist. The therapist does not blame or condemn clients; rather, he or she teaches them how to avoid rating and condemning themselves. The therapist functions as a teacher; the client functions as a student. As clients begin to understand how they continue to contribute to their problems, they need to actively practice changing their self-defeating behavior and converting it into rational behavior.

Cognitive therapy emphasizes a collaborative effort. Together, the therapist and client frame the client's conclusions in the form of a testable hypothesis. Cognitive therapists are continuously active and deliberately interactive with the client; they also strive to engage the client's active participation and collaboration throughout all phases of therapy.

## Techniques and Procedures

Rational emotive behavior therapists are eclectic in that they use a variety of cognitive, affective, and behavioral techniques, tailoring them to individual clients. The approach borrows many methods from behavioral therapy. Cognitive techniques include disputing irrational beliefs, cognitive homework, changing one's language, and the use of humor. Emotive techniques include rational-emotive imagery, role playing, and shame-attacking exercises. Behavioral techniques include operant conditioning, self-management strategies, and modeling. Techniques are designed to induce clients to critically examine their present beliefs and behavior.

With respect to techniques and therapeutic style, there are some differences between REBT and cognitive therapy. REBT is highly directive, persuasive, and confrontive. Cognitive therapy emphasizes a Socratic dialogue and helping clients discover their misconceptions for themselves. Through a process of guided discovery, the therapist functions as a catalyst and guide who helps clients understand the connection between their thinking and the ways they feel and act.

## Applications

Applications of REBT include individual therapy, ongoing group therapy, marathon encounter groups, brief therapy, marriage and family therapy, sex therapy, and classroom situations. REBT is applicable to clients with moderate anxiety, neurotic disorders, character disorders, psychosomatic problems, eating disorders, poor interpersonal skills, marital problems, poor parenting skills, addictions, and sexual dysfunctions. It is most effective with those who can reason well and who are not seriously disturbed.

The most common application of cognitive therapy is in the treatment of depression and anxiety. CT has been applied successfully in treating a broad range of problems with children, adolescents, and adults. Cognitive methods have also been very useful in managing stress, in parent training, and in treating various clinical disorders.

## Contributions

Cognitive behavior therapy has wide applicability. Counseling is brief and places value on active practice in experimenting with new behavior so that insight is carried into doing. It discourages dependence on the therapist and stresses the client's capacity to control his or her own destiny. REBT is a comprehensive, integrative approach to therapy that uses cognitive, emotive, and behavioral methods to try to change disturbances in thinking, feeling, and behaving. REBT has shed much light on how people can change their emotions by changing the content of their thinking. It is in many ways the forerunner of other increasingly popular cognitive behavioral approaches.

With respect to cognitive therapy, Beck has made pioneering efforts in the treatment of anxiety, phobias, and depression, and this approach has received a great deal of attention by clinical researchers. He developed specific cognitive procedures that are useful in challenging a depressive client's assumptions and beliefs and in teaching clients how to change their thinking.

## Limitations

REBT does not provide a rationale for or clear explanation of why one tends to reindoctrinate oneself with irrational beliefs or why one clings to those beliefs. It does not apply to persons with limited intelligence. Possible dangers are the imposition of the therapist's own philosophy on the client and the psychological harm done to the client by the therapist who is overly confrontive or persuasive. In general, the cognitive behavioral approaches have the limitation of not emphasizing the exploration of emotional issues. Their focus on the role of thinking can lead to an intellectualized approach to therapy.

## GLOSSARY OF KEY TERMS

**A-B-C model** Temporal sequence of antecedents, behavior, and consequences. The theory that people's problems do not stem from activating events but, rather, from their beliefs about such events. Thus, the best route to changing problematic emotions is to change one's beliefs about situations.

**Automatic thoughts** Maladaptive thoughts that appear to arise reflexively, without conscious deliberation.

**Cognitive behavior therapy** A treatment approach that aims at changing cognitions that are leading to psychological problems.

**Cognitive errors** In cognitive therapy, the client's misconceptions and faulty assumptions. Examples include arbitrary inference, selective abstraction, overgeneralization, magnification, polarized thinking, and personalization.

**Cognitive restructuring** A process of actively altering maladaptive thought patterns and replacing them with constructive and adaptive thoughts and beliefs.

**Cognitive structure** The organizing aspect of thinking, which monitors and directs the choice of thoughts; implies an "executive processor," one that determines when to continue, interrupt, or change thinking patterns.

**Cognitive therapy** An approach and set of procedures that attempts to change feelings and behavior by modifying faulty thinking and believing.

**Collaborative empiricism** A strategy of viewing the client as a scientist who is able to make objective interpretations. The process in which therapist and client work together to phrase the client's faulty beliefs as hypotheses and design homework so that the client can test these hypotheses.

**Constructivism** A recent development in cognitive therapy that emphasizes the subjective framework and interpretations of the client rather than looking to the objective bases of faulty beliefs.

**Coping skills program** A behavioral procedure for helping clients deal effectively with stressful situations by learning to modify their thinking patterns.

**Distortion of reality** Erroneous thinking that disrupts one's life; can be contradicted by the client's objective appraisal of the situation.

**Internal dialogue** The sentences that people tell themselves and the debate that often goes on "inside their head"; a form of self-talk, or inner speech.

**Irrational belief** An unreasonable conviction that leads to emotional and behavioral problems.

**Musturbation** A term coined by Ellis to refer to behavior that is absolutist and rigid. We tell ourselves that we *must, should,* or *ought to* do or be something.

**Rationality** The quality of thinking, feeling, and acting in ways that will help us attain our goals. Irrationality consists of thinking, feeling, and acting in ways that are self-defeating and that thwart our goals.

**Rational emotive imagery** A form of intense mental practice for learning new emotional and physical habits. Clients imagine themselves thinking, feeling, and behaving in exactly the way they would like to in everyday situations.

**Relapse prevention** Procedure for promoting long-term maintenance that involves identifying situations in which clients are likely to regress to old patterns and to develop coping skills in such situations.

**Self-instructional therapy** An approach to therapy based on the assumption that what people say to themselves directly influences the things they do. Training consists of learning new self-talk aimed at coping with problems.

**Self-talk** What people "say" to themselves when they are thinking. The internal dialogue that goes on within an individual in stressful situations.

**Shame-attacking exercises** An REBT strategy of encouraging people to do things despite a fear of feeling foolish or embarrassed. The aim of the exercise is to teach people that they can function effectively even if they might be perceived as doing foolish acts.

**Stress-inoculation training** A form of cognitive behavior modification developed by Donald Meichenbaum that involves an educational, rehearsal, and application phase. Clients learn the role of thinking in creating stress, are given coping skills for dealing with stressful situations, and practice techniques aimed at changing behavior.

**Therapeutic collaboration** A process whereby the therapist strives to engage the client's active participation in all phases of therapy.

## QUESTIONS FOR REFLECTION AND DISCUSSION

1. Do you agree with the assumption of REBT that the basis for emotional disturbance lies in irrational beliefs and thinking? To what degree do you accept the notion that events themselves do not cause emotional and behavioral problems but, rather, that it is our cognitive evaluation and beliefs about life events that lead to our problems?

2. According to Ellis, effective psychotherapy can take place without personal warmth from the therapist. He contends that too much warmth and understanding can be counterproductive by fostering dependence on the therapist for approval. Beck contends that the therapeutic relationship is important and emphasizes the collaborative

nature of the work. Which of these views comes closer to your thinking about the role of the client–therapist relationship?

3. REBT tends to be highly directive, persuasive, and confrontive and focuses on the teaching role of the therapist. In contrast, cognitive therapy places more stress on a Socratic dialogue, a process of posing open-ended questions to clients and letting them arrive at their own conclusions. If you were a client, which style do you think would be more effective with you? As a counselor, which role might you favor? Why?

4. In Beck's cognitive therapy the assumption is that a client's internal dialogue plays a major role in behavior. For him, how individuals monitor themselves, how they give themselves praise or criticism, how they interpret events, and how they make predictions of future behavior are directly related to emotional disorders. How could you apply his ideas to counseling a depressed client? How might you teach such a client to challenge his or her own thinking and develop new thinking?

5. Beck maintains that systematic errors in reasoning lead to faulty assumptions and misconceptions, which he terms "cognitive distortions." After reviewing his list of cognitive distortions, which, if any, apply to you? Which CT procedures might be of value to you in examining your faulty assumptions?

6. In Meichenbaum's cognitive behavior modification, cognitive restructuring is vital in teaching people how to deal effectively with stress. Part of his program involves teaching clients cognitive and behavioral strategies to cope with stressful situations. If you had a client who wanted to learn self-management techniques to reduce stress, what are some specific steps you would teach the client?

7. What do you consider to be some of the major contributions of the cognitive behavioral approaches? How do you think cognitive factors influence one's emotions and behaviors?

8. Think of situations in which you might encounter clients with culturally diverse backgrounds. What aspects of cognitive behavioral therapy do you think might work well in multicultural counseling? How might you have to modify some of your techniques so that they would be appropriate for the client's cultural background?

9. Homework is a part of all of the cognitive behavioral approaches. What are some ways in which you might attempt to incorporate homework in your counseling practice? Can you think of ways to increase the chances of your client cooperating and carrying out the homework?

10. Can you think of ways to incorporate exploration of feelings in the cognitive behavioral approaches? Of the theories you've studied so far, what approaches might you want to blend with cognitive behavioral therapy? What are a few experiential techniques that you might want to add to the cognitive and behavioral techniques?

## ISSUES AND QUESTIONS FOR PERSONAL APPLICATION

The following questions and some of the underlying issues can be applied personally to help you get a better grasp of cognitive behavior therapy. Bring the questions to class for discussion.

1. Are you aware of reindoctrinating yourself with certain beliefs and values that you originally accepted from your parents or from society? Make a list of some of your beliefs and values. Do you want to keep them? Do you want to modify them?

2. Are you able to accept yourself in spite of your limitations and imperfections? Do you blame yourself or others for your limitations?

3. Review Ellis's list of irrational ideas. How many can you identify with? How do you think your life is affected by your irrational beliefs? How do you determine *for yourself* whether your beliefs are rational or irrational?

To help focus your thinking on the above issues, put a check (✓) before each of the following irrational beliefs that you see as applying to you:

_____ a. "I must be thoroughly competent in everything I do."

_____ b. "Others must treat me fairly and in ways that I want them to."

_____ c. "I must have universal approval, and if I don't get this approval from everyone, it's horrible and I feel depressed."

_____ d. "Life must be the way I want it to be, and if it isn't, I can't tolerate it."

_____ e. "If I fail at something, the results will be catastrophic."

_____ f. "I should feel eternally guilty and rotten and continue to blame myself for all of my past mistakes."

_____ g. "Because all of my miseries are caused by others, I have no control over my life, and I can't change things unless *they* change."

List a few other statements you tend to make that might pinpoint your core irrational ideas:

_____

_____

_____

_____

4. Select one of your beliefs that causes you trouble. Then review the A-B-C model of personality and attempt to apply that method to changing your irrational belief. What is the experience like for you? Do you think the method holds promise for helping you lead a less troubled life? How can you apply the approach to your daily life?

5. How can you challenge your own irrational beliefs and attitudes? Once you are aware of some basic problems or difficulties, what do you see that you can do *for yourself* to change toward a more rational system?

6. REBT practitioners are highly active and directive, and they often give their own views without hesitation. Does that style fit you personally? Could you adopt it and feel comfortable? Why or why not?

7. The REBT practitioner acts as a model. What implications do you see for self-development of the client? Can the client grow to become his or her own person, or does he or she become a copy of the therapist?

8. In being a model for clients, it is important that therapists not be highly emotionally disturbed, that they live rationally, that they not be worried about losing their clients' love and approval, and that they have the courage to confront clients directly. Would you have any difficulty in being that type of model? Explain.

9. Consider the applications of REBT to school counseling or to counseling in community mental health clinics. Assume that a practitioner who employs the principles and methods of REBT does not have a doctorate, has not had any supervised internship, and has not had extensive training in REBT. What cautions do you think need to be applied? What are the potential misuses of the approach? How can the approach have more potentially harmful results than, for example, the person-centered approach?

10. If you were to be a client in counseling, which approach might you favor for yourself—Ellis's REBT or Beck's cognitive therapy? What specific features of REBT might be useful in helping you cope with your problems? And what aspects of cognitive therapy could you use?

11. According to Meichenbaum's cognitive theory of behavior change, there are three relevant phases. Clients are asked to (1) observe and monitor their own behavior, identifying negative thoughts and feelings; (2) begin to create a new internal dialogue by substituting positive and constructive self-statements for negative ones; and (3) ac-

quire more effective coping skills that they can practice both in the therapy session and in real-life situations. For at least one week, identify some behavior you would like to change, and apply this three-phase process. Can you think of ways to use this strategy with your clients? In what counseling situations might you use Meichenbaum's cognitive restructuring techniques?

12. Assume that you are working with a small group of college students who have problems with test anxiety and fears relating to failure. If you were to employ *cognitive methods* to change their mental set and expectations, what are some things you might say to these students? In what ways might thoughts, self-talk, self-fulfilling prophecies, and attitudes of failure (all examples of cognitive processes) influence these students' *behavior* in test-taking situations?

   a. How would you set up your program?

   b. What cognitive techniques would you use? What other behavioral techniques would you employ to change these students' cognitive structures and their behavior?

   c. What are some ways by which you might evaluate the effectiveness of your program?

13. Complete the REBT Self-Help Form on page 130 by making it a homework assignment for a week. After you complete the form, look for patterns in your thinking. What connections do you see between your beliefs and the way you feel? Focus especially on creating *disputing* statements.

## PRACTICAL APPLICATIONS

REBT is based on the assumption that people create their own emotional disturbances. It places the individual squarely in the center of the universe and gives individuals almost full responsibility for choosing to make or not to make themselves seriously disturbed. It follows logically that if people have the capacity to make themselves disturbed by foolishly and devoutly believing in irrational assumptions about themselves and others, they can generally make themselves undisturbed again. REBT assumes that change can best be accomplished through rational emotive procedures and that to effect behavioral change, hard work and active practice are essential.

The homework assignment method is one good way of assisting clients in putting new behavior into practice. The method encourages clients to actively attack the irrational beliefs at the roots of their problems. In this exercise, suggest what you consider might be an appropriate homework assignment for each situation described.

1. The client, a college sophomore, wants to overcome his shyness around women. He does not date and even does his best to keep away from women because he is afraid they will reject him. But he does want to change that pattern. What homework might you suggest? _____

_____

_____

2. The client says that because she feels depressed much of the time she tries to avoid facing life's difficulties or anything about her that might make her feel more depressed. She would like to feel happy, but she is afraid of doing much. What homework might you suggest? _____

_____

_____

3. The client feels that he must win everyone's approval. He has become a "super nice guy" who goes out of his way to please everyone. Rarely does he assert himself, for fear

# RATIONAL EMOTIVE BEHAVIOR THERAPY
## SELF-HELP FORM

### A  (Activating Event)

[ ]

- Briefly summarize the situation you are disturbed about (what would a camera see?).
- An A can be internal or external, real or imagined.
- An A can be an event in the past, present, or future.

### C  (Consequences)

Major unhealthy negative **emotions**:

Major self-defeating **behaviors**:

**Unhealthy negative emotions include:**

- Anxiety
- Depression
- Low Frustration Tolerance
- Shame/ Embarrassment
- Hurt
- Rage
- Guilt
- Jealousy

---

| IBs (IRRATIONAL BELIEFS) | D (DISPUTING IBs) | RBs (RATIONAL BELIEFS) | E (NEW EFFECT) |
| --- | --- | --- | --- |

- _____
- _____
- _____
- _____

D:
- _____
- _____
- _____
- _____

RBs:
- _____
- _____
- _____
- _____

New healthy **negative behaviors:**

New constructive **behaviors:**

**To identify IBs, look for:**

- **Dogmatic Demands** (musts, absolutes, shoulds)
- **Awfulizing** (It's awful, terrible, horrible)
- **Low Frustration Tolerance** (I can't stand it)
- **Self/Other Rating** (I'm/he/she is bad, worthless)

**To dispute, ask yourself:**

- Where is holding this belief getting me? Is it *helpful* or *self-defeating*?
- Where is the evidence to support the existence of my irrational belief? Is it consistent with reality?
- Is my belief *logical*? Does it follow from my preferences?
- Is it really *awful* (as bad as it could be)?
- Can I really not stand it?

**To think more rationally, strive for:**

- **Non-Dogmatic Preferences** (wishes, wants, desires)
- **Evaluating Badness** (It's bad, unfortunate)
- **High Frustration Tolerance** (I don't like it, but I can stand it)
- **Not Globally Rating Self or Others** (I—and others—are fallible human beings)

**Healthy negative emotions include:**

- Disappointment
- Concern
- Annoyance
- Sadness
- Regret
- Frustration

*Source:* Dryden, W. (1995a). *Brief Rational Emotive Behaviour Therapy.* London: Wiley. Reprinted by Permission of Albert Ellis.

that he might displease someone who then would not like him. He says he would like to be less of a nice guy and more assertive. What homework might you suggest?

_____

_____

_____

4. The client would like to take a course in creative writing, but she fears that she has no talent. She is afraid of failing, afraid of being told that she is dumb, and afraid to follow through with taking the course. What homework might you suggest?

_____

_____

_____

5. The client continually accepts blame by telling himself what a rotten louse he is because he does not give his wife enough attention. He feels totally to blame for the marital problems between himself and his wife, and he says he cannot let go of his terrible guilt. What homework might you suggest? _____

_____

_____

_____

6. Each week the client comes to his sessions with a new excuse for why he has not succeeded in following through with his homework assignments. Either he forgets, gets too busy, gets scared, or puts it off—anything but actually *doing* something to change what he *says* he wants to change. Instead of really doing much of anything, he whines each week about how rotten he feels and how he so much would like to change but just doesn't know how. What homework might you suggest? _____

_____

_____

_____

## JERRY COREY'S WORK WITH RUTH FROM A COGNITIVE BEHAVIORAL PERSPECTIVE

In working with Ruth as a cognitive behavior therapist, I tend to employ a directive and action-oriented approach. In many ways the client–therapist relationship is like the student–teacher relationship. I view therapy as a learning process that will afford Ruth the opportunity to explore ways of changing her thinking, feeling, and behaving. I assist Ruth in identifying a number of her core beliefs, many of which she acquired from her parents. Once we have identified some of her major beliefs, I will ask her to begin thinking about the decisions she made about herself, others, and the world. I will also ask her to reflect on the direction her early decisions are taking her.

To achieve the goal of assisting Ruth in achieving a constructive set of beliefs and acquiring a self-enhancing internal dialogue, I perform several tasks as her therapist. First, I challenge Ruth to critically evaluate the self-defeating beliefs she originally accepted without questioning. Throughout the therapeutic process, I attempt to actively teach Ruth that being self-critical is the basis of many of her emotional and behavioral problems. Basically, Ruth tells herself that she must be perfect at everything. She has to be the supermother, superwife, and superstudent, to mention just a few. She berates herself when she does not measure up to expectations that others have set for her. She is beginning to realize that she is performance-oriented and rarely allows herself to enjoy the process.

I suggest a cognitive role-play situation in which I take on the role of Ruth's critical self and Ruth assumes the role of the side of her that would like to relax and let up on her demands.

RUTH: [*playing her more accepting side*] You don't need to drive yourself so hard. Be kinder to yourself, and give yourself room to be imperfect.

JERRY: [*playing Ruth's self-critical side*] Oh, but it's up to me to take care of everything—and perfectly well! If I don't, things will fall apart at home.

RUTH: Well, others in my family can take more responsibility. I'm tired of being the only one who is responsible for everything in the family.

JERRY: But if I let down, my family is going to suffer. So it's all up to me to do everything!

After engaging in a process of argumentation where Ruth tries to convince me that she has a right to lighten up, she becomes emotional. She realizes how exhausting it is to demand perfection of herself in all things. Listening to me as I played her critical side, Ruth becomes aware of the price she pays for driving herself. She is now in a position where she can actively challenge her self-talk and work toward replacing some faulty beliefs that influence what she does.

My major focus with Ruth is on her thinking. Only through learning to apply rigorous self-challenging methods will she succeed in freeing herself from the defeatist thinking that led to her problems. I am concerned that Ruth not only recognize her self-defeating thought patterns and the resultant feelings but also take steps to challenge and change them. Ruth's real work consists of doing homework in everyday situations and bringing the results of these assignments to our sessions for analysis and evaluation.

## You Continue Working With Ruth

1. What are a few of Ruth's faulty beliefs that you would want to target for intervention? How would you proceed in assisting her to challenge her thinking?

2. From what you know of Ruth, what kinds of homework might you suggest that would likely result in her examining her self-talk and core beliefs?

3. What are some cognitive and behavioral techniques that you are likely to employ in working with Ruth?

4. Refer to *Case Approach to Counseling and Psychotherapy* (Chapter 8) for examples of two different cognitive-oriented approaches to working with Ruth: Albert Ellis's rational emotive behavior therapy and Frank Dattilio's cognitive behavioral approach in couples and family therapy. In this chapter, I also show my style of applying cognitive behavioral techniques in working with Ruth. What aspects of the approaches of Ellis and Dattilio might you incorporate in counseling Ruth?

5. See the *CD-ROM for Integrative Counseling* (the session dealing with a cognitive focus) for a demonstration of how to utilize cognitive behavioral techniques in addressing Ruth's faulty thinking. Do you identify with any of Ruth's faulty beliefs? How might cognitive therapy help you?

 MARION: A Woman Who Lives by "Oughts" and "Shoulds"

## Some Background Data

Marion, age 37, is an African American physician who has lived by a series of "shoulds" and "oughts" for most of her life. Among the things she is now telling herself is that she *must* succeed in her profession. From her perspective, succeeding means being far better than most of her colleagues in her professional specialty, family medicine. Marion constantly berates herself for not being able to publish more research articles, for not keeping up with all the reading in her field, and for sometimes failing to live up to the expectations her patients have for her. One of her beliefs is that she should take care of everyone: her family, her friends, her colleagues, and her patients. It is essential for her to always be in control. Even without the benefit of therapy, Marion is aware that a key motivating force in her life is to demonstrate her success both as an African American and as a woman.

There is not much room in Marion's life for making mistakes. Her perfectionistic strivings are literally making her sick. She experiences frequent migraine headaches, chronic constipation, stomach pains, and dizziness. Although her body is sending her clear messages that she is driving herself relentlessly, she keeps forging ahead, thinking that she must meet all of her standards. Unfortunately, these standards are unrealistically high, and she will never be able to attain them. No matter what she achieves, she is chronically self-critical for not having done better or done more. On top of all this, Marion feels guilty about having all of her physical symptoms. As a physician, she thinks she should be in better control of her physical and mental state.

Marion judges herself constantly in all areas of her life. She gives herself grades for her performances, and her grades are typically low because she demands so much of herself. Marion struggles with feeling uncomfortable in social situations. She tells herself that she is not an interesting person and wonders how other people could enjoy her.

The reality is that Marion is deeply committed to her medical practice in a community health center. Both her colleagues and her patients have a great deal of respect for her. She puts in long hours and rarely takes any time off from work. When she is not working or achieving something, it is almost unbearable for her. The drive to accomplish more and more in a shorter amount of time keeps her from being able to relax. She often says she cannot afford the luxury of free time because there are so many important things to do.

In her family of origin Marion learned that it was not enough for African Americans to be simply good or even excellent, they must be *outstanding* in everything they attempt. Her parents frequently told her that if she followed through with her plans to go to medical school she would certainly encounter more than her share of discrimination on the grounds of both her race and her gender. She would have to prove herself time and again. Marion has accepted this view of life; moreover, she feels a great deal of pressure to live up to the high expectations of her parents and not to disappoint them.

## Jerry Corey's Way of Working With Marion From a Cognitive Behavioral Perspective

Marion presents herself voluntarily for therapy because she recognizes that her pressurized lifestyle is self-destructive. She would like to continue doing her best, but she does not want to feel that she always has to be the best in every aspect of her personal and professional life. It has finally come down to her feeling desperate. Marion feels miserable both physically and emotionally and has not been able to change her situation in spite of her most determined efforts. Marion says that she wants to learn to challenge her perfectionism and begin accepting herself as a worthwhile person in spite of her limitations. She would like very much to be able to enjoy her work without telling herself that she should and must do more. Marion has told herself that she ought to be less judgmental of herself than she is, yet this does little good.

### Exploring Marion's Self-Defeating Beliefs

Drawing on some of Beck's notions in cognitive therapy, I focus on Marion's internal communications. I assume that she monitors her thoughts, wishes, feelings, and actions. In social situations she probably keeps score of how other people are reacting to her. Her thinking is also polarized in many respects. She sees things in terms of good or bad, wonderful or horrible. Further, Marion engages in some "catastrophizing," in which she anticipates negative outcomes of her ventures. In sum, she is contributing to her emotional problems by what she is telling herself, by the assumptions she is making, and by her belief system.

To more clearly identify Marion's faulty cognitions, I use the REBT Self-Help Form as one of the main homework assignments. First of all, I ask her to write down an activating event (A), such as one of the times she made a mistake. Next she writes down the consequence (C), which is her guilty feelings or the self-defeating behavior she would like to change. Then, using the REBT form, I ask her to keep track of all of her irrational beliefs (IBs) that led to the consequence. The activating event was a situation in which one of her patients got upset and complained to her that she was not helping him and that he would be switching physicians. Initially, Marion says, she felt devastated. Although she had tried as hard as she could, her patient was a chronic complainer. Yet her beliefs about his displeasure over his medical care led her to feel depressed and inadequate.

### A Typical Session

During a typical session, Marion and I follow through with a critical evaluation of one of her irrational notions. She relates several situations in which older, White, male patients have expressed doubts about her ability to help them. She believes she has had to face and struggle with the reality of prejudice and discrimination all of her life and that she must still contend with prejudice from some of her patients. Together we explore this reality and begin to sort out realistic and unrealistic conclusions.

Given the reality of prejudice and discrimination against minorities, I still challenge Marion to change her thinking when it is not possible to change her environment. After discussing the many instances of discrimination she has experienced and her reactions to these events, we proceed to explore her belief that she must be an outstanding physician largely because she is an African American woman. I ask her to show me the evidence for her conclusion that because she is an African American woman she must constantly prove herself.

### Employing Techniques of Cognitive Behavior Modification

Marion continues to monitor her thoughts during a typical week by writing down specific situations that produce stress for her. She is getting better at noticing those factors, and she is also improving her ability to detect self-statements that increase her level of stress. As part of her homework, Marion records what she tells herself in problematic situations, what she then does, and how she feels. During her sessions, we go over her written analysis of her thinking, behaving, and feeling patterns in various situations. We then discuss alternative statements that she could make to herself, as well as ways that she could actually behave differently.

The beginning step in Marion's therapy consists of continued observation of her behavior in interpersonal situations. We go over her week as she recorded it to see what we can learn about the ways she is contributing to her fears in social situations through her negative thoughts. Marion reports that she has become aware of how many times in various social situations she sets herself up for failure by telling herself that people will not be interested in her.

The second step in changing Marion's cognitive processes involves my teaching her how to substitute *adaptive behavioral responses* for the maladaptive behaviors she now displays. If she hopes to change, what she says to herself must initiate a new behavioral chain—one that is incompatible with her maladaptive behaviors. Thus, we look at positive self-talk that can help her generate new expectations. She considers saying to herself: "Even though I'm nervous about meeting new people, I will challenge my assumption that people find me boring. I can learn to relax, and I can tell myself that I do have something to say." Marion is beginning to learn some new internal dialogues, and she is learning how to create positive expectations to guide new behavior.

The third phase of Marion's cognitive modification consists of learning more effective coping skills, which can be practiced in real-life situations. I teach her a standard *relaxation exercise* used in the cognitive behavioral approaches. I ask her to practice it twice a day for about 20 minutes each session. I teach her some training procedures in breathing and deep-muscle relaxation that she can apply to many of the situations she encounters that bring about anxiety. As Marion practices more effective coping skills, she notices that she is getting different reactions from others. This encourages her to continue with new patterns of behavior.

### Follow-Up: You Continue as Marion's Therapist

Consider the concepts and techniques I drew on and the style in which I did so as you think about how you might work with Marion. What would you do differently?

1. Do any of Marion's "shoulds," "oughts," and "musts" remind you of messages you tell yourself? How successful are you in identifying and working through some of your major irrational beliefs?

2. Are there any ways in which you might work with Marion differently than you would with a White female physician? with a White male physician? What special issues might you want to explore with her that are related to her gender and race?

3. How might you react if Marion were to say to you: "How can you understand my problems if you are not an African American woman who happens to be involved in a male-dominated medical profession?" What problems, if any, do you think you'd have in establishing an effective therapeutic relationship with her?

4. Most of Marion's work with me consists of identifying self-defeating notions and learning to dispute them, both in the therapy sessions and through activity-oriented homework assignments. I am trying to get Marion to see how her faulty beliefs lead to self-defeating thoughts, feelings, and actions. Do you think the cognitive behavioral approach is sufficient to produce lasting change? If not, what else do you think might be needed?

## QUIZ ON COGNITIVE BEHAVIOR THERAPY

### A Comprehension Check

Score _____%

**Note:** Refer to Appendix 1 for the scoring key.

**True/false items:** Decide if the following statements are "more true" or "more false" as they apply to REBT or other cognitive behavioral approaches.

T (F) 1. REBT makes use of both cognitive and behavioral techniques, but it does not use emotive techniques.

(T) F 2. REBT stresses the importance of the therapist demonstrating unconditional positive regard for the client.

T (F) 3. Cognitive therapy for depression was developed by Meichenbaum.

(T) F 4. REBT is a form of cognitive behavior therapy.

T (F) 5. Ellis shares Rogers's view of the client–therapist relationship as a condition for change to occur within clients.

T (F) 6. Beck developed a procedure known as stress-inoculation training.

T (F) 7. To feel worthwhile, human beings need love and acceptance from *significant* others.

(T) F 8. Ellis maintains that events themselves do not cause emotional disturbances; rather, it is our evaluation of and beliefs about these events that cause our problems.

T  F  9. A difference between Beck's cognitive therapy and Ellis's REBT is that Beck places more emphasis on helping clients discover their misconceptions for themselves than does Ellis.

T  F  10. According to Beck, people become disturbed when they label and evaluate themselves by a set of rules that are unrealistic.

**Multiple-choice items:**  Select the *one best answer* of those alternatives given. Consider each question within the framework of cognitive behavior therapy.

____ 11. Rational emotive behavior therapy stresses

   a. support, understanding, warmth, and empathy.
   b. awareness, unfinished business, impasse, and experiencing.
   c. thinking, judging, analyzing, and doing.
   d. subjectivity, existential anxiety, self-actualization, and being.
   e. transference, dream analysis, uncovering the unconscious, and early experiences.

____ 12. REBT is based on the philosophical assumption that human beings are

   a. innately striving for self-actualization.
   b. determined by strong unconscious sexual and aggressive forces.
   c. potentially able to think rationally but have a tendency toward irrational thinking.
   d. trying to develop a lifestyle to overcome feelings of basic inferiority.
   e. determined strictly by environmental conditioning.

____ 13. REBT stresses that human beings

   a. think, emote, and behave simultaneously.
   b. think without emoting.
   c. emote without thinking.
   d. behave without emoting or thinking.

____ 14. REBT views neurosis as the result of

   a. inadequate mothering during infancy.
   b. failure to fulfill our existential needs.

   c. excessive feelings.
   d. irrational thinking and behaving.

____ 15. According to REBT, what is the core of most emotional disturbance?

   a. self-blame
   b. resentment
   c. rage
   d. unfinished business
   e. depression

____ 16. REBT contends that people

   a. have a need to be loved and accepted by everyone.
   b. need to be accepted by most people.
   c. will become emotionally sick if they are rejected.
   d. do not need to be accepted and loved.
   e. need to be accepted and will become sick if they are rejected.

____ 17. According to REBT, we develop emotional disturbances because of

   a. a traumatic event.
   b. our beliefs about certain events.
   c. abandonment by those we depend on for support.
   d. withdrawal of love and acceptance.

____ 18. According to REBT, a personal client–therapist relationship is

   a. necessary, but not sufficient, for change to occur.
   b. necessary and sufficient for change to occur.
   c. neither necessary nor sufficient for change to occur.

____ 19. REBT includes all of the following methods except for

   a. persuasion.
   b. counterpropaganda.

c. confrontation.

d. logical analysis.

e. analysis of the transference relationship.

_C_ 20. Cognitive therapy is based on the assumption that

a. our feelings determine our thoughts.

b. our feelings determine our actions.

c. cognitions are the major determinants of how we feel and act.

d. the best way to change thinking is to reexperience past emotional traumas in the here-and-now.

e. insight is essential for any type of change to occur.

_C_ 21. In cognitive therapy techniques are designed to

a. assist clients in substituting rational beliefs for irrational beliefs.

b. help clients experience their feelings more intensely.

c. identify and test clients' misconceptions and faulty assumptions.

d. enable clients to deal with their existential loneliness.

e. teach clients how to think only positive thoughts.

_B_ 22. The type of cognitive error that involves thinking and interpreting in all-or-nothing terms or categorizing experiences in either-or extremes is known as

a. magnification and exaggeration.

b. polarized thinking.

c. arbitrary inference.

d. overgeneralization.

e. none of the above.

_E_ 23. Beck's cognitive therapy differs from Ellis's REBT in that Beck emphasizes

a. a Socratic dialogue.

b. helping clients discover their misconceptions by themselves.

c. working with the client in collaborative ways.

d. more structure in the therapeutic process.

e. all of the above.

_D_ 24. Beck's cognitive therapy has been most widely applied to the treatment of

a. stress symptoms.

b. anxiety reactions.

c. phobias.

d. depression.

e. cardiovascular disorders.

_B_ 25. In Meichenbaum's self-instructional therapy, which of the following is given primary importance?

a. detecting and debating irrational thoughts

b. the role of inner speech

c. learning the A-B-C theory of emotional disturbances

d. identifying cognitive errors

e. exploring feelings that are attached to early decisions

# Chapter 11

# Reality Therapy

 PRECHAPTER SELF-INVENTORY

**Directions:** Refer to page 41 for general directions. Use the following code:

5 = I *strongly agree* with this statement.

4 = I *agree,* in most respects, with this statement.

3 = I am *undecided* in my opinion about this statement.

2 = I *disagree,* in most respects, with this statement.

1 = I *strongly disagree* with this statement.

_____ 1. The underlying problem of most clients is the same: they are either involved in a present unsatisfying relationship or lack a significant relationship.

_____ 2. Therapy is literally teaching clients how to make better choices in dealing with the people they need in their lives.

_____ 3. Responsibility implies meeting one's own needs in such a way that others are not deprived of fulfilling their needs.

_____ 4. Our behavior, which is internally motivated and chosen, is always our best attempt to get what we want to satisfy our needs.

_____ 5. Insight is *not* essential to producing change.

_____ 6. There can be no basic personal change unless the client makes an evaluation of his or her behavior and then decides that a change is important.

_____ 7. It is clients' responsibility, not the therapist's, to evaluate their current behavior.

_____ 8. What is important is not the real world but the way we perceive the world.

_____ 9. When people say they are depressed, have a headache, are angry, or are anxious, it is more accurate for them to refer to themselves as depressing, headaching, angering, and anxietying, which implies responsibility for these conditions.

_____ 10. The notion of transference is both false and misleading. It can keep the therapist hidden, and it can be used to avoid discussing one's current behavior.

_____ 11. It is not productive for therapists to listen very long to a client complaining, blaming, and criticizing.

_____ 12. Essentially we choose all we do, which means we are responsible for what we choose.

_____ 13. The past is over, and revisiting it is not a productive use of therapy time.

_____ 14. Therapy should focus on *present behavior,* not on the past, not on attitudes, and not on feelings.

_____ 15. Unless the therapist creates an involvement with the client, no motivation for therapy exists.

_____ 16. Early in counseling it is essential to discuss with clients the overall direction of their lives, including where they are going and where their behavior is taking them.

_____ 17. For therapy to be effective, clients must decide on a plan for action and make a commitment to implement this plan in daily life.

_____ 18. Therapy can be considered a mentoring process in which the therapist is the teacher and the client is the student.

_____ 19. Much of the significant work of the counseling process focuses on helping clients identify specific ways to fulfill their wants and needs.

_____ 20. The core of the therapy process involves challenging clients to evaluate their behavior.

## OVERVIEW OF REALITY THERAPY/CHOICE THEORY

### Key Figures and Major Focus

Key figures: William Glasser and Robert Wubbolding. The approach was developed in the 1950s and 1960s. Originally it had no systematic theory but emphasized that individuals are responsible for what they do. In the 1970s and 1980s Glasser began teaching control theory, which states that all people have choices about what they are doing. By 1996 Glasser had revised this theory and renamed it *choice theory*, which provides a framework of why and how people behave. Choice theory is concerned with the phenomenological world of the client and stresses the subjective way in which clients perceive and react to their world from an internal locus of evaluation. Behavior is viewed as our best attempt to get what we want. Behavior is purposeful; it is designed to close the gap between what we want and what we perceive we are getting. Specific behaviors are always generated from this discrepancy. Our behaviors come from the inside, and thus we choose our own destiny.

### Philosophy and Basic Assumptions

Reality therapy is grounded on the basic premises of choice theory, which asserts that we are self-determining beings. Because we choose our total behavior, we are responsible for how we are acting, thinking, feeling, and for our physiological states. A major premise of choice theory is that all behavior is aimed at satisfying the needs for survival, love and belonging, power, freedom, and fun. Acting and thinking are chosen behaviors, which should be the focus of therapy. When we change our acting and thinking, we also indirectly influence how we are feeling as well as our physiological state. Choice theory explains how we attempt to control the world around us and teaches us ways to satisfy our wants and needs more effectively.

### Key Concepts

The main idea is that behavior is our attempt to control our perceptions of the external world so they fit our internal and need-satisfying world. Total behavior includes four inseparable but distinct components of acting, thinking, feeling, and the physiology that accompanies all our actions. Although we all possess the same five human needs, each of us fulfills them differently. We develop an inner "mental picture album" (or quality world) of wants, which contains precise images of how we would best like to fulfill our needs. A core principle of reality therapy/choice theory is that no matter how dire the circumstances, people always have a choice. The emphasis of reality therapy is on assuming personal responsibility and on dealing with the present. Reality therapy rejects many of the themes in psychoanalytic therapy, such as the medical model, the focus on the past, the exploration of dreams, dwelling on feelings or insight, transference, and the unconscious.

## Therapeutic Goals

The overall goal of this approach is to help people find better ways to meet their needs for survival, love and belonging, power, freedom, and fun. Changes in behavior should result in the satisfaction of basic needs. Other goals besides behavioral change include personal growth, improvement, enhanced lifestyle, and better decision making. Therapists help clients gain the psychological strength to accept personal responsibility for their lives and assist them in learning ways to regain control of their lives and to live more effectively. Clients are challenged to examine what they are doing, thinking, and feeling to figure out if there is a better way for them to function. Clients conduct explicit self-evaluations of each component of behavior to determine if they want to change.

## Therapeutic Relationship

The therapist initiates the therapeutic process by becoming involved with the client and creating a warm, supportive, and challenging relationship. Clients need to know that the therapist cares enough about them to accept them and to help them fulfill their needs in the real world. Both *involvement with* and *concern for* the client are demonstrated throughout the entire process. Once this involvement has been established, the counselor confronts clients with the reality and consequences of their actions. Throughout therapy the counselor avoids criticism, refuses to accept clients' excuses for not following through with agreed-on plans, and does not easily give up on clients. Instead, therapists continually assist clients to evaluate the effectiveness and appropriateness of their behavior.

## Techniques and Procedures

The practice of reality therapy can best be conceptualized as the cycle of counseling, which consists of two major components: (1) the counseling environment and (2) specific procedures that lead to change in behavior. These procedures are based on the assumption that human beings are motivated to change (1) when they determine that their current behavior is not getting them what they want and (2) when they believe they can choose other behaviors that will get them closer to what they want. Some of the specific procedures in the practice of reality therapy are summarized in the "WDEP" model, which refers to the following clusters of strategies:

> W = wants: exploring wants, needs, and perceptions.
>
> D = direction and doing: focusing on what clients are doing and the direction that this is taking them.
>
> E = evaluation: challenging clients to make an evaluation of their total behavior.
>
> P = planning and commitment: assisting clients in formulating realistic plans and making a commitment to carry them out.

(For a more detailed summary of the procedures that lead to change, see the two-page chart "Cycle of Managing, Supervising, Counseling and Coaching" on pages 142 and 143.)

## Applications

Originally designed for working with youthful offenders in detention facilities, choice theory and reality therapy are applicable to people with a variety of behavioral problems.

The approach can be applied to individual counseling, marital and family counseling, and group counseling. It has found wide application in military clinics that treat alcohol and drug abusers. Used on both the elementary and secondary school levels, the approach has been applied to teaching and administration. Choice theory is also applicable to social work, crisis intervention, institutional management, and community development.

## Contributions

As a short-term approach, reality therapy can be applied to a wide range of clients. It provides a structure for both clients and therapists to evaluate the degree and nature of changes. It consists of simple and clear concepts that are easily understood by many in the human services field, and the principles can be used by parents, teachers, ministers, educators, managers, consultants, supervisors, social workers, and counselors. As a positive and action-oriented approach, it appeals to a variety of clients who are typically viewed as "difficult to treat." The heart of reality therapy consists of accepting personal responsibility and gaining more effective control. People take charge of their lives rather than being the victims of circumstances beyond their control. This therapy approach teaches clients to focus on what they are able and willing to do in the present to change their behavior.

## Limitations

Reality therapy does not give enough emphasis to feelings, the unconscious, the therapeutic value of dreams, the place of transference in therapy, the effect of early childhood trauma, and the power of the past to influence one's present personality. There is a tendency for this approach to play down the crucial role of one's social and cultural environment in shaping behavior. It may foster a treatment that is symptom-oriented and discourage an exploration of deeper emotional issues.

## GLOSSARY OF KEY TERMS

**Autonomy**   The state that exists when individuals accept responsibility for what they do and take control of their lives.

**Commitment**   The act of sticking to a realistic plan aimed at change.

**Choice theory**   The view that humans are internally motivated and behave to control the world around them according to some purpose within them. We are basically self-determining and create our own destiny.

**Cycle of counseling**   Specific ways of creating a positive climate in which counseling can occur. The proper environment is based on personal involvement and specific procedures aimed at change.

**Involvement**   Therapist interest in and caring for the client.

**Paining behaviors**   Choosing misery by developing symptoms (such as headaching, depressing, and anxietying) because these seem like the best behaviors available at the time.

**Perceived world**   The reality that we experience and interpret subjectively.

**Psychological needs**   The needs for belonging, power, freedom, and fun; these are the forces that drive humans and explain behavior.

**Quality world**   The perceptions and images we have of how we can fulfill our basic psychological needs.

**Responsibility**   Satisfying one's needs in ways that do not interfere with others' fulfilling their needs.

**Self-evaluation**   Clients' assessment of current behavior to decide whether it is working and if what they are doing is meeting their needs.

**Total behavior**   The integrated components of doing, thinking, feeling, and physiology. Choice theory assumes that all elements of behavior are interrelated.

**WDEP system**   The key procedures applied to the practice of reality therapy groups. The strategies help clients identify their wants, determine the direction their behavior is taking them, make self-evaluations, and design plans for change.

# CYCLE OF MANAGING, SUPERVISING, COUNSELING AND COACHING

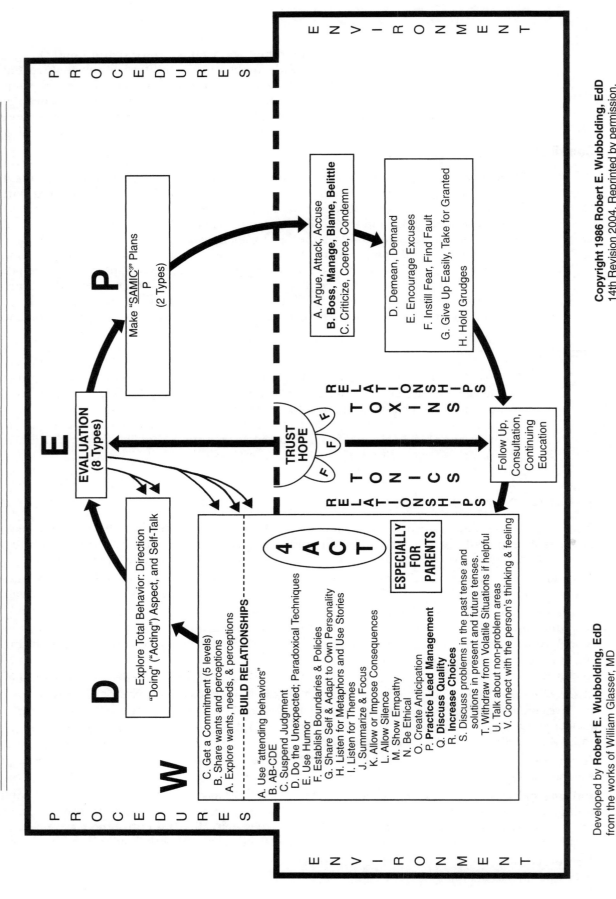

Developed by **Robert E. Wubbolding, EdD**
from the works of William Glasser, MD

**PROCEDURES**

**ENVIRONMENT**

**E**

**P**
Make "SAMIC³" Plans
P
(2 Types)

A. Argue, Attack, Accuse
**B. Boss, Manage, Blame, Belittle**
C. Criticize, Coerce, Condemn

D. Demean, Demand
E. Encourage Excuses
F. Instill Fear, Find Fault
G. Give Up Easily, Take for Granted
H. Hold Grudges

**EVALUATION**
**(8 Types)**

RELATIONSHIPS
TRUST
HOPE
F F F
RELATIONSHIPS

Follow Up,
Consultation,
Continuing
Education

**D**

Explore Total Behavior: Direction
"Doing" ("Acting") Aspect, and Self-Talk

**W**

C. Get a Commitment (5 levels)
B. Share wants and perceptions
A. Explore wants, needs, & perceptions

- - - - BUILD RELATIONSHIPS - - - -

A. Use "attending behaviors"
B. AB-CDE
C. Suspend Judgment
D. Do the Unexpected; Paradoxical Techniques
E. Use Humor
F. Establish Boundaries & Policies
G. Share Self & Adapt to Own Personality
H. Listen for Metaphors and Use Stories
I. Listen for Themes
J. Summarize & Focus
K. Allow or Impose Consequences
L. Allow Silence
M. Show Empathy
N. Be Ethical
O. Create Anticipation
P. **Practice Lead Management**
Q. **Discuss Quality**
R. **Increase Choices**
S. Discuss problems in the past tense and
   solutions in present and future tenses.
T. Withdraw from Volatile Situations if helpful
U. Talk about non-problem areas
V. Connect with the person's thinking & feeling

**4**
**A**
**C**
**T**

**ESPECIALLY**
**FOR**
**PARENTS**

**ENVIRONMENT**

# SUMMARY DESCRIPTION OF THE
## "CYCLE OF MANAGING, SUPERVISING, COUNSELING AND COACHING"

The Cycle is explained in detail in books by Robert E. Wubbolding:
*Employee Motivation, 1996: Reality Therapy for the 21st Century, 2000*
*A Set of Directions for Putting and Keeping Yourself Together, 2001*

## Introduction:

The Cycle consists of two general concepts: Environment conducive to change and Procedures more explicitly designed to facilitate change. This chart is intended to be a **brief** summary. The ideas are designed to be used with employees, students, clients as well as in other human relationships.

## Relationship between Environment & Procedures:

1. As indicated in the chart, the Environment is the foundation upon which the effective use of Procedures is based.

2. Though it is **usually** necessary to establish a safe, friendly Environment before change can occur, the "Cycle" can be entered at any point. Thus, the use of the cycle does **not** occur in lock step fashion.

3. Building a relationship implies establishing and maintaining a professional relationship. Methods for accomplishing this comprise some efforts on the part of the helper that are Environmental and others that are Procedural.

## ENVIRONMENT:

**Relationship Tonics:** a close relationship is built on TRUST and HOPE through friendliness, firmness and fairness.

A. Using Attending Behaviors: Eye contact, posture, effective listening skills.

B. AB = "Always **B**e . . ." **C**onsistent, **C**ourteous & **C**alm, **D**etermined that there is hope for improvement, **E**nthusiastic (Think Positively).

C. Suspend Judgment: View behaviors from a low level of perception, i.e., acceptance is crucial.

D. Do the Unexpected: Use paradoxical techniques as appropriate; Reframing and Prescribing.

E. Use Humor: Help them fulfill need for fun within reasonable boundaries.

F. Establish boundaries: the relationship is professional.

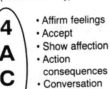

- Affirm feelings
- Accept
- Show affection
- Action consequences
- Conversation (WDEP)
- Time together

G. Share Self: Self-disclosure within limits is helpful; adapt to own personal style.

H. Listen for Metaphors: Use their figures of speech and provide other ones. Use stories.

I. Listen to Themes: Listen for behaviors that have helped, value judgements, etc.

J. Summarize & Focus: Tie together what they say and focus on them rather than on "Real World."

K. Allow or Impose Consequences: Within reason, they should be responsible for their own behavior.

L. Allow Silence: This allows them to think, as well as to take responsibility.

M. Show Empathy: Perceive as does the person being helped.

N. Be Ethical: Study Codes of Ethics and their applications, e.g., how to handle suicide threats or violent tendencies.

O. Create anticipation and communication hope. People should be taught that something good will happen if they are willing to work.

P. **Practice lead management, e.g., democracy in determining rules**.

Q. **Discuss quality.**

R. **Increases choices.**

S. Discuss problems in the past tense, solutions in present and future tenses.

T. Withdraw from volatile situations if helpful.

U. Talk about non-problem areas.

V. Connect with the person's thinking and feeling.

## Relationship Toxins:

Argue, **Boss Manage,** or Blame, Criticize or Coerce, Demean, Encourage Excuses, Instill Fear, or Give up easily, Hold Grudges.

Rather, stress what they **can** control, accept them as they are, and keep the confidence that they can develop more effective behaviors. Also, continue to use "WDEP" system without giving up.

Follow Up, Consult, and Continue Education:

Determine a way for them to report back, talk to another professional person when necessary, and maintain ongoing program of professional growth.

## PROCEDURES:

Build Relationships:

A. Explore **W**ants, Needs & Perceptions: Discuss picture album or quality world, i.e., set goals, fulfilled & unfulfilled pictures, needs, viewpoints and "locus of control."

B. Share Wants & Perceptions: Tell what you want from them and how you view their situations, behaviors, wants, etc. This procedure is secondary to A above.

C. Get a Commitment: Help them solidify their desire to find more effective behaviors.

Explore Total Behavior:

Help them examine the **D**irection of their lives, as well as specifics of how they spend their time. Discuss ineffective & effective self talk.

**E**valuation – The Cornerstone of Procedures:

Help them evaluate their behavioral direction, specific behaviors as well as wants, perceptions and commitments. Evaluate own behavior through follow-up, consultation and continued education.

Make **P**lans: Help them change direction of their lives.

Effective plans are **S**imple, **A**ttainable, **M**easurable, **I**mmediate, **C**onsistent, **C**ontrolled by the planner, and **C**ommitted to. The helper is **P**ersistent. Plans can be linear or paradoxical.

---

**Note:** The "Cycle" describes specific guidelines & skills. Effective implementation requires the artful integration of the guidelines & skills contained under Environment & Procedures in a spontaneous & natural manner geared to the personality of the helper. This requires training, practice & supervision. Also, the word "client" is used for anyone receiving help: student, employee, family member, etc.

---

### For more information contact:

Robert E. Wubbolding, EdD, Director

Center for Reality Therapy
7672 Montgomery Road, #383
Cincinnati, Ohio 45236

(513) 561-1911 • FAX (513) 561-3568
E-mail: wubsrt@fuse.net • www.realitytherapy.com

The Center for Reality Therapy provides counseling, consultation, training and supervision including applications to schools, agencies, hospitals, companies and other institutions. The Center is a provider for many organizations which award continuing education units.

## QUESTIONS FOR REFLECTION AND DISCUSSION

1. Choice theory is based on the premise that although outside events influence us we are not determined by them. To what degree do you agree with the assumption that our actions, thoughts, and emotions are the product of our choices? What are the implications for counseling practice of the way you answer this question?

2. Choice theory rests on the assumption that everything we do, think, and feel is generated by what happens inside us. What are the implications of this perspective for counseling practice? How would this view influence the interventions you may make?

3. What is the importance of defining and clarifying wants or "pictures"? What are the implications of counselors' helping clients express realistic wants?

4. If you were working with a man who was depressing and he insisted he couldn't help the way he felt, how would you deal with him by teaching him choice theory? Assume that he told you he was coming to you because he was not capable of getting out of his pit of depression. How would you proceed?

5. In what specific areas or situations might you have trouble allowing your clients to make self-evaluations? Might you be inclined to impose your values or perceptions on your clients? Would you be inclined to make evaluations for certain clients?

6. How would you proceed with a client who consistently refused to make any plans to change? How would you intervene with a client who made plans but then did not carry them out?

7. What are your reactions to reality therapy's focus on current behavior and its lack of interest in exploring the past? Compare and contrast this view of the role of the past with the psychoanalytic view.

8. Although reality therapists do not ignore feelings, they do not encourage clients to focus on feelings as if they were separate from actions and thoughts. What is your reaction to this approach?

9. If you were working with a culturally diverse population, how well do you think the concepts of choice theory and the practices of reality therapy might work? Assume that your clients want to focus on factors such as institutional racism, environmental barriers, and economic injustices that they are dealing with daily. How would it be for you (and for your clients) if you worked exclusively with reality therapy?

10. Assume that you are working with involuntary clients, mostly youths associated with gangs. Also assume that your clients are not particularly motivated to change their behavior but are motivated only to keep out of the courtroom. In what ways might you apply the principles of reality therapy?

## PRACTICAL APPLICATIONS OF CHOICE THEORY AND REALITY THERAPY

This set of exercises is based on a modification of the WDEP model as developed by Dr. Robert Wubbolding. One of the best ways to learn how to work with clients from a reality therapy perspective is for you to apply the procedures to your own life. Take time to engage in this self-reflection and self-evaluation. Doing so could help you make some significant changes in your life as well as enhance your skills in applying the WDEP model in your work with clients.

### W = What Is It That You Want?

Explore your wants, needs, and perceptions. If you had what you wanted now, how would your life be different?

Reflect on what you most want from yourself, friends, spouse or partner, religion or spirituality, work, and the world around you. Select *one* area as a target for further exploration. Apply this specific target example to the following questions.

1. What are you doing now to get what you say you want? How much effort are you devoting to get what you want?

2. How do you perceive yourself and significant others in your life?

3. How are you meeting your basic needs?

Reflect on the ways in which your needs are being met, as well as how you see them influencing your daily behavior. Rank the five basic needs in the order of their priority for you. As you reflect on your needs, ask yourself in what areas you would like to make changes.

*Survival.* To what degree are you maintaining vitality and good health, rather than merely surviving?

*Belonging.* What do you do to meet your needs for meaningful relationships? In what ways do you feel a sense of belonging?

*Power or achievement.* When do you feel a sense of power? In what areas of your life are you making significant achievements? When do you feel recognized?

*Freedom or independence.* To what degree do you feel that you are in charge of your life and are moving in the direction that you want?

*Fun or enjoyment.* What are those activities that you do for fun? Do you have as much fun as you would like?

Choose one specific need that you would like to change. For example, if you are not having as much fun in your life as you would like, what specifically would you like to be doing by way of fun that you are not? Reflect on what you are willing to do to change this aspect of your life.

## D = What Are You Doing?

Explore the *direction* in which your total behavior is moving you. What are you currently doing, and to what degree is it working for you?

1. Where is the overall direction of your life leading you? Where is your overall journey taking you? Is your destination taking you in a place you want to be? If you continue in the direction you are going now, where will you be in one year? five years?

2. Is the general direction of your life in your own best interest? Are you getting closer to your core goals? Is your overall direction moving you closer to the people with whom you want to be involved?

3. Is your behavior congruent with what you say you want? To what degree are your present actions in line with your core values?

4. How satisfied are you with most of your actions? Are there some ways you'd like to be acting that you are not? How would your life be different if you were acting the way you want?

5. More specifically, is your present specific behavior helping you get what you want? To what degree are your current actions helping or hurting you and your significant others?

6. Are your wants realistic and attainable? If you had in your life what you wanted at this point, what would that be like?

## E = How Willing Are You to Make a Searching Self-Evaluation?

Total behavior is composed of action, thinking, feelings, and physiology in an attempt to meet your needs and fulfill wants. You have most control over your actions, so let's focus on the acting dimension. Engage in a comprehensive self-evaluation to determine if you are getting what you want. As you review your behavior on a given day, think about what you would most want to change about yourself. Make a global self-assessment first.

1. What would you most want to accomplish in your life in the next few years in these areas: physically? emotionally? socially? spiritually? intellectually? professionally? in area of family relationships? contributing to humanity? financially?

2. What specific actions or thoughts would you like to change because they are not working for you?

3. To what degree do you think you are getting what you want?

4. Select one area that you are willing to invest time and effort in to bring about change. Reflect on the specific kinds of changes you most want to make in this particular area. To what degree are your current actions, cognitions, and feelings helping you?

5. What are you willing to do to make the changes you want?

6. Are you committed to taking action to change?

## P = Are You Ready to Make Plans to More Effectively Meet Your Needs?

Make plans designed to change the direction of your life. Take a particular target area that you have decided is important enough to you that you are willing to actually make a plan that will result in change. Think about a particular behavior you want to change and are willing to change. One of the best ways to understand the process of formulating personal plans is to develop such a plan yourself. In making your plan, consider these aspects of an effective plan:

- Make your plan simple.
- Determine if your plan is realistic and within your ability to follow through.
- Make your plan specific and measurable so you will be able to determine the degree to which you are succeeding.
- Design a long-range plan with specific short-range steps you can take to attain your overall goals.
- Work out the details of your plan.
- Be ready to make a commitment to sticking to a plan that is important to you and one you have decided you want to implement.

Apply these questions to developing your plan.

1. What kind of specific plan would you be interested in developing as a way to enhance your life?

2. How can you design a specific plan for change?

3. What will help you follow through with your plan and make a commitment to change?

4. If you follow through on your plan, how might your life be different?

## Using WDEP as an Approach to Self-Improvement

Select a number of specific aspects of your life that you are interested in changing and apply the WDEP model to your self-improvement program. For example, if you are not satisfied with your current level of exercise or the way you feel physically, consider what kinds of action plans you would be willing to incorporate in your daily life. It is important to be specific and begin with those areas you are willing to expend effort in exploring. Once you have made some concrete changes in the direction that is satisfying to you, it will be easier to tackle other areas of thinking, feeling, and acting that you want to modify. If you can do this kind of personal change, the chances are far greater that you will be able to inspire and motivate your clients to identify what they want, to assess the overall direction of their lives, to make a searching self-inventory of their total behavior, and to make workable plans aimed at change.

## JERRY COREY'S WORK WITH RUTH FROM A REALITY THERAPY PERSPECTIVE

As a reality therapist I do not tell Ruth what she should change but encourage her to examine what she wants and determine if what she is doing is meeting her needs. It is up to Ruth to decide how well her current behavior is working for her. Once Ruth makes her own evaluation about what she is actually doing, she can take some significant steps toward making changes for herself. She has a tendency to complain of feeling victimized and controlled, and my intention is to help her see how her behavior actually contributes to this perceived helplessness. Rather than focusing on her feelings of depression and anxiety, I choose to focus on what she does from the time she wakes up to the time she goes to bed. Through a self-observational process, Ruth gradually assumes more responsibility for her actions.

In applying reality therapy with Ruth, much of what we do consists of developing realistic and specific plans and then talking about how she might carry them out in everyday life. After Ruth becomes clearer about certain patterns of her behavior, I encourage her to develop a specific plan of action that can lead to the changes she desires. Broad and idealistic plans are bound to fail, so we work on a concrete plan for change that she is willing to commit herself to. When she does not stick with a subgoal or carry out a plan for the week, I am not likely to listen to any excuses. Eventually, Ruth gets better at setting smaller goals and makes more realistic plans. She stops and says, "Now I wonder if I really want to do this, or am I hearing someone else tell me that I should want it?"

### You Continue Working With Ruth

1. Refer to *Case Approach to Counseling and Psychotherapy* (Chapter 9) for examples of two different reality therapists' perspectives (William Glasser and Robert Wubbolding) on Ruth's case. In this chapter, I also show my style of applying reality therapy concepts in working with Ruth.

2. See the *CD-ROM for Integrative Counseling* (the session with a behavioral focus) for a demonstration of developing plans with Ruth that she can carry out in everyday life.

3. If Ruth were your client, how would you assist her in establishing specific action plans?

4. What might you say to Ruth if she did not follow through with some of her commitments in implementing her plan?

5. I expect Ruth to engage in self-evaluation. It is not my place as her counselor to evaluate her behavior; rather, it is my job to provide a structure that will enable her to make evaluations of what she is doing. How might you work with Ruth to ensure that she would make her own assessment of what she is currently doing and how well it is working for her?

## MANNY: A LOSER FOR LIFE?

### Some Background Data

The scene is a U.S. Army base in Germany. The army has a mandatory counseling program for drug and alcohol rehabilitation of personnel with addictive personalities. Manny is sent to me for mandatory counseling. Manny, at 27, has made the military his career. He approaches the session in a high state of anxiety and displays many nervous bodily mannerisms. In our first session I attempt to create a working relationship. My aim is to help Manny acquire a new perspective about a situation in which he sees himself as an involuntary client, so that he might perceive some payoffs in choosing to participate in counseling.

## Jerry Corey's Way of Working With Manny From a Reality Therapy Perspective

Initially, Manny does not want to be in the office. Rather than fighting his resistance, I go with it by engaging him in a discussion of the possible consequences of both seeing me and not seeing me. My hope is that he will find it easy enough to talk with me, that I will not appear overly threatening to him, and that I will be able to lay the foundations for more meaningful *involvement* with him. Even though he sees himself as an involuntary client, I challenge him a bit on the fact that he did indeed choose to come and see me rather than suffer the consequences of not keeping his appointment.

At another point Manny reminds me that he does not want to attend therapy sessions. I tell him then what we will be doing in the sessions and what he can expect of me. But I also tell him what I expect of him. I am not willing to see him unconditionally, nor am I willing to sit with him silently or try to pry things out of him. I suggest that I see him three times to explore the possibilities of what counseling can offer him. He agrees to come in for three sessions to learn about the counseling process, to look at what he is *doing* now, and to decide how well it is working for him. Notice that I am not determining what he will talk about, but I insist that on some level he address his present behavior. We then proceed with the first session.

Manny sees his locus of control as being outside of himself. Part of creating the involvement process consists of helping Manny find ways of gaining more effective control of his life. My aim is to help him look at what specific areas he has control over and what areas are outside of his control. I facilitate this process by encouraging him to explore his wants, needs, and perceptions.

MANNY: Sure, I've got my share of problems. You'd have some problems if you grew up the way I did. My old man kicked me out of the house when I was a kid, and I had to go and live with an uncle in East Los Angeles. I got in with a gang and started being a loser then. I got kicked out of school for peddling dope and gang activity. Never was able to hold a job. I mean, man, I've had a rough life. If you had all the things happen to you that I've had to go through, you might not have made it as far as I have.

JERRY: I haven't been through all that you have. I'm not sure I'd have survived. That doesn't necessarily mean I can't understand you. I'd like for you to give me that chance. Even though I've had different life experiences from yours, I may have some feelings that are similar to yours, and I may be able to see things the way you do. I'd like an opportunity to make contact with you, even for this single meeting.

MANNY: Well, before you can understand the way I am, you need to know about what I've lived through. My old man was never there, I got beat up all the time, I failed at everything I tried—I was a real loser. A loser from the word go. And it's mostly because I never had the things in life most normal kids have.

JERRY: You know, the way I work, I prefer to look at what you're doing *right now* in your life and what this behavior is actually getting you. I think we can easily get sidetracked if we go back into your past with all the details of the negative things that happened to you. I'm not so much interested in hearing about the loser you've been all your life as I am in getting you to think about the winner you can be in your future. I'd like to hear you talk about what you can have *some* control over *now*.

## Where I'd Proceed With Manny From Here

Assuming that Manny is willing to at least take a look at the results of his behavior, I ask him if he is committed to a better life for himself and how much he really wants change in his life. I ask him to talk more about some of the ways in which he has been a failure, and I challenge him to see if there are any ways in which he has contributed to his setbacks. However, my focus is on helping him see what steps he can now take toward becoming a successful person. Thus, our work together is grounded on the assumption that his behavior is an attempt to fulfill his basic needs for belonging, power, freedom, and fun. It is crucial that I do not judge his present behavior for him but that I continue to challenge Manny to do this himself. Thus, I will try to get Manny to realistically appraise his behavior.

My main concern at this point is for Manny to simply see that nothing in his life will change unless *he* sees the need for change. He says that although there are times when he would like to be different he does not know how to go about it. This provides an excellent lead for a discussion of specific plans that could lead to constructive changes for him. Therefore, I will at least begin by exploring with him some of the things he can do well, some of the things he likes, and some of the ways he would like to be different. This includes encouraging him to talk about the mental pictures he has about the life he would like. My hope is that he will begin to consider possibilities for himself that he has previously ruled out.

My job is to help Manny make plans that are immediate and realistic. Such plans can even begin during the session. Manny says he would like to specialize in electronics and that he has some talent in this area. I hope that before our session ends, he will at least have some plan for checking out the army's electronics program. This could even involve his making a phone call during the session to inquire about it. It is a good idea to write these plans down. If he agrees to short-range plans, we can discuss how he can best carry them out and what he might do if he encounters difficulties in doing what he says he would like to do. It would also be a good idea to ask him to consider what he might get from some further counseling sessions.

As part of the planning process, I would certainly refer Manny to a professional with expertise in addictions counseling. Once he has had some short-term counseling and made some decisions about wanting to change some of his behaviors, Manny is more likely to be open to getting specialized help in working on his addiction problem.

## Follow-Up: You Continue as Manny's Therapist

Assume that Manny does do something about his life and decides to give short-term counseling a try. He consults you and asks you to continue where he and I left off. Using reality therapy as a base, how might you proceed with him?

1. How do you perceive Manny? What are your personal reactions to him? Would you want to work with him? Why or why not?

2. To what degree have you had life experiences that would allow you to identify with Manny's drug problem and his failures? If you have not had similar feelings of being a loser, do you think you could be effective with him? Would you be inclined to refer Manny to a professional with expertise in addictions counseling from the very beginning? Why or why not?

3. Manny wants to talk about his past and the experiences he thinks contributed to the person he is today. I keep focusing him on the present and on what he might do about his future. What do you think of such an approach? What are its possible merits and limitations?

4. This approach stresses the importance of a concrete plan of action and a commitment from the client to follow the plan. What might you say and do if Manny neither

developed a concrete plan for change nor committed himself to the process of behavioral change?

5. In my session with Manny I make it clear that I am interested mainly in his actions, not in his feelings, not in changing his attitudes and beliefs, and not in helping him to acquire insight. What do you think of an approach that focuses so directly on one domain—in Manny's case, what he is doing today?

6. Manny was not identified with respect to cultural and ethnic background or to his race. Consider how you might work with him differently depending on his specific cultural and ethnic background. What variables might you attend to if his background were different from yours?

 # QUIZ ON REALITY THERAPY

## A Comprehension Check

Score _____%

**Note:** Refer to Appendix 1 for the scoring key.

**True/false items:** Decide if the following statements are "more true" or "more false" as they apply to reality therapy.

**(T)** F    1. What is important is not the way the real world exists but, rather, the way we perceive the world to exist.

**(T)** F    2. Choice theory is the framework for the practice of reality therapy.

T **(F)**    3. A good way to change behavior is for us to be self-critical.

T **(F)**    4. It is important to explore the past as a way to change current behavior.

T **(F)**    5. One of the therapist's functions is to make judgments about clients' present behavior.

T **(F)**    6. The focus of reality therapy is on attitudes and feelings.

**(T)** F    7. The use of contracts is often part of reality therapy.

**(T)** F    8. Reality therapy is grounded on some existential concepts.

**(T)** F    9. It is the client's responsibility to decide on the goals of therapy.

T **(F)**   10. Appropriate punishment is an effective way to change behavior.

**Multiple-choice items:** Select the *one best answer* of those alternatives given. Consider each question within the framework of reality therapy.

___E___ 11. The founder of reality therapy is
   a. Albert Ellis.
   b. Albert Bandura.
   c. Joseph Wolpe.
   d. William Wheeler.
   e. none of the above.

___B___ 12. According to this approach, insight
   a. is necessary before behavior change can occur.
   b. is not necessary for producing behavior change.
   c. will come only with changed attitudes.
   d. can be given to the client by the teachings of the therapist.

   e. will be discovered by the client alone.

___D___ 13. The view of human nature underlying reality therapy is
   a. that we have a need for identity.
   b. that we have the need to feel loved and to love others.
   c. that we need to feel worthwhile to ourselves and others.
   d. all of the above.
   e. none of the above.

___B___ 14. Which is *not* a key concept of reality therapy?
   a. focus on the present
   b. unconscious motivation

c. self-evaluations

d. involvement as part of the therapy process

e. responsibility

_E_ 15. Which of the following is *not* true of reality therapy?

a. Punishment is eliminated.

b. Clients must make commitments.

c. Therapists do not accept excuses or blaming.

d. Therapy is a didactic process.

e. Working through the transference relationship is essential for therapy to occur.

_B_ 16. Regarding the goals of reality therapy,

a. it is the therapist's responsibility to decide specific goals for clients.

b. it is the client's responsibility to decide goals.

c. the goals of therapy should be universal to all clients.

d. society must determine the proper goals for all clients.

e. both (c) and (d) are true.

_B_ 17. Concerning the role and place of making evaluations in reality therapy,

a. it is the therapist's function to make an evaluation concerning the morality of the client's behavior.

b. clients should make an evaluation concerning their own behavior.

c. value judgments should not be a part of reality therapy.

d. therapist evaluations should be made only when clients ask for such feedback.

_B_ 18. Which statement is *not* true of reality therapy?

a. It is based on a personal relationship.

b. It focuses on attitude change as a prerequisite for behavior change.

c. Planning is essential.

d. The focus is on the client's strengths.

_B_ 19. Reality therapy was designed originally for working with

a. elementary schoolchildren.

b. youthful offenders in detention facilities.

c. alcoholics.

d. drug addicts.

e. people with marital conflicts.

_E_ 20. Which of the following would *not* be used by a reality therapist?

a. analysis of the transference relationship

b. hypnosis

c. the analysis of dreams

d. the search for causes of current problems

e. all of the above

_D_ 21. Which of the following statements is true as it applies to choice theory?

a. Behavior is the result of external forces.

b. We are controlled by the events that occur in our lives.

c. We can control the behavior of others by learning to actively listen to them.

d. We are motivated completely by internal forces, and our behavior is our best attempt to get what we want.

e. We can control our feelings more easily than our actions.

_A_ 22. According to Glasser, all of the following are basic psychological needs except for

a. competition.

b. belonging.

c. power.

d. freedom.

e. fun.

_B_ 23. Choice theory tends to focus on

a. feeling and physiology.

b. doing and thinking.

c. coming to a fuller understanding of the past.

d. the underlying causes for feeling depressed or anxious.

e. how the family system controls our decisions.

_D_ 24. Sometimes it seems as though people actually choose to be miserable (depressed). Glasser explains the dynamics of *depressing* as being based on

a. keeping anger under control.
b. getting others to help us.
c. excusing our unwillingness to do something more effective.
d. all of the above.
e. none of the above.

_C_ 25. All of the following are procedures in reality therapy that are said to lead to change except for

a. exploring wants, needs, and perceptions.
b. focusing on current behavior.
c. the therapist's evaluating of the client's behavior.
d. the client's evaluating of his or her own behavior.
e. the client's committing to a plan of action.

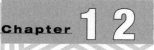

# Chapter 12

# Feminist Therapy

 PRECHAPTER SELF-INVENTORY

**Directions:** Refer to page 41 for general directions. Use the following code:

5 = I *strongly agree* with this statement.

4 = I *agree,* in most respects, with this statement.

3 = I am *undecided* in my opinion about this statement.

2 = I *disagree,* in most respects, with this statement.

1 = I *strongly disagree* with this statement.

_____ 1. Ideally, psychotherapy involves a partnership between equals.

_____ 2. Therapy practice needs to shift from its reliance on an intrapersonal psychopathology perspective to a focus on understanding the pathological forces in the culture that damage and constrain women.

_____ 3. The appropriate aims of therapy are social transformation and individual change.

_____ 4. The socialization of women inevitably affects their identity development, self-concept, goals and aspirations, and emotional well-being.

_____ 5. Feminist therapists are committed to monitoring their own biases and distortions, especially the social and cultural dimensions of women's experiences.

_____ 6. Although the therapeutic relationship is important, the relationship, in and of itself, is not sufficient to produce change.

_____ 7. Appropriate self-disclosure by the counselor can be therapeutic.

_____ 8. Therapists should actively work to demystify the counseling process.

_____ 9. It is important that clients tell their stories and give voice to their experiencing.

_____ 10. As much as possible, clients should be included in the assessment and treatment process.

_____ 11. Including the client in the therapeutic process increases the chances that interventions will be culturally appropriate.

_____ 12. Social action is an essential part of the therapy process.

_____ 13. The therapist should be viewed as one source of information rather than as the best or "expert" source.

_____ 14. The environment is a major source of pathology in the lives of women and men.

_____ 15. Gender is an essential consideration in effective therapy practice.

_____ 16. It is appropriate for therapists to help clients come to an understanding of how they are influenced by gender-role expectations and socialization.

_____ 17. An appropriate aim of therapy is to confront institutional policies that discriminate on any grounds.

_____ 18. Therapists would do well to empower clients to live according to their own values and to rely on an internal locus of control in determining what is right for them.

_____ 19. Therapist and client should take active and equal roles, working together to determine goals and procedures of therapy.

_____ 20. The therapist should strive to develop a collaborative relationship in which the client can become an expert on her- or himself.

## OVERVIEW OF FEMINIST THERAPY

### Key Figures and Major Focus

Although feminist therapy does not have a founder, or a single individual who developed the approach, women who have made significant contributions include Jean Baker Miller, Carol Gilligan, Carolyn Enns, Laura Brown, Lillian Comas-Diaz, and Olivia Espin. Feminist therapy has developed in a grassroots manner, responding to the emerging needs of women. Gender is the central focus of this approach. A central concept in this perspective is the concern for the psychological oppression of women and the socialization of women that affects their identity development.

### Philosophy and Basic Assumptions

Practitioners interpret the basic tenets of therapy in different ways depending on the feminist philosophy they espouse. Currently, there are at least eight basic philosophies underlying feminist practice: liberal, cultural, radical, socialist, postmodern, women of color, lesbian, and global/international. These various philosophies each have a different view on the sources of oppression and what is needed to bring about substantial social transformation. All of these theoretical perspectives focus on issues of diversity, the complexity of sexism, and the centrality of social context in understanding gender issues. Feminist therapists have challenged the male-oriented assumptions regarding what constitutes a mentally healthy individual. The underlying philosophy of feminist theory can be described as being gender-neutral, flexible, interactional, and life-span-oriented. Feminist therapists emphasize that gender-role expectations profoundly influence our identity from birth onward. Thus, therapy has the task of bringing to one's awareness how gender-role socialization is deeply ingrained in adult personality.

### Key Concepts

Feminist therapy is based on six interrelated principles:

- The personal is political.
- Personal and social identities are interdependent.
- Definitions of distress and mental illness are reformulated.
- Feminist therapists use an integrated analysis of oppression.
- The counseling relationship is egalitarian.
- Women's perspectives are valued.

A key concept of feminist therapy is the notion that societal gender-role messages influence how individuals view themselves and behave. Through therapy the impact of these socialization patterns are identified so that clients can critically evaluate and modify early messages pertaining to appropriate gender-role behavior. Most feminist therapists believe gender is always an important factor, but they realize that ethnicity, sexual orientation, and class may be more important factors in given situations and across situations for many women. The practice of contemporary feminist therapy is based on the assumption that gender cannot be considered apart from other identity areas such as race, ethnicity, class, and sexual orientation. A key concept pertaining to understanding symptoms is that problematic symptoms can be viewed as coping or survival strategies rather than as evidence of pathology. Although individuals are not to blame for personal problems largely caused by dysfunctional social environments, they are responsible for working toward change.

## Therapeutic Goals

Five goals for feminist therapy have been proposed: equality, balancing independence and interdependence, empowerment, self-nurturance, and valuing diversity. Feminist therapists believe gender is central to therapeutic practice and that understanding a client's problems requires adopting a sociocultural perspective. Both individual transformation and societal changes are crucial goals of therapy. At the individual level, therapists work to help women and men recognize, claim, and embrace their personal power. As a consciously political enterprise, another goal is social transformation. The aim is to replace the current patriarchy with a feminist consciousness, thus creating a society that values equality in relationships, that stresses interdependence rather than dependence, and that encourages both women and men to define themselves rather than being defined by societal demands.

## Therapeutic Relationship

The therapeutic relationship is based on empowerment, deliberately equalizing the power base between client and therapist. Empowerment and egalitarianism are guiding principles. The structure of the client–therapist relationship models how to identify and use power responsibly. Emphasis is given to mutuality, or a condition of authentic connection between client and therapist. The therapist works to demystify therapy and to include the client as an active partner in the assessment and treatment process. Therapists teach clients to recognize that how they define themselves and how they relate to others are inevitably influenced by gender-role expectations.

## Techniques and Procedures

Feminist therapy incorporates techniques from many of the traditional approaches, such as the use of therapeutic contracts, homework, bibliotherapy, therapist self-disclosure, empowerment, role playing, cognitive restructuring, reframing, relabeling, and assertiveness training. In addition, feminist procedures include gender-role analysis and intervention, power analysis and intervention, and social action. Feminist therapists have challenged assessment and diagnostic procedures on the grounds that they are often influenced by subtle forms of sexism, racism, ethnocentrism, heterosexism, ageism, or classism. In the feminist therapy process, diagnosis of distress becomes secondary to identification and assessment of strengths, skills, and resources.

## Applications

Feminist therapy can be applied to individual therapy with both women and men, couples therapy, family therapy, group counseling, and community intervention. The basic concepts of feminist therapy can be applied to most of the other theories of counseling.

## Contributions

A key contribution of feminist therapy is the potential for integration of feminist therapy principles and concepts with other therapeutic systems. Theories can be evaluated against the criteria of being gender-free, flexible, interactionist, and life-span-oriented. Therapists of any orientation can infuse feminist practices in their work if they conduct therapy with a positive, egalitarian attitude toward both women and men and are willing to confront patriarchal systems. The feminist approach emphasizes the importance of considering the context of women's lives rather than focusing narrowly on symptoms and behaviors. Feminism has done a great deal to sensitize therapists to the gendered uses of power in relationships, which can be applied to counseling with women and men. In addition, feminist therapy groups actively worked to establish shelters for battered women, rape crisis centers, and women's health and reproductive health centers. Along with multicultural therapists, feminist therapists have worked to establish policies that lessen the opportunities for discrimination of all types—gender, race, culture, sexual orientation, ability, and age. Feminist principles can be applied to supervision, teaching, consultation, ethics, research, and theory building, as well as to the practice of psychotherapy. Building community, providing authentic mutual empathic relationships, creating a sense of social awareness, and the emphasis on social change are all significant strengths of this approach.

## Limitations

Feminist therapists do not take a neutral stance; they advocate for change in social structures. A potential limitation pertains to therapists who may impose their values on clients regarding the need to challenge the status quo. However, culturally competent feminist therapists look for ways to work within the clients' culture by exploring consequences and alternatives, but not making decisions for clients. There is an appreciation of the complexities involved in changing within one's culture. Another criticism is that feminist therapy was developed by White, middle-class, heterosexual women and that its underlying assumptions are biased due to this narrow viewpoint.

 GLOSSARY OF KEY TERMS

**Androcentric theory**   A theory that uses male-oriented constructs to draw conclusions about human nature.

**Egalitarian relationship**   Power should be balanced in a relationship. In feminist therapy the voices of the oppressed are acknowledged as authoritative and valuable sources of knowledge.

**Ethnocentrism**   The idea that one's own cultural group is superior to others and that other groups should be judged based on one's own standards.

**Gendercentrism**   The idea that there are two separate paths of development for women and men.

**Gender-neutral theory**   Explains differences in the behavior of women and men in terms of socialization processes rather than viewing gender differences as fixed in nature.

**Gender-role analysis**   Used to help clients understand the impact of gender-role expectations in their lives.

**Gender-role intervention**   Provides clients with insight into the ways social issues affect their problems.

**Gender schema**   An organized set of mental associations people use to interpret their perceptions about gender.

**Heterosexism**   Views a heterosexual orientation as normative and desirable and devalues same-sex relationships.

**Life-span perspective**   Assumes that human development is a lifelong process and that personality patterns and behavioral changes can occur at any time.

**Personal is political**   Individuals' personal problems have social and political causes. Therapy is aimed at helping clients change their own behavior and become active participants in transforming society.

**Power analysis**   Emphasis is on the power difference between men and women in society. Clients are helped to recognize different kinds of power they possess and how they and others exercise power.

**Reframing**   A technique whereby the counselor changes the frame of reference for looking at an individual's behavior. There is a shift from an intrapersonal (or "blaming the victim") stance to a consideration of social factors in the environment that contribute to a client's problem.

**Relabeling**   An intervention that changes the label or evaluation applied to the client's behavioral characteristics. Generally, the focus is shifted from a negative to a positive evaluation.

**Relational-cultural theory**   A perspective suggesting that a woman's sense of identity and self-concept develop in the context of relationships.

**Self-in-relation**   The idea that a woman's sense of self depends largely on how she connects with others.

**White privilege**   An invisible package of unearned assets White people enjoy that are not extended to people of color.

## QUESTIONS FOR REFLECTION AND DISCUSSION

1. Feminist therapists teach their clients that uncritical acceptance of traditional roles can greatly restrict their range of freedom to define the kind of person they want to be. What are your thoughts about this?

2. The principle "the personal is political" holds that clients' problems have social and political causes. This implies that therapy should focus not only on individual change but social change as well. If you accept this principle, how would this affect your way of working with clients?

3. Feminist therapists do not restrict their practice to women; they also work with men, couples, families, and children. What are some ways feminist therapy concepts can be applied to counseling men?

4. Do you think a male therapist can be a feminist therapist? Why or why not?

5. In feminist therapy the therapeutic relationship is based on empowerment and egalitarianism. If you were to practice from this perspective, how could you work to actively break down the hierarchy of power in the therapy relationship? What interventions would you make to increase the empowerment of clients?

6. What are some ways you could demystify the therapeutic process at the initial session? What kinds of information would you most want to give to your clients? What would you do to promote a collaborative partnership?

7. Feminist therapists do not use diagnostic labels, or they use them reluctantly. They are critical of traditional assessment and diagnosis because of the belief that these procedures are often based on sexist assumptions. What are your thoughts concerning the feminist critique of assessment and diagnosis?

8. How could you apply what you have learned in your study of the previous eight traditional theories to the practice of feminist therapy? Do you see any basis for integrating some of the concepts and techniques of the traditional models with feminist therapy? What concepts and techniques of traditional therapy conflict with a feminist orientation?

9. What are your reactions to the feminist critique of family therapy? In what ways can family therapy be practiced with a focus on appreciating gender, power, and cultural variables?

10. What do you consider to be the major contributions of the feminist approach to the counseling profession? What are some criticisms or shortcomings of this approach?

## Quick Discrimination Index*

This social-attitude survey is designed to assess sensitivity, awareness, and receptivity to cultural diversity and gender equity. It is a self-assessment inventory, and it is essential that you strive to respond to each item as honestly as possible. This inventory is not designed to assess how you *should* think about cultural diversity and gender equity issues; rather, its aim is to assess subtle racial and gender bias. You can use this inventory to become more aware of your attitudes and beliefs pertaining to these issues.

**Directions:** Remember there are no right or wrong answers. Please circle the appropriate number to the right.

| | Strongly disagree | Disagree | Not sure | Agree | Strongly agree |
|---|---|---|---|---|---|
| 1. I do think it is more appropriate for the mother of a newborn baby, rather than the father, to stay home with the baby (not work) during the first year. | 1 | (2) | 3 | 4 | 5 |
| 2. It is as easy for women to succeed in business as it is for men. | 1 | (2) | 3 | 4 | 5 |
| 3. I really think affirmative-action programs on college campuses constitute reverse discrimination. | 1 | 2 | (3) | 4 | 5 |
| 4. I feel I could develop an intimate relationship with someone from a different race. | 1 | 2 | 3 | (4) | 5 |
| 5. All Americans should learn to speak two languages. | 1 | (2) | 3 | 4 | 5 |
| 6. It upsets (or angers) me that a woman has never been president of the United States. | 1 | 2 | (3) | 4 | 5 |
| 7. Generally speaking, men work harder than women. | 1 | (2) | 3 | 4 | 5 |
| 8. My friendship network is very racially mixed. | 1 | (2) | 3 | 4 | 5 |
| 9. I am against affirmative-action programs in business. | 1 | (2) | 3 | 4 | 5 |
| 10. Generally, men seem less concerned with building relationships than women. | 1 | 2 | (3) | 4 | 5 |
| 11. I would feel OK about my son or daughter dating someone from a different race. | 1 | 2 | 3 | (4) | 5 |
| 12. It upsets (or angers) me that a racial minority person has never been president of the United States. | 1 | 2 | (3) | (4) | 5 |

---

* The Quick Discrimination Index (QDI) is copyrighted by Joseph G. Ponterotto, Ph.D. No further reproduction or xeroxing of this instrument is permitted without the written permission of Dr. Ponterotto. If you are interested in using this instrument for any purpose, write to Joseph G. Ponterotto, Ph.D. (at the Division of Psychological and Educational Services, Fordham University at Lincoln Center, Room 1008, 113 West 60th Street, New York, NY 10023-7478) and request the "User Permission Form," the QDI itself, and the latest reliability and validity information.

|  | Strongly disagree | Disagree | Not sure | Agree | Strongly agree |
|---|---|---|---|---|---|
| 13. In the past few years, too much attention has been directed toward multicultural or minority issues in education. | 1 | 2 | (3) | 4 | 5 |
| 14. I think feminist perspectives should be an integral part of the higher education curriculum. | 1 | 2 | (3) | 4 | 5 |
| 15. Most of my close friends are from my own racial group. | 1 | 2 | 3 | (4) | 5 |
| 16. I feel somewhat more secure that a man rather than a woman is currently president of the United States. | 1 | (2) | 3 | 4 | 5 |
| 17. I think that it is (or would be) important for my children to attend schools that are racially mixed. | 1 | 2 | 3 | (4) | 5 |
| 18. In the past few years too much attention has been directed toward multicultural or minority issues in business. | 1 | 2 | (3) | 4 | 5 |
| 19. Overall, I think racial minorities in America complain too much about racial discrimination. | 1 | (2) | 3 | 4 | 5 |
| 20. I feel (or would feel) very comfortable having a woman as my primary physician. | 1 | 2 | 3 | (4) | (5) |
| 21. I think the president of the United States should make a concerted effort to appoint more women and racial minorities to the country's Supreme Court. | 1 | 2 | (3) | 4 | 5 |
| 22. I think White people's racism toward racial-minority groups still constitutes a major problem in America. | 1 | 2 | 3 | (4) | 5 |
| 23. I think the school system, from elementary school through college, should encourage minority and immigrant children to learn and fully adopt traditional American values. | 1 | 2 | (3) | 4 | 5 |
| 24. If I were to adopt a child, I would be happy to adopt a child of any race. | 1 | 2 | 3 | 4 | (5) |
| 25. I think there is as much female physical violence toward men as there is male physical violence toward women. | 1 | (2) | 3 | 4 | 5 |
| 26. I think the school system, from elementary school through college, should promote values representative of diverse cultures. | 1 | 2 | 3 | (4) | 5 |
| 27. I believe that reading the autobiography of Malcolm X would be of value. | 1 | 2 | (3) | 4 | 5 |
| 28. I would enjoy living in a neighborhood consisting of a racially diverse population (Asians, Blacks, Latinos, Whites). | 1 | 2 | (3) | 4 | 5 |

| | Strongly disagree | Disagree | Not sure | Agree | Strongly agree |
|---|---|---|---|---|---|
| 29. I think it is better if people marry within their own race. | 1 | (2) | 3 | 4 | 5 |
| 30. Women make too big a deal out of sexual-harassment issues in the workplace. | 1 | (2) | 3 | 4 | 5 |

The total score measures overall sensitivity, awareness, and receptivity to cultural diversity and gender equality. Of the 30 items on the QDI, 15 are worded and scored in a positive direction (high scores indicate high sensitivity to multicultural/gender issues), and 15 are worded and scored in a negative direction (where low scores are indicative of high sensitivity). Naturally, when tallying the total score response, these latter 15 items need to be *reverse-scored*. Reverse scoring simply means that if a respondent circles a "1" they should get five points; a "2" four points, a "3" three points, a "4" two points, and a "5" one point.

The following QDI items need to be *reverse-scored*: 1, 2, 3, 7, 9, 10, 13, 15, 16, 18, 19, 23, 25, 29, 30.

Score range = 30 to 150, with high scores indicating more awareness, sensitivity, and receptivity to racial diversity and gender equality.

*98*

## Follow-Up to Self-Inventory of Your Beliefs on Cultural Diversity and Gender Equity Issues

**Directions:** Fill in the blanks with your responses based on your answers to the "Quick Discrimination Index" self-inventory. Remember that there are no "correct" answers and that the point of the exercise is to stimulate you to reflect on your own attitudes pertaining to gender-role socialization and gender equity. Now that you have finished the self-inventory and completed the follow-up questions, discuss what you've learned about yourself with others in your class. How will your own gender-role socialization affect the manner in which you counsel others? What are some of your gender biases that are likely to influence your counseling practice?

1. Go over the 30 items you've rated in the Quick Discrimination Index and list at least 3 statements where you have concerns about your responses. *There are none that really concern me, it might just change my answer if I knew more information such a 1 because if the baby is breast fed I do think the mother should stay home. Another two are 23, 27.*

2. Identify any of your responses that reveal either gender bias or cultural bias on your part. *I think any question that dealt with females, because I am a strong believer that women are just as able or equal to men. Some of these are 1, 6, 7.*

3. What are your thoughts about the price women must pay for accepting traditional gender roles? *I think that it's rediculous because men are able to do these roles just as well as we are. I do think though that some things are starting to change and have reversed roles*

4. Give your reaction to this statement: "Women have been restricted by their cultural conditioning and by accepting gender-role stereotypes that keep them in an inferior position." _I think that it is not true, because you are able to say this about any stereotype and it is their fault for accepting it._

5. How do you view feminist therapy with respect to addressing cultural diversity and gender equity issues in the therapy process? _I think that you would need to fully understand the other culture before addressing the feminist perspective so that you do not say or suggest something out of line._

6. Write down the characteristics you see as essential to your view of yourself as being a woman or being a man. _I think some characteristics would be caring, loving, independent/strong will, determination and confidence._

7. How did you acquire your gender views, and to what degree are you satisfied with them? _I think I have acquired them through family and being the only girl with two brothers I think has been and influence, I feel that I am satisfied with them_

8. How might your own views about gender influence your counseling practice? _I hope that they won't but some issues to women I feel strong about and it could impact my clients._

 ## JERRY COREY'S WORK WITH RUTH FROM A FEMINIST PERSPECTIVE

I use contracts as a way to make the goals and processes of therapy overt rather than covert and mysterious. This is in keeping with the feminist perspective of striving to make the client a therapeutic partner. When I first mention to Ruth that our work will be defined by a therapeutic contract, she seems resistant. She thinks it sounds so formal and legalistic, and she wonders why it is necessary.

JERRY: A contract sets the focus for therapy. As the client, you decide what specific beliefs, emotions, and behaviors you plan to change to reach your stated goals.

RUTH: But I'm not quite sure what I want to change. I was counting on you to point out to me what I should work on. There's so much to change, and frankly I'm at a loss where to begin.

JERRY: Part of our work here will entail determining where in your life you want to take on more responsibility.

At this point Ruth and I discuss this issue in some detail. I let her know that my approach to therapy is based on the expectation that clients focus on their goals and make a commitment. It emphasizes the division of responsibility and provides a point of departure for working.

RUTH [*after some exploration*]: I just want to be me. I want to be happy. I'm tired of taking care of everyone else, and I want to take care of me.

JERRY: That's a start, but can you narrow this down? What would make you happy? What do you mean by taking care of yourself? How will you do this? And in what ways are you not being you?

I work with Ruth until she eventually comes up with clear statements of what she wants from therapy, what steps she will take to get what she wants, and how she will determine when her contract is fulfilled. After much discussion and a series of negotiations, Ruth comes up with a list of changes she is willing to make.

RUTH: For one, I'm willing to approach my husband and tell him what I feel about our relationship. I know you say I can't change him and that I can only change myself, so I'll tell him what I intend to do differently. And later, I would like to deal directly with my four children. They all take advantage of me, and I intend to change that. I can begin by telling them what I'm willing to do and what I'm no longer willing to do.

Although this list is more specific than her original goals, there is still a need for greater specificity.

I ask Ruth exactly what she does want to change about each area she has mentioned, including what she intends to do differently. One part of Ruth's contract involves asking her husband to attend at least one of the sessions so that she can tell him the specific things she most wants to change in their relationship.

For most of her life Ruth has been programmed to believe she should be what others expect her to be, that she should not voice what she wants, and that she should go along with the program others have for her. I will employ some assertiveness training strategies at this point, and we will spend considerable time exploring where Ruth acquired her views about the "proper role of women." As Ruth begins to restructure some of her core beliefs, she recognizes she has a right to be different. Once Ruth begins to think differently, she is more amenable to learning specific skills for being assertive.

## You Continue Working With Ruth

1. What would you want to tell Ruth about the therapy process from the beginning? How would you obtain her informed consent?

2. If you were to continue counseling Ruth, what direction would you likely follow?

3. If Ruth and John were to attend a session with you, what would be your interventions with them as a couple?

4. Refer to *Case Approach to Counseling and Psychotherapy* (Chapter 10) for a comprehensive illustration of three feminist therapists (Kathy Evans, Susan Seem, and Elizabeth Kincade) who collaboratively work with Ruth. See also Pam Remer's (also a feminist therapist) approach with Ruth as a survivor of sexual violence. I also demonstrate my version of counseling Ruth from a feminist perspective. Would you use one of these approaches in counseling Ruth? Why or why not?

5. See the *CD-ROM for Integrative Counseling* (first three sessions) and analyze my attempt to incorporate feminist principles and concepts in my beginning work with Ruth. How would you work with Ruth in these early sessions?

## MARIA: Torn Between Herself and Her Culture

### Some Background Data

Maria is a 32-year-old Latina whose parents were born in Mexico. She and her parents now live in Arizona, where she is pursuing graduate study in social work. Her ultimate goal is to make her home in Mexico and work in the management of social service agencies. She sees a great need for counseling and social work in Mexico, and she is committed to helping her people. Maria has completed all her course work in the doctoral program in social work. To get her degree, she needs to complete her doctoral dissertation, which she has been putting off for well over a year.

Maria is seeking therapy with me because she wants to work on her fears of succeeding and her struggles with her parents over the fact that they are not accepting of her professional ambitions. During the intake interview, Maria tells me that a negative experience she had with another male therapist made it extremely difficult for her to seek help again. She feels that her former therapist was not at all sensitive to her cultural background and did not understand the nature of her struggles as a woman.

## Jerry Corey's Way of Working With Maria From a Feminist Perspective

Because I am not Mexican American and Maria's experiences with her previous therapist were not satisfactory, she is concerned about my ability to relate to her situation. She lets me know that she places great value on her family, on respect for her parents, and on remaining true to the values espoused by her religion. Although she struggles with her parents, she has no intention of cutting them out of her life. Assuming a feminist orientation, I will describe how I work with Maria and her significant others.

In Maria's case, a general goal from a feminist perspective is to empower her to make choices pertaining to her identity as a woman. From the outset I stress a therapeutic contract, setting the focus for counseling. Maria will have to decide what specific beliefs, feelings, and behaviors she wants to change. In her family she has been told what is best for her, which makes it difficult for her to identify what she wants for herself. Early in the sessions I will encourage her to explore her wants within the context of her culture. I hope Maria will gradually begin to identify what she hopes to change about herself and how she can accomplish her stated goals. However, Maria is vague in stating what she wants. She tells me she is confused about her desires. She finally says that she wants to "be myself around my father" and also to "feel free to live my own life, rather than doing what my family expects of me." One way I can assist Maria in becoming more concrete is to ask her specific questions that call on her to use descriptive language.

We work together to narrow down her goals, and Maria finally comes up with a clearer statement of her personal goals. Maria recognizes her pattern of avoiding completion of projects. She is aware that she initiates diverse projects, yet she does not allow herself to do what is necessary to complete them. As part of her therapeutic work, she wants to explore the meaning and the implications of this pattern in her life. She hopes to become her own person and still maintain a relationship with her family.

Early in our therapy sessions, Maria begins exploring the meaning of her failure to complete projects, which leads us to discuss her role in her family of origin. She has accepted and learned definite roles, and she now rehearses and acts out these roles according to the expectations of her parents. I am likely to raise questions of Maria such as: "In what type of family did you grow up?" "In reviewing your early years, what are a few events that seem most significant to you now, and why?"

In working with Maria in the context of her family and cultural background, I take into account certain cultural values that she expresses early in the course of our work together. Her culture has contributed to her view of herself as a woman. She has clear expectations of appropriate gender-role behavior that separates women from men. In her culture women are traditionally expected to be submissive, docile, intuitive, feeling, gentle, caring, sentimental, and dependent. Her culture taught her that men are supposed to be strong, determined, authoritarian, independent, courageous, rational, objective, and forceful.

Maria is willing to explore the ways in which her "family rules" and gender-role socialization have affected her. Maria has probably heard many verbal and direct messages, as well as some subtle ones that she inferred from her parents' actions. Examples of these messages are:

- Men need to be taken care of.
- Men are more important than women.
- Women must silently endure the hardships of life and marriage.
- A woman's place is at home with the children, creating the perfect environment for her husband.

We will certainly take into account the power that cultural messages about appropriate gender-role behavior continue to wield in her life today. For instance, simply coming to therapy proved to be extremely difficult. It is considered highly inappropriate for her to seek help with her problems outside of the church or her family. Merely coming to therapy goes against her cultural norms.

Although it is acceptable for Maria to study psychotherapy and practice it with others as a helper, she feels it is not acceptable for her to need this help or to reveal her deeper problems to others. Her negative experience with her previous therapist has compounded her reluctance to explore her own psychological world.

Maria is caught between two cultures. If she does accept some of the values of the dominant culture, she wants to do so without losing her Mexican American cultural traits. She is having a difficult time balancing the demands of her traditional family against the dominant culture in which she lives, and she is experiencing even more trouble defining what she expects for herself. Whether Maria marries into her culture will be a key to which direction she will go. However, given her present leanings, it will be quite surprising if she can live in a strictly traditional environment without resentment and frustration. Our work together consists of discovering ways in which her family and culture influence her now and how she might begin to initiate a process of personal change.

If Maria hopes to change, she will have to take action and do something, rather than merely talk about the prospects of change. Because feminist therapy is action-oriented, Maria and I think of ways she can practice some behaviors that will challenge the early decisions she made. We collaboratively design plans for how she can actually complete a very meaningful project—in the situation at hand, her doctorate. The therapy involves going through each of the steps and practicing what she has typically done to procrastinate and what she can do differently now to overcome the barriers that will prevent her from completing this important task. We explore her fears of the board of examiners and predict the worst outcomes she can imagine. She is convinced of the importance of finishing her dissertation, and she makes a commitment to stick to her contract.

I also use a future-projection technique and ask Maria to imagine talking to each member of her family, letting them know that she has completed her doctorate. I ask her to talk to me as her father, mother, and each of her brothers. I also ask her to "become each family member" and say to me what she expects they might tell her; then she also says what she hopes each of them would say. This provides fertile ground for discussion, and it is a way of working with Maria in the environmental context. As a suggested homework assignment, Maria agrees to write a letter to each family member—but not to send the letter. She is taking steps to open doors that could lead to enhanced communication.

An important aspect of therapy is to help Maria find some way that satisfactorily blends her Mexican American cultural values and the dominant cultural values into a new synthesis. If Maria wants to pursue a profession, she will probably have to come to grips with the reality that her culture does not put a great deal of emphasis on women achieving individual professional goals. It is likely that she will experience conflicts as she attempts to integrate some of her new ways when she encounters significant people in her life. In our sessions we practice various ways to respond when others do not accept the changes she is making. Ultimately, Maria is the expert on her life, and she will make the choices that change her life.

## Follow-Up: You Continue as Maria's Therapist

Assume that Maria continues counseling with the goal of working toward making decisions that are best for her, even if they are different from those her family expects. On my referral she comes to see you. Show how you would work with her from a feminist perspective.

1. Maria really lives in two cultures. How might you help her work through what seem to her to be insurmountable conflicts? How might you help her respect and appreciate the values she acquired from her family and culture?

2. If what Maria wanted was diametrically opposed to what would be acceptable in her culture, how would you proceed? What might you suggest if you saw that her progress in attaining her personal goals would result in alienating her from her family and from her culture?

3. What specific feminist therapy strategies are you likely to employ with Maria? Can you see ways of blending a feminist and a systemic perspective? What techniques from other approaches might you utilize?

4. What specific knowledge would you want to have about Mexican American traditions and the culture in which Maria grew up as a child and as a youth? What mistakes might you make if you attempted to counsel her without taking into account her family and cultural background?

5. Do any of Maria's early experiences and decisions touch off any associations with your life? To what degree have you faced, or do you now face, similar issues? How do you think this will either facilitate or interfere with your work with her?

## QUIZ ON FEMINIST THERAPY

### A Comprehension Check

Score _____%

**Note:** Please refer to Appendix 1 for the scoring key.

**True/false items:** Decide if the following statements are "more true" or "more false" as they apply to feminist therapy.

T  F  1. Although feminist therapy addresses social and political issues pertaining to gender-role stereotyping, this approach does not address most other forms of oppression.

T  F  2. One of the goals of feminist therapy is to help women understand how sexist and oppressive societal beliefs and practices influence them in negative ways.

T  F  3. A criticism of feminist therapy is that it was developed by White, middle-class, heterosexual women.

T  F  4. Therapist self-disclosure is rarely used in feminist therapy.

T  F  5. Gender-role analysis involves a cooperative exploration by client and therapist of the impact of gender on the client's distress.

T  F  6. In feminist therapy, clients are viewed as active participants in redefining themselves in the context of the therapeutic relationship rather than the therapist being viewed as the best or "expert" source.

T  F  7. Feminist therapy is an approach that is applicable to women but not to men.

T  F  8. Instead of being diverse, feminist practice is a single and unified approach to therapy.

T  (F)  9. Because women are assuming positions of leadership in government and business, this can be interpreted to mean that women no longer have difficulty making life choices.

T  ( F )  10. It is probably accurate to say that in today's society barriers no longer stand in the way of gender equity.

**Multiple-choice items:** Select the *one best answer* of those alternatives given. Consider each question within the framework of feminist therapy.

___A___  11. Which branch of feminist therapy provides a model for critiquing the value of other traditional and feminist approaches?

a. postmodern feminism
b. women of color feminism
c. lesbian feminism
d. global/international feminism
e. none of the above

___d___  12. All of the following are considered aspects of the "third wave" of feminist perspectives except for

a. postmodern feminism.
b. women of color feminism.
c. lesbian feminism.
d. cultural feminism.
e. global/international feminism.

___c___  13. All of the following are ways feminist therapy differs from traditional therapy except for

a. viewing problems in a sociopolitical and cultural context.
b. demystifying the therapeutic process.
c. accepting the premise that diagnosis is a basic prerequisite for effective treatment.
d. creating a therapeutic relationship that is egalitarian.
e. recognition that clients know what is best for their life and are experts in their own life.

___A___  14. Which of the following interventions is least likely to be used by a feminist therapist?

a. analysis and interpretation of transference
b. sex-role analysis and intervention
c. power analysis and intervention
d. encouraging clients to take social action
e. assertiveness training

___d___  15. Which of the following is considered to be a major contribution feminists have made to the field of counseling?

a. pioneering research in the therapy process
b. creation of a brief, solution-focused therapy approach
c. integrating a diagnostic perspective in counseling practice
d. paving the way for gender-sensitive practice
e. all of the above

___b___  16. The principle of "the personal is political" implies that women's problems are

a. primarily due to unresolved intrapsychic conflicts.
b. mainly socially, culturally, and politically caused.
c. due to the fact that women have traditionally been denied political power.
d. best solved through adjustment to social and political norms and expectations.

___b___  17. All of the following are considered to be constructs of feminist theory except being

a. gender-neutral.
b. androcentric.
c. life-span-oriented.
d. interactionist.
e. flexible.

___b___  18. The feminist philosophy that emphasizes the differences between women and men and views the goal of therapy as being the infusion of cooperative values in society is

a. liberal feminism.
b. cultural feminism.
c. postmodern feminism.
d. social feminism.

_A_ 19. The feminist philosophy that emphasizes helping individual women overcome the limits and constraints of their socialization problems is

a. liberal feminism.
b. cultural feminism.
c. global/international feminism.
d. social feminism.

_D_ 20. This approach to feminism focuses on multiple oppressions and has the goals of transforming social relationships and institutions.

a. liberal feminism
b. cultural feminism
c. radical feminism
d. social feminism

_C_ 21. The philosophy that focuses on the oppression of women that is embedded in patriarchy and seeks to change society through activism is known as

a. women of color feminism.
b. cultural feminism.
c. radical feminism.
d. social feminism.

_E_ 22. Part of the feminist critique of assessment and diagnosis is that these procedures

a. are often based on sexist assumptions.
b. minimize the effect of environmental factors that influence behavior.
c. provide different treatments to women and men who display similar symptoms.
d. tend to reinforce gender-role stereotypes and encourage adjustment to the status quo.
e. do all of the above.

_C_ 23. Which of the following is not considered to be a basic principle of feminist therapy?

a. Women's experiences are honored.
b. Therapy involves an integrated analysis of oppression.
c. Definitions of distress and mental illness are based on the DSM-IV-TR.
d. Counseling is based on a relationship that is egalitarian.
e. The personal is political.

_b_ 24. What perspective calls for feminist theory to include an analysis of multiple identities and their relationship to oppression?

a. postmodern feminism
b. lesbian feminism
c. radical feminism
d. cultural feminism
e. liberal feminism

_b_ 25. Which of the following statements about feminist therapy is _not_ true?

a. Therapy is relatively short term.
b. The model underlying practice tends to be static.
c. A goal is to replace the current patriarchal system with feminist consciousness.
d. Women are encouraged to define themselves rather than being defined by societal demands.
e. Feminist therapy differs from traditional therapy in a number of ways.

# Postmodern Approaches

 PRECHAPTER SELF-INVENTORY

**Directions:** Refer to page 41 for general directions. Use the following code:

5 = I *strongly agree* with this statement.
4 = I *agree,* in most respects, with this statement.
3 = I am *undecided* in my opinion about this statement.
2 = I *disagree,* in most respects, with this statement.
1 = I *strongly disagree* with this statement.

_____ 1. Assessments and provisional diagnoses are best arrived at in a collaborative conversation with clients.

_____ 2. Changing the direction in therapy from a problem-focus to a solution-focus can dramatically change clients' beliefs about their life situation.

_____ 3. An appropriate aim of therapy is to create conversations with clients that allow for developing new meanings for problematic thoughts, feelings, and behaviors.

_____ 4. A not-knowing position allows therapists to follow, affirm, and be guided by the stories of their clients.

_____ 5. People live their lives according to the stories people tell about them and the stories they tell themselves.

_____ 6. The client should be viewed as the expert on his or her own life.

_____ 7. Clients are often stuck in a pattern of living a problem-saturated story that is not working for them.

_____ 8. Clients are able to build more satisfying lives in a relatively short period of time in the context of an effective therapeutic relationship.

_____ 9. It is important that clients tell their stories and give voice to their experiencing.

_____ 10. A problem-focused approach to therapy is likely to cement unhelpful modes of behavior.

_____ 11. Including the client in the therapeutic process increases the chances that interventions will be culturally appropriate.

_____ 12. Rather than dwelling on what is wrong with people, it is more useful to view the client as resourceful and competent.

_____ 13. The therapist should be viewed as one source of information rather than as the best or "expert" source.

_____ 14. Collaboration, compassion, respect, reflection, and discovery are characteristic of effective therapeutic relationships.

_____ 15. The therapist's role of being respectfully curious encourages clients to explore the impact of the problem on them.

_____ 16. As clients become free of problem-saturated stories, they become more able to envision and plan for a less problematic future.

_____ 17. An appropriate aim of therapy is assist clients in creating a more satisfying story.

_____ 18. A useful strategy is to attempt to separate a problem from a person's identity.

_____ 19. For therapy techniques to effectively be implemented, it is essential that a quality relationship exists between client and therapist.

_____ 20. Empathy and the collaborative partnership in the therapeutic process are more important than assessment or technique.

## OVERVIEW OF POSTMODERN APPROACHES

### Key Figures and Major Focus

The postmodern approaches do not have a single founder. Rather, these approaches represent a collective effort by many. Two co-founders of solution-focused brief therapy are Insoo Kim Berg and Steve de Shazer. Two co-founders of narrative therapy are Michael White and David Epston. Some of the major postmodern approaches include social constructionism, solution-focused brief therapy, and narrative therapy. In these approaches the therapist disavows the role of expert, preferring a more collaborative and consultative stance. The focus is not on discussing problems but on creating solutions. In narrative therapy the focus is on searching for times when clients were strong or resourceful and on helping clients separate from the dominant cultural narratives they have internalized so as to open space for the creation of alternative life stories.

### Philosophy and Basic Assumptions

From the viewpoint of social constructionism, the stories that people tell are about the creation of meaning. There may be as many stories of meaning as there are people who tell stories, and each of these stories is true for the individual who is telling the story. Postmodernists assume that realities are socially constructed. There is no absolute reality, and therapists should not impose their vision of reality or their values on an individual. Both solution-focused brief therapy and narrative therapy are based on the optimistic assumption that people are healthy, competent, resourceful, and possess the ability to construct solutions and alternative stories that can enhance their lives. Complex problems do not necessarily require complex solutions. The expertise of the therapist involves helping clients recognize the competencies they possess. Attention is given to what clients are doing that is working and helping them to build on their potential, strengths, and resources. Narrative therapists strive to avoid making assumptions about people out of respect for each client's unique story and cultural heritage.

### Key Concepts

Key concepts of solution-focused brief therapy include a movement from problem-talk to solution-talk and a focus on keeping therapy simple and brief. There are exceptions to every problem, and by talking about these exceptions, clients are able to conquer what seem to be gigantic problems. Therapists pay attention to what is working, and then do more of this. Change is constant and inevitable, and small changes pave the way for larger changes. Little attention is paid to pathology or to giving clients a diagnostic label. A therapist's not-knowing stance creates an opportunity for the client to construct a solution.

Some key concepts of narrative therapy include a discussion of how a problem has been disrupting, dominating, or discouraging the person. The therapist attempts to separate clients from their problems so that they do not adopt a fixed view of their identities. Clients are invited to view their stories from different perspectives and eventually to co-create an alternative life story. Clients are asked to find evidence to support a new view of themselves as being competent enough to escape the dominance of a problem and are encouraged to consider what kind of future could be expected from the competent person that is emerging.

## Therapeutic Goals

The solution-focused model emphasizes the role of clients establishing their own goals and preferences. This is done when a climate of mutual respect, dialogue, inquiry, and affirmation are a part of the therapeutic process. Working together in a collaborative relationship, both the therapist and client develop useful treatment goals. Through the use of the miracle question, solution-focused therapists help clients identify goals and potential solutions. The heart of the therapeutic process from the postmodern perspectives involves identifying how societal standards and expectations are internalized by people in ways that oftentimes constrain and narrow the kind of life they are capable of living. The general theme of narrative therapy is to invite clients to describe their experience in fresh language, which tends to open up new vistas of what is possible.

## Therapeutic Relationship

From the social constructionist viewpoint, therapy is a collaborative venture; the therapist strives to carry out therapy *with* an individual, rather than doing therapy *on* an individual. Instead of aiming to *make* change happen, the therapist attempts to create an atmosphere of understanding and acceptance that allows individuals to tap their resources for making constructive changes. Both solution-focused and narrative therapists adopt a "not-knowing" position to put clients in the position of being the experts about their own lives. The therapist-as-expert is replaced by the client-as-expert. Therapists do not assume that they know more about the lives of clients than they do. Clients are the primary interpreters of their own experiences. Therapists attempt to create collaborative relationships based on the assumption that collaboration opens up a range of possibilities for present and future change. One way of creating a working therapeutic partnership is for the therapist to show clients how they can use the strengths and resources they already possess to construct solutions. In the narrative approach, the therapist seeks to understand clients' lived experience and avoid efforts to predict, interpret, or pathologize. Narrative therapists collaborate with clients in assisting them to experience a heightened sense of agency or ability to act in the world.

## Techniques and Procedures

Social constructionists use a range of techniques, depending on the therapist's orientation. Some therapists ask the client to externalize the problem and focus on strengths or unused resources. Others challenge clients to discover solutions that might work. Their techniques focus on the future and how best to solve problems rather than on understanding the cause of problems.

The solution-focused approach represents a different perspective from most of the traditional therapy models with respect to thinking about and doing brief therapy. A number of solution-focused brief therapy techniques are frequently used, including pretherapy change, exception questions, the miracle question, scaling questions, homework, and summary feedback.

Solution-focused brief therapists often ask clients at the first session, "What have you done since you called for an appointment that has made a difference in your problem?" Asking about pretherapy change tends to encourage clients to rely less on the therapist and more on their own resources to reach their goals.

Exception questions direct clients to those times in their lives when their problems did not exist. Exploring exceptions offers clients opportunities for evoking resources, engaging strengths, and creating possible solutions. Illustrations of questions looking for exceptions are: "When was the last time that things were better? Talk about times when things were going well for you? What were you doing then? What are some things that you have done that helps with your problem? How will you know when you are handling your problem well?"

The miracle question allows clients to describe life without the problem. This question involves a future focus that encourages clients to consider a different kind of life than one dominated by a particular problem. The miracle question focuses clients on searching for solutions. Examples are: "How will you know when things are better? What will be some of the things you will notice when life is better?"

Scaling questions require clients to specify, on a scale of zero to 10, improvement on a particular dimension. This technique enables clients to see progress being made in specific steps and degrees.

Homework often consists of asking clients to observe events that they would like to see occur more frequently in the future.

Therapists may provide summary feedback in the form of genuine affirmations or pointing out particular strengths that clients have demonstrated.

Narrative therapy emphasizes the quality of the therapeutic relationship and the creative use of techniques within this relationship. In narrative therapy the therapy process provides the sociocultural context where clients are assisted in separating themselves from their problems and are afforded the opportunity of authoring new stories. Some specific narrative techniques include externalizing, mapping the effects, deconstruction, co-authoring alternative stories, and building an audience as a witness to the emerging preferred story. Narrative therapy's most distinctive feature is captured by the statement, "The person is not the problem, but the problem is the problem." Conversations are aimed at separating the problem from the person rather than insisting that the person own the problem. The assumption is that clients can develop alternative and empowering stories once they have distanced themselves from the problems and cultural notions they have internalized. In narrative therapy it is through a systematic process of careful listening, coupled with curious, persistent, and respectful questioning that the therapist works with clients to explore the impact of the problem on them and what they are doing to reduce the effects of the problem. It is through this process that the client and therapist co-construct enlivening alternative stories.

## Applications

Solution-focused brief therapy can be applied to individual therapy in a wide array of settings, including inpatient treatment centers, schools, and medical settings. The approach has been used to address diverse clinical problems, including substance abuse, depression, sexual abuse, child abuse, and spousal abuse.

Narrative therapy has been applied to a broad range of human problems, including relationship problems, depression, eating disorders, and problems in childhood and adolescence. Narrative ideas are applied in various areas, some of which include, school counseling, maritial and family therapy, mediation, substance abuse counseling, and clinical supervision.

## Contributions

A key contribution of all the postmodern approaches is the optimistic orientation that views people as being competent and able to create better solutions and more life-affirming stories. The nonpathologizing stance taken by postmodern practitioners moves away from dwelling on what is wrong with a person to emphasizing creative possibilities. Problems are not viewed as pathological manifestations but as ordinary difficulties and challenges of life. As therapists listen to a client's story, they pay attention to details that give evidence of a client's competence in taking a stand against an oppressive problem. A strength of both solution-focused and narrative therapies is the use of questioning, especially future-oriented questions that challenge clients to think about how they might solve potential problems in the future.

## Limitations

Many of the limitations of both solution-focused and narrative therapies pertain to lack of skill on the part of the therapist to implement techniques. Some inexperienced or untrained therapists may be enamored by any number of techniques: the miracle question, scaling questions, the exception question, and externalizing questions. Although a number of techniques are available to both solution-focused and narrative therapists, the attitude of the therapist is critical to the success of outcomes. To effectively practice solution-focused brief therapy it is essential that therapists are skilled in brief interventions. This means that in a relative short time practitioners are able to make quick assessments, assist clients in formulating specific goals, and effectively use appropriate interventions. In the practice of narrative therapy, there is no recipe, no set agenda, and no formula that the therapist can follow to assure desired outcomes.

## GLOSSARY OF KEY TERMS

**Alternative story**    The story that develops in counseling in contradiction to the dominant story that is embedded in a client's problem.

**Co-authoring**    The process by which both therapist and client share responsibility for the development of alternative stories.

**Deconstruction**    The exploration of meaning by taking apart, or unpacking, the taken-for-granted categories and assumptions underlying social practices that pose as truth.

**Dominant story**    A way of understanding a situation that has been so widely accepted within a culture that it appears to represent "reality." Growing out of conversations in a social and cultural context, dominant stories shape reality in that they construct and constitute what people see, feel, and do.

**Exception questions**    Solution-focused therapists inquire about those times in clients' lives when the problems they identify have not been problematic. Exploring these exceptions reminds clients that problems are not all-powerful and have not existed forever.

**Externalizing conversation**    A way of speaking in which the problem may be spoken of as if it is a distinct entity that is separate from the person. Externalization is based on the notion that when clients view themselves as "being" the problem they are greatly limited in the ways they can effectively deal with the problem.

**Formula first session task**    A form of homework a therapist might give clients to complete between their first and second therapy sessions. Clients are asked to simply observe what is happening in their lives that they want to continue happening.

**Mapping-the-influence questions**    A series of questions asked about a problem that a client has internalized as a means of understanding the relationship between the person and the problem.

**Miracle question**  A solution-focused technique that asks clients to imagine how their life would be different if they woke up tomorrow and they no longer had their problem.

**Narrative**  A social constructionist conceptualization of how people create "storied" meaning in their lives.

**Narrative therapy**  A postmodern approach to therapy that is based on the therapist's personal characteristics that allow for creating a climate that encourages clients to see their stories from different perspectives. Grounded in a philosophical framework, narrative practices assist clients in finding new meanings and new possibilities in their lives.

**Not-knowing position**  A therapist's stance that invites clients to become the experts who are informing the therapist about the significant narratives of their lives.

**Postmodernism**  A philosophical movement across a variety of disciples that has aimed at critically examining many of the assumptions that are part of the established truths of society. The postmodern worldview acknowledges the complexity, relativity, and intersubjectivity of all human experience.

**Postmodernist**  A believer in subjective realities that cannot exist independently of the observational processes used. Problems exist when people agree that there is a problem that needs to be addressed.

**Pretherapy change**  At the first therapy session, solution-focused therapists often inquire about presession improvements, or anything clients have done since scheduling the appointment that has made a difference in their problems.

**Problem-saturated story**  People often come to therapy feeling overwhelmed by their problems to which they are fused. Narrative therapists assist clients in understanding that they do not have to be reduced by these totalizing descriptions of their identity.

**Re-authoring**  A process in narrative therapy in which client and therapist jointly create an alternative life story.

**Scaling questions**  A solution-focused technique that asks clients to observe changes in feelings, moods, thoughts, and behaviors. On a scale of zero to 10, clients are asked to rate some change in their experiences.

**Social constructionism**  A therapeutic perspective within a postmodern worldview that stresses the client's reality without disputing the accuracy or validity of this reality. Social constructionism emphasizes the ways in which people make meaning in social relationships.

**Solution-focused brief therapy**  A postmodern approach to therapy that provides a context whereby individuals focus on recovering and creating solutions rather than talking about their problems.

**Totalizing descriptions**  A categorical description of people that constricts them to a single dimension that purports to capture their identity.

**Unique outcome**  Aspects of lived experience that lie outside the realm of dominant stories or in contradiction to the problem-saturated story.

## QUESTIONS FOR DISCUSSION AND EVALUATION

1. The social constructionist perspective emphasizes collaborating with people rather than directing them. What are some basic differences of this perspective from many of the traditional approaches you have studied?

2. The postmodern therapies are based on the assumption that the therapist takes a not-knowing position and clients are viewed as the experts on their own lives. To what degree do you think you could assume this stance as a therapist? What role would you assume if you were not the expert?

3. Solution-focused brief therapy eschews the past in favor of both the present and the future. What implications does this time perspective have for the practice of therapy? What are your thoughts about getting clients to work toward present and future solutions?

4. Solution-focused brief therapists strive to get their clients away from talking about their problems and instead emphasizes talking about solutions. How does solution-oriented therapy differ from problem-oriented therapy? How natural might it be for you to focus on constructing solutions with clients rather than resolving problems?

5. What thoughts do you have about the value of asking clients to talk about the exceptions to their problems and to adopt a positive focus on what they are doing that is working in their lives? If you build your therapy practice on the notion of helping clients recognize their strengths and resources, what implication does this have for the way you would work with clients?

6. Solution-focused therapists often ask clients the miracle question. What value do you see in asking clients to imagine their problems would vanish one night when they were asleep? How does the miracle question enable clients to focus on ways of creating solutions? What are some specific ways that you might make therapeutic use of how they respond to this question?

7. In narrative therapy, the emphasis is on being able to listen to the problem-saturated story of the client without getting stuck. What are your thoughts about the narrative approach of separating the person from the problem as you listen and respond to your client? To what extent do you think you might be able to engage your clients in externalizing conversations, where they are able to experience their problems as something distinct from their identities?

8. Both narrative therapists and solution-focused therapists are very concerned with establishing truly collaborative relationships with their clients. Clients are co-creators of solutions and are co-authors in the process of re-authoring their life stories. As a therapist, what kind of collaborative partnership would you want to form with your clients?

9. In practicing narrative therapy, there is no recipe, no set agenda, and no formula for practice. Instead, the attitudes of the therapist are at least as important as the therapist's techniques. What are some therapist attitudes that you see as being most important in encouraging clients to share their stories and discover ways to create alternative stories?

10. What are some specific ways that you think the postmodern approaches can be applied to working with culturally diverse client populations? How would you compare the postmodern approaches with the traditional approaches you have studied with respect to working from a multicultural perspective?

## ISSUES AND QUESTIONS FOR PERSONAL APPLICATION

Imagine yourself being a client in therapy and address the following issues and questions as a way for you to get a sense of your experience of both solution-focused brief therapy and narrative therapy.

1. Assume your therapist asks you what you most want to accomplish from your therapy [or to state your major therapeutic goal]. In concrete terms, what would be one important goal you want to accomplish? _____

   _____

   _____

   _____

   _____

2. How might you react if your therapist said: "Although I have expertise, I am not the expert on your life. You are the expert on your life." _____

   _____

   _____

   _____

3. To what degree would you appreciate the shift from problem-talk to solution-talk?

_____

_____

_____

_____

4. How ready would you be for a collaborative relationship with your therapist? What kind of resources do you have that you could draw from in making the changes you most desire? _____

_____

_____

_____

5. If your therapist told you that she was opposed to formal diagnosis because of her belief that diagnosis leads to pathologizing and labeling clients, how would you react?

_____

_____

_____

6. If your therapist informed you that he eschewed the past in favor of both the present and the future and had little interest in gaining an understanding of the problem, what might you say? _____

_____

_____

_____

7. Assume your therapist asks you: "If a miracle happened and the problem you have was solved overnight, how would you know it was solved, and what would be different?" How might you reply? _____

_____

_____

_____

8. If you were asked to externalize a problem you have, by considering the problem as something that is separate from who you are, what would this be like for you?

_____

_____

_____

9. What do you think the process would be like for you to re-author a new story?

_____

_____

_____

10. Finding an appreciative audience to support you in the changes you are making is a critical aspect of narrative therapy. Who would you most want to include in this audience that would appreciate your new story? _____

_____

_____

_____

_____

11. As clients become free of problem-saturated stories of the past, they are then able to envision and plan for a less problematic future. If your therapist asked you what you would most want in your future, what would you say? _____

_I would say that I want a stable job, a house and a healthy family._

12. Questions are often used in both solution-focused and narrative therapy. What are a few questions that you think would be timely and useful for you to consider as a client? 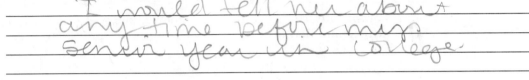 _Question from the past about family and issues relating to the current and what I want for myself._

13. Imagine a problem that you might want to address. If your therapist said, "Tell me about a time when your problem did not exist," what would you say? _____

_I would tell her about any time before my senior year in college._

_____

14. Again, imagine a problem that you would bring to your therapy. Your therapist asks you: "Was there ever a time in which [your problem] wanted to take you over and you resisted? What was that like for you? How did you do it?" Your reply: 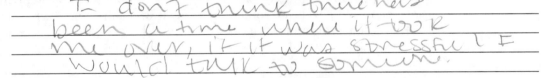 _I don't think there has been a time when it took me over, if it was stressful I would talk to someone._

15. With these approaches your therapist would encourage you to decide when to terminate therapy. What specific criteria would you use to determine when it was timely and appropriate for you to end your therapy? _I think it would be a good to end when I have figured out what and when I am going to solve my issue._

## JERRY COREY'S WORK WITH RUTH FROM A NARRATIVE PERSPECTIVE

Narrative therapy emphasizes the value of devoting time to listening to clients' stories and to looking for events that can open up new stories. Ruth's life story influences what she notices and remembers, and in this sense her story influences how she will face the future. Although I am somewhat interested in Ruth's past, we will certainly not dwell on her past problems. Instead, our focus will be on what Ruth is currently doing and on her strivings for her future. One of my tasks is to help Ruth rewrite the story of her life.

Working within a narrative approach, I am influenced by the notion that our collaboration will be aimed at freeing Ruth from the influence of oppressive elements in her social environment and empowering her to become an active agent who is directing her own life. Part of our work together will be to look for personal resources Ruth has that will enable her to create a new story for herself.

A method of supporting Ruth with the challenges she faces is to get her to think of her problems as external to the core of her selfhood. A key concept of narrative therapy is that the problem does not reside in the person. Even during the early sessions, I encourage Ruth to separate her being from her problems by posing questions that externalize her problem. I view Ruth's problems as something separate from her, even though her problems are influencing her thoughts, feelings, and behaviors. Ruth presents many problems that are of concern to her, yet we cannot deal with all of them at once. When I ask her what one problem most concerns her right now, she replies, "Anxiety. I feel anxious so often over so many things. No matter what I do, I often worry a great deal." Ruth feels anxious when she is faced with making a decision, largely because of her self-doubts.

My intention is to help Ruth come to view her problem of anxiety as being separate from who she is as a person. I ask Ruth how her anxiety occurs and ask her to give examples of situations where she experiences anxiety. I am interested in charting the influence of the problem of anxiety. I also ask questions that externalize the problem, such as the following: "How does anxiety get you, and what are you doing to let it become so powerful?" "How has anxiety dominated and disrupted your life?" "What ways does anxiety and self-doubt attempt to trip you up?"

In this narrative approach, I follow up on these externalizing questions with further questions aimed at finding exceptions: "Has there ever been a time when anxiety could have taken control of you, but didn't? What was it like for you? How did you do it?" "How is this different from what you would have done before?" "What does it say about you that you were able to do that?" "How do you imagine your life would be different if you didn't have anxiety and you did not doubt your every decision?"

My questioning is aimed at discovering moments when Ruth hasn't been dominated or discouraged by the problem of anxiety. When we identify times when Ruth's life was not disrupted by anxiety, we have a basis for considering how life would be different if anxiety were not in control. As our therapy proceeds, I expect that Ruth will gradually come to see that she has more control over her problem of anxiety than she believed. As she is able to distance herself from defining herself in terms of problematic themes (such as anxiety and self-doubt), she will be less burdened by her problem-saturated story and will discover a range of options. She will likely focus more on the resources within herself to construct the kind of life she wants.

## You Continue Working With Ruth

1. Narrative therapists are very cautious about using formal diagnosis. If they do make use of diagnosis, they make this a joint process with the client. What do you think about working with Ruth to collaboratively establish a diagnosis?

2. What are some of the advantages to the approach of externalizing the problem from the client? How might you get Ruth to see anxiety as something separate from herself as a person?

3. Asking clients to think of exceptions to their problems often gets them to think about a time when a particular problem did not have such intense proportions. What are some of the advantages you can see in asking Ruth to talk about a time when she did not have a given problem? How might you build on times of exceptions?

5. Refer to *Case Approach to Counseling and Psychotherapy* (Chapter 11) for a comprehensive illustration of three postmodern therapists (Jennifer Andrews, David Clark, and Gerald Monk) who each demonstrate their own approaches in working with Ruth.

6. See the *CD-ROM for Integrative Counseling* (sessions on an integrative perspective and also the session on working toward decisions and behavior change). What concepts and techniques from narrative therapy are you likely to draw upon in counseling Ruth?

# QUIZ ON POSTMODERN APPROACHES

## A Comprehension Check

Score _____%

**Note:** Please refer to Appendix 1 for the scoring key.

**True/false items:** Decide if the following statements are "more true" or "more false" as they apply to social constructionism, solution-focused brief therapy, and narrative therapy.

T   F   1. Narrative therapists believe new stories take hold only when there is an audience to appreciate and support such stories.

T   F   2. One of the functions of a narrative therapist is to ask questions of the client and, based on the answers, generate further questions.

T   F   3. The effective application of narrative therapy is primarily a function of a therapist being polished in the use of techniques.

T   F   4. Narrative practitioners encourage clients to avoid being reduced by totalizing descriptions of their identity.

T   F   5. Narrative therapists pay more attention to a client's past than they do to the client's present and future.

T   F   6. In solution-focused therapy, gathering extensive information about a problem is a necessary step in helping clients to find a solution to the problem.

T   F   7. Solution-focused therapists assist clients in paying attention to the exceptions to their problem patterns.

T   F   8. Solution-focused therapists use questions that presuppose change, posit multiple answers, and remain goal-directed and future-oriented.

T   F   9. In solution-focused therapy, the role of the client is to create, explore, and co-author his or her evolving story.

T   F   10. Because solution-focused therapy is designed to be brief, it is essential that therapists teach clients specific strategies for understanding their problems.

**Multiple-choice items:** Select the *one best answer* of those alternatives given. Consider each question within the framework of the postmodern therapies.

_____ 11. Which of the following is true of narrative therapy and solution-focused therapy?
   a. The client is an expert on his or her own life.
   b. The therapeutic relationship should be hierarchical.
   c. The therapist is the expert on a client's life.
   d. Clients should adjust to social and cultural norms.
   e. For change to occur, clients must first acquire insight into their problems.

_____ 12. A major goal of narrative therapy is to
   a. shift from problem-talk to solution-talk.
   b. assist clients in designing creative solutions to their problems.
   c. invite clients to describe their experience in new and fresh language, and in doing this opening up new vistas of what is possible.
   d. uncover a client's self-defeating cognitions.
   e. enable clients to gain clarity about the ways their family of origin still affects them today.

_____ 13. All of the following are true of narrative therapy except for

a. viewing problems in a sociopolitical and cultural context.
b. assisting clients in developing an alternative life story.
c. accepting the premise that diagnosis is a basic prerequisite for effective treatment.
d. creating a therapeutic relationship that is collaborative.
e. recognizing that clients know what is best for their life and are experts in their own life.

_____ 14. Which of the following interventions is least likely to be used by a narrative therapist?

a. externalizing conversations
b. mapping the influence of a problem
c. power analysis and intervention
d. the search for unique outcomes
e. documenting the evidence

_____ 15. Which of these techniques is *not* used in solution-focused therapy?

a. using the reflecting team
b. scaling questions
c. the miracle question
d. formula-first-session task
e. exception questions

_____ 16. A major strength of both solution-focused and narrative therapies is the

a. empirical evidence that has been conducted on both approaches.
b. attention given to how one's early history sheds light on understanding current problems.
c. history taking procedures used during the intake interview.
d. use of questioning.

_____ 17. Two of the major founders of solution-focused brief therapy are

a. Michael White and David Epston.
b. Insoo Kim Berg and Steve de Shazer.
c. Harlene Anderson and Harold Goolishian.
d. Tom Andersen and Bill O'Hanlon.
e. John Walter and Jane Peller.

_____ 18. Two of the major founders of narrative therapy are

a. Michael White and David Epston.
b. Insoo Kim Berg and Steve de Shazer.
c. Marlene Anderson and Harold Goolishian.
d. Tom Andersen and Bill O'Hanlon.
e. John Walter and Jane Peller.

_____ 19. The therapeutic process in solution-focused brief therapy involves all of the following except for the notion

a. of creating collaborative therapeutic relationships.
b. of asking clients about those times when their problems were not present or when the problems were less severe.
c. that clients are the experts on their own lives.
d. that solutions evolve out of therapeutic conversations and dialogues.
e. that therapists are experts in assessment and diagnosis.

_____ 20. Which of the following is *not* a basic assumption guiding the practice of solution-focused brief therapy?

a. Individuals who come to therapy have the ability to effectively cope with their problems.
b. There are advantages to a positive focus on solutions and on the future.
c. Clients want to change, have the capacity to change, and are doing their best to make change happen.
d. Using techniques in therapy is a way of discounting a client's capacity to find his or her own way.

_____ 21. In solution-focused therapy, which kind of relationship is characterized by the client and therapist jointly identifying a problem and a solution to work toward?

a. customer-type relationship
b. the complainant
c. a visitor
d. a compliant client

_____B_____ 22. Pretherapy change is a solution-focused therapy technique that

    a. is arrived at by asking clients about exceptions to their problems.

    b. asks clients to address changes that have taken place from the time they made an appointment to the first therapy session.

    c. is based on a series of tests that the client takes prior to beginning therapy to get baseline data.

    d. involves comparing the use of both pretest and posttest data from instruments that report client satisfaction with therapy.

_____B_____ 23. Which of these solution-focused therapy techniques involves asking clients to describe life without the problem?

    a. pretherapy change

    b. the miracle question

    c. exception questions

    d. scaling

    e. formula-first-session task

_____D_____ 24. In narrative therapy, the process of finding evidence to bolster a new view of the person as competent enough to have stood up to or defeated the dominance or oppression of the problem refers to

    a. the initial assessment.

    b. exploring problem-saturated stories.

    c. objectifying the problem.

    d. the search for unique outcomes.

_____B_____ 25. Which of the following statements about creating alternative stories is *not* true?

    a. Constructing new stories goes hand in hand with deconstructing problem-saturated narratives.

    b. The narrative therapist analyzes and interprets the meaning of a client's story.

    c. The therapist works with clients collaboratively by helping them construct more coherent and comprehensive stories that they live by.

    d. The development of alternative stories is an enactment of ultimate hope.

    e. The narrative therapist listens for openings to new stories.

# Chapter 14

# Family Systems Therapy

 ## PRECHAPTER SELF-INVENTORY

**Directions:** Refer to page 41 for general directions. Use the following code:

5 = I *strongly agree* with this statement.

4 = I *agree,* in most respects, with this statement.

3 = I am *undecided* in my opinion about this statement.

2 = I *disagree,* in most respects, with this statement.

1 = I *strongly disagree* with this statement.

_____ 1. Individuals are best understood through assessing the interactions between and among family members.

_____ 2. Symptoms of an individual's problems are best understood within the context of a dysfunctional system.

_____ 3. Because an individual is connected to a living system, change in one part of that system will result in change in other parts.

_____ 4. To focus primarily on studying the internal dynamics of an individual without adequately considering interpersonal dynamics yields an incomplete picture of the person.

_____ 5. Significant changes within an individual are not likely to be made or maintained unless the client's network of intimate relationships is taken into account.

_____ 6. Family therapy needs to include an examination of how one's culture has influenced each member.

_____ 7. Actions by any individual family member will influence all the others in the family, and their reactions will have a reciprocal effect on the individual.

_____ 8. It is not possible to accurately assess an individual's concerns without observing the interaction of the other family members.

_____ 9. Differentiating oneself from one's family of origin is best viewed as a lifelong developmental process.

_____ 10. Rather than losing sight of the individual, family therapists understand the person as specifically embedded in larger systems.

_____ 11. Family therapy serves a valuable function in challenging patriarchy and other forms of dominant culture privilege, bias, or discrimination.

_____ 12. Family therapists can no longer ignore their personal influence as part of their therapy.

_____ 13. Because the larger social structure affects the organization of a family, it is essential that the influence of the community on the family be considered.

_____ 14. Effective family therapy tends to be brief, focuses on solutions, and deals with the here-and-now interactions within a family.

_____ 15. It is the family therapist's responsibility to plan a strategy for resolving clients' problems.

_____ 16. A family therapist needs to be active and sometimes directive in working with a family.

_____ 17. A multilensed approach to family therapy is best supported by a collaborative therapist–client relationship in which mutual respect, caring, and empathy are primary.

_____ 18. Change is facilitated by staying present and not trying to change anything at all.

_____ 19. An appropriate goal of family therapy is the growth of individuals and the family rather than merely stabilizing the family.

_____ 20. Family therapists begin to form a relationship with clients from the moment of first contact.

## OVERVIEW OF FAMILY SYSTEMS THERAPY

### Key Figures and Major Focus

Key figures of Adlerian family therapy are Alfred Adler and Rudolf Dreikurs.

The key figure of the multigenerational approach to family therapy is Murray Bowen. He stresses exploring patterns from one's family of origin.

The key figure of the human validation process model is Virginia Satir. This form of therapy focuses on the interpersonal relationship between the therapist and the family members.

The key figure associated with experiential family therapy is Carl Whitaker. His approach assumes that it is experience that changes families, not education.

The key figure associated with the structural approach is Salvador Minuchin. His theory focuses on the family as a system and its subsystems, boundaries, and hierarchies.

The key figures associated with strategic family therapy are Cloe Madanes and Jay Haley. This therapy stresses parental hierarchies and cross-generational coalitions.

### Philosophy and Basic Assumptions

If we hope to work therapeutically with people, family therapists believe it is critical to consider clients within their family system. An individual's dysfunctional behavior grows out of the interactional unit of the family as well as the larger community and societal systems. Almost all of these theories view the family from an interactive and systemic perspective, which sees an individual's dysfunctional behavior as a manifestation of dysfunctional behavior within the system or as affecting the system negatively.

Family therapy is a diverse field, comprising various theories of how change occurs within the family and an equally diverse set of intervention strategies. The theories of family therapy share a common philosophy of the importance of dealing with all parts of a system if change is to take place and be maintained. The family systems therapy models are grounded on the assumptions that a client's problematic behavior may (1) serve a function or purpose for the family, (2) be a function of the family's inability to operate productively, especially during developmental transitions, or (3) be a symptom of dysfunctional patterns handed down across generations. All these assumptions challenge the more traditional intrapsychic frameworks for conceptualizing human problems and their formation.

These multiple frameworks provide eight lenses representing different perspectives in working with any family. The goal is to provide the therapist with multiple perspectives for tailoring therapy to the needs and situations of a family.

## Key Concepts

Because there are so many separate schools of family therapy, it is difficult to identify general concepts that cut across all of these orientations. Each school of therapy has its own key concepts:

- Adlerian family therapists focus on a relationship based on mutual respect, investigation of birth order and mistaken goals, and re-education.
- Bowenians focus on extended-family patterns. This multigenerational approach is based on a number of key ideas, two of which are differentiation of the self and triangulation.
- Satir's human validation process model utilizes a communication process to assist a family in moving from status quo through chaos to new possibilities and new integrations.
- The experiential family therapists take a developmental perspective in explaining individual growth in a systemic context.
- Structuralists emphasize the family as a system, subsystems, boundaries, and hierarchies. The therapist joins the family in a leadership role and changes these structures.
- Strategic therapists base their interventions on a communications model, which focuses on stuck interactional sequences in a family. Change occurs through action-oriented directives and paradoxical interventions.
- The multiple lenses provide a context for developing an integrative approach in working with families.

## Therapeutic Goals

Most family therapists share some general goals, but specific goals are determined by the practitioner's theoretical orientation or by a collaborative process between the therapist and the family. Global goals include intervening in ways that enable individuals and the family to relieve their distress. Although many family therapists agree on the goals, their interventions differ.

Here is a summary of the therapeutic goals associated with some of the various theories of family therapy:

- Adlerians emphasize unlocking mistaken goals and interactional patterns in the family and promotion of effective parenting.
- Bowenian (multigenerational) therapy seeks to (1) decrease anxiety and bring about relief from distressing symptoms and (2) bring about the maximum self-differentiation for each family member within his or her family and cultural context.
- The goals and the process of therapy of Satir's approach parallel her view of the process of change. Specific goals include generating self-esteem and hope, identifying and strengthening coping skills, and facilitating movement toward health and actualization.
- The goals for experiential family therapy include increasing awareness of one's present experiencing, facilitating individual growth and more effective interactional patterns, and promoting authenticity.
- Structural family therapy aims at both treating symptoms and changing dysfunctional transactional patterns within the family. Rules are identified that govern interactions among family members, with the purpose of helping them develop clear boundaries and appropriate hierarchies.

- In strategic family therapy insight is considered unimportant. The central goal of this approach is to resolve a family's presenting problem (or symptoms) by focusing on changing its current behavioral sequences.
- Using a perspective of multiple lenses, the best way to assess the client is to match a client's needs with the specific therapeutic perspective.

## Therapeutic Relationship

In the strategic and structural approaches to family therapy, the therapeutic relationship is not emphasized. But the experiential and human validation models are based on the quality of that relationship. Many family therapists are primarily concerned with solution-focused therapy and with teaching members how to modify dysfunctional interactional patterns and change stereotypical patterns. Some family therapists are more concerned with implementation of techniques designed to solve presenting problems than with the quality of the therapeutic relationship. Others realize that their relationship with family members is temporary, and thus they focus more on the quality of relationships within a family.

## Role and Function of Family Therapists

Here are some central roles associated with the major approaches to family therapy.

- Adlerian family therapists assume the roles of educators, motivational investigators, and collaborators.
- In Bowen's multigenerational therapy, therapists function as guides and objective researchers. Therapists monitor their own reactions and take on an active role in facilitating change in a family. Once individuals have gathered information about their family of origin, the therapist coaches each person in developing strategies for dealing with significant others outside of the therapy sessions.
- In Satir's approach to family therapy, the fundamental function of the therapist is to guide the individual family members through the process of change. The therapist provides the family with new experiences and teaches members how to communicate openly. In this model the therapist is an active facilitator who models congruence and serves as a resource person.
- The experiential family therapist functions as a family coach, challenger, and model for change through play. Therapists have various functions at different points in therapy, including being a stress activator, a growth activator, and a creativity stimulator.
- Structural family therapists function as stage directors. They join the system and attempt to manipulate family structure for the purpose of modifying dysfunctional patterns. The therapist's central task is to deal with the family as a unit, in the present, with the goal of initiating a restructuring process.
- In the strategic model therapists function in active and directive ways. Working as consultants and experts, they are manipulative and authoritarian in dealing with resistive behaviors. The therapist is the agent responsible for changing the organization of a family and resolving the family's presenting problems.
- In the integrative approach to family therapy, therapists look at a family from multiple perspectives and collaboratively work out with a family specific processes and practices that will lead to change.

## Techniques and Procedures

The techniques and procedures family therapists employ are best considered in conjunction with their personal characteristics. Although techniques are tools for achieving therapeutic goals, these intervention strategies do not make a family therapist. Personal characteristics such as respect for clients, compassion, empathy, and sensitivity are qualities that influence the degree to which techniques are effective. Faced with meeting the demands of clinical practice, family therapists need to be flexible in selecting intervention strategies.

An integrative approach to the practice of family therapy includes guiding principles that help the therapist organize goals, interactions, observations, and ways to promote change. Certain family systems therapy models focus on perceptual and cognitive change, others deal mainly with changing feelings, and still other theories emphasize behavioral change. The multiple lenses allow the therapist to draw on a variety of perspectives in working with a family rather than being limited to a single viewpoint. Regardless of the lens that a family therapist operates from, change needs to happen relationally, not just intrapsychically.

There is a diversity of techniques, depending on the therapist's theoretical orientation, and a considerable degree of flexibility in applying them, even among practitioners within a school. Family therapists tend to be active, directive, oriented toward the solution of problems, and open to using techniques borrowed from various approaches. Here are some of the primary intervention strategies associated with the various schools of family therapy.

- Adlerian family therapists employ techniques such as family constellation, reporting of a typical day, goal disclosure, and logical consequences.
- Multigenerational family therapy focuses on asking questions, tracking interactional sequences, assigning homework, and educating.
- Throughout the process of Satir's human validation model, various techniques are used to facilitate enhanced interpersonal communication within the family, a few of which are drama, reframing, humor, touch, family reconstruction, role playing, family life-fact chronology, and family sculpture.
- Experiential family therapists utilize themselves as their best therapeutic technique, creating interventions that grow out of the phenomenological context in working with a family.
- Structural family therapists engage in tracking transactional sequences, reframing, issuing directives, joining and accommodating a family, restructuring, and enactment.
- Strategic therapists utilize reframing, directives, and paradoxical interventions, and they also track interactional sequences.

## Contributions

The main contribution of a family systems approach is the inclusion of all parts of the system rather than being limited to the "identified patient." Rather than blaming either the "identified patient" or the family, the entire family has an opportunity to (a) examine the multiple perspectives and interactional patterns that characterize the unit and (b) participate in finding solutions. Because an individual's problems are relational, it makes sense to focus on all of the interactions and external factors that impinge on the person.

## Limitations

A major limitation of systemic approaches is the potential to lose sight of the individual by focusing on the broader system. If a family comes in for therapy, there are some real advantages to working with the entire unit. However, the language and focus of systems have often placed a primary emphasis on the family whole at the expense of individuals. Postmodern thinking and the natural development of the profession are beginning to integrate the person back into the system.

GLOSSARY OF KEY TERMS

**Boundary**   In structural family therapy an emotional barrier that protects individuals within a system.

**Coaching**   Bowen's and Whitaker's view of the role of the therapist in assisting clients in the process of differentiating the self.

**Differentiation of self**   Bowen's concept of psychological separation of intellect and emotions and of independence of the self from others. The greater one's differentiation, the better one's ability to keep from being drawn into dysfunctional patterns with other family members.

**Disengagement**   Minuchin's term for a family organization characterized by psychological isolation that results from rigid boundaries.

**Enactment**   In structural family therapy an intervention consisting of a family playing out its relationship patterns during a therapy session so that the therapist can observe and then change transactions that make up the family structure.

**Enmeshment**   Minuchin's term referring to a family structure in which there is a blurring of psychological boundaries, making autonomy very difficult to achieve.

**Experiential therapy**   A therapeutic approach that emphasizes the value of the therapist's realness in interacting with a family.

**Family dysfunction**   The inability of a family to attain harmonious relationships and to achieve interdependence.

**Family life cycle**   The series of events that marks an individual's life within a family, from separation from one's parents to marriage to growing old and dying.

**Family life-fact chronology**   Satir's experiential technique in which clients retrace their family history for the purpose of gaining insight into current family functioning.

**Family of origin**   The original nuclear family into which one was born or adopted.

**Family rules**   The implicit agreements that prescribe the rights, duties, and range of appropriate behaviors within the family.

**Family sculpting**   A nonverbal experiential technique that consists of physically arranging members of a family in space, which reveals significant aspects of their perceptions and feelings about one another.

**Family structure**   The functional organization of a family, which determines interactional patterns among members.

**Functional family**   A family in which the needs of the individual members are met and there is a balance of interdependence and autonomy among members.

**Genogram**   A schematic diagram of the family system, usually including at least three generations; employed by many family therapists to identify recurring behavior patterns within the family.

**Identified patient**   A family member who carries the symptom for a family and who is identified by the family as the person with the problem. In genograms this person is the index person.

**Joining**   In structural family therapy, accommodating to a family's system to help the members change dysfunctional patterns.

**Metaframeworks**   An approach to integration of family theories aimed at transcending the various family therapy models.

**Multigenerational transmission process**   The way in which dysfunctional patterns are passed from one generation to the next.

**Multilensed process of family therapy**   This perspective consists of eight lenses that serve as a basic structure for assessment. The multilensed perspective presupposes certain assumptions about families, the therapist, and family therapy.

**Paradoxical directive**   A technique in strategic family therapy whereby the therapist directs family members to continue their symptomatic behavior. Change occurs through defying the directive.

**Reframing**   Relabeling a family's description of behavior by putting it into a new and more positive perspective.

**Strategic therapy**   A therapeutic approach whereby the therapist develops a specific plan and designs interventions geared toward solving a family's presenting problems.

**Structural therapy**   A therapeutic approach directed at changing or realigning the organization of a family to modify dysfunctional patterns and clarify boundaries.

**Triangle**    A three-person system; the smallest stable emotional unit of human relations.

**Triangulation**    A pattern of interaction consisting of detouring conflict between two people by involving a third person.

## QUESTIONS FOR DISCUSSION AND EVALUATION

1. What are some of the main differences between family systems approaches and individual counseling approaches?

2. A basic assumption of Bowen's multigenerational family therapy is that unresolved emotional issues, such as an individual's failure to differentiate from the family, will be passed on from generation to generation. As you study your own family, are you aware of any patterns you have "inherited"?

3. Whitaker typically makes use of the co-therapy model in doing family therapy. What are the advantages of such an approach? Are there any disadvantages?

4. The core of Satir's human validation process model is the therapist's use of self as a facilitator of change whereby the family moves from being psychologically stuck to a place of wellness. To what extent do you agree (or disagree) with the notion that the use of the therapist's self is more important than any technique? How does this model differ from strategic therapy in this respect?

5. Minuchin's structural family therapy model emphasizes the therapist's role in joining and accommodating the family. As you picture yourself as a family therapist, what difficulties, if any, do you imagine you might have in these two areas with certain families?

6. In strategic family therapy the therapist is expected to be in charge of the session, which often includes issuing directives and planning a strategy to solve the client's problems. How comfortable would you be in carrying out this role? With what specific clients do you think strategic approaches would be best suited?

7. What are some ways in which you could apply what you learned in your study of the previous theories to the practice of family therapy? To what degree do you see a basis for integrating some of the concepts and techniques of the individual counseling models with family systems therapy models?

8. How useful do you find the multilensed process of family therapy as a framework for understanding a family? Of the eight lenses described in this chapter, which lens (or perspective) do you find the most useful?

9. To practice with families in an ethical and effective manner, what kind of education, training, and supervision would you need? Do you have any ideas about how you might seek competence in working with families?

10. What do you consider to be the main contribution of the family therapy perspective? What are the main limitations of family therapy?

## SUGGESTED ACTIVITIES AND EXERCISES FOR PERSONAL APPLICATION

1. **How Your Past Influences Your Present**

   When you counsel an individual, a couple, or a family, you are not always perceiving them with a fresh and unbiased perspective. When a new person whom you encounter represents some unresolved relationship with someone from your past, you can unconsciously attempt to deal with old relationships through your current relationships. The more you are aware of your patterns with your own family members, the greater is the benefit to your clients. It is crucial that you know to whom you are responding: to the individual in front of you or to a person from your past.

Try this exercise Satir used to demonstrate that we are constantly revisiting significant people and family members in our lives: Stand in front of someone (Person A) in your current life who interests you or with whom you are having some difficulty. This individual might be a client, an associate, a family member, or a friend. If the person is not present, you can imagine him or her. Take a good look at this person, and form a picture on the screen of your mind. Now, let a picture of someone in your past come forward (Person B). Who comes to mind? How old are you and how old is Person B? What relationship do you, or did you, have with this individual you are remembering? What feelings are linked with this relationship? What did you think about Person B?

Now, examine again your current emotional reactions to Person A. Do you see any connection between what Person A is evoking in you and the past feelings that Person B has evoked? You can apply this exercise by yourself through the use of imagery when you have intense emotional reactions to other people, especially if you do not know them well. This exercise can help you begin to recognize how your past relationships may sometimes affect the here-and-now reactions you are having toward people that you initially encounter. Perhaps what is most important is simply to be aware of ways in which you are carrying your past into present interactions.

2. Understanding Your Family Structure

Family structure also includes factors such as birth order and the individual's perception of self in the family context. A facet of family structure is a particular pattern such as nuclear, extended, single-parent, divorced, and blended. As you reflect on these questions, identify what is unique in the structure of your family.

- In what type of family structure did you grow up? It might be that the structure of your family changed over time. If so, what were these changes? What do you most remember about growing up in your family? What were some of the most important values? What most stands out for you about your family life? In what ways do you think these experiences have a continuing influence on the person you are today?

- What is your current family structure? Are you still primarily involved in your family of origin? If your current family is different, what roles do you play that you also enacted in your original family? Have you carried certain patterns from your original family to your current family? How do you see yourself as being different in the two families?

- Draw a genogram of your family of origin. Include all the members of your family, and identify significant alliances among the various members. Identify the relationship you had as a child with each person and your relationship with each member now.

- Make a list of the siblings from oldest to youngest. Give a brief description of each (including yourself). What most stands out for each sibling? Which sibling(s) is (are) most different from you, and how? Which is most like you, and how?

- Review some key dimensions of your experiences as a child growing up in your family. How would you describe yourself as a child? What were some of your major fears? hopes? ambitions? What was school like for you? What was your role in your peer group? Were there any significant events in your physical, sexual, and social development during childhood?

- Identify one of your personal problems. How do you think your relationship with your family has contributed to the development and perpetuation of this problem? Besides blaming your family for this problem, what options are open to you for making substantial changes in yourself? What are a few ways you can be different in your family?

3. A Balance of Being Separate and of Belonging to a Family

- In what significant ways, if any, do you see yourself as having a distinct identity and being psychologically separate from your family of origin? And in what ways, if any, are you still psychologically fused with your family of origin? Are there any aspects of this that you want to change?

- In some cultures autonomy is not a cherished value. Instead, children are viewed as having an obligation not to emerge too distinctly from the rest of the family. A collective sense is given more value than individual independence. What cultural values influenced the degree to which you have striven toward autonomy? Are there any values that stem from your culture that you want to retain? Any that you want to challenge or to modify?

- The concept of *boundaries* as used in family therapy refers to emotional barriers that protect and enhance the integrity of members of a system. It also refers to a delineation between members that is governed by implicit or explicit rules pertaining to who can participate and in what manner. Apply the notion of boundaries to your development. In growing up in your family, what boundaries existed between you and your parents? Between your parents and the siblings? Among the siblings? Between your parents? What did you learn about boundaries? Do you have any problems with boundaries today?

## 4.  Understanding the Rules of Your Family

Rules or messages that were delivered by our parents and parent substitutes are often couched in terms of "Do this or that." Consider the following "do" messages: "Be obedient." "Be practical at all times." "Be the very best you can be." "Be appropriate." "Be perfect." "Be a credit to your family." At this point, reflect on the rules that seemed apparent in your family. What were some of the major rules that governed your family? What were some unspoken rules between the adults? What rules did you learn about appropriate sex-role behavior? What did you learn about femininity? about masculinity? To what degree did you abide by all these rules? Were there any that you challenged? How did unspoken rules affect you? Were there rules surrounding what could not be mentioned? If there were secrets in your family, how did this affect the family atmosphere?

Consider some of the major "do's" and "don'ts" that you heard growing up in your family, and your reactions to them.

- What are a few messages or rules that you did accept?
- What were some rules that you fought against?
- Which of your early decisions do you deem to be most significant in your life today? What was the family context in which you made these decisions? If you grew up in your family thinking "I am never enough," how has this conclusion about yourself played out in your current relationships in various aspects of your life?
- Do you ever hear yourself giving the same messages to others that you heard from your parents?
- Consider for a moment the overall impact of the messages that you have been exposed to, both from your parents and from society. How have these messages influenced your self-worth? your view of yourself as a woman or as a man? your trust in yourself? your ability to be creative and spontaneous? your ability to receive love and give love? your willingness to make yourself vulnerable? your sense of security? your potential to succeed?

## 5.  Significant Developments in Your Family

You might find it useful to describe your family of origin's life cycle. Chart significant turning points that characterize its development. One way is to look at family albums and see what the photos are revealing. Let these pictures stimulate your memories, and see what you can learn. As you view photos of your parents, grandparents, siblings, and other relatives, look for patterns that can offer clues to family dynamics. In charting transitions in the development of your family, reflect on these questions:

- What were any crisis points for your family?
- Can you recall any unexpected events that affected your family?
- Were there any periods of separation due to employment, military service, or imprisonment?
- Who tended to have problems within the family? How were these problems manifested? How did others in the family react to the person with problems?
- In what ways did births affect the family?
- Were there any serious illnesses, accidents, divorces, or deaths in your family of origin? If so, how did they affect individual members in the family and the family as a whole?

6. Applying the Multiple Lenses to Yourself
Using the eight lenses described in Chapter 14, apply these multiple perspectives to your own family by considering these questions:

- How would these lenses be applied to your own family?
- What lens would be most relevant in working with your family?
- What parts are most evident when you return home?
- What goals do you most often have when you interact with members of your family?
- Where do you see yourself in the family life cycle?
- What did it mean to you in growing up as a woman or a man in your family?
- Do you know what cultural influences are present in your family? How do they influence routines in your family?

## JERRY COREY'S WORK WITH RUTH FROM A FAMILY SYSTEMS PERSPECTIVE

In Ruth's individual sessions it becomes evident that many of her current issues pertain to relationships in her family. She has concerns about several of her children, and she is greatly troubled about her present relationship with her husband, John. I recommend that Ruth bring her entire family into the therapeutic process. Because changes that occur in any one part of the system will change other parts, changes in Ruth have affected the equilibrium of this family. It is important to have the whole family enter treatment so that the changes that occur are productive for Ruth's family as well as for her.

After an initial session with Ruth's family, several tentative conclusions are formed. (See Mary Moline's piece in Chapter 12 of *Case Approach to Counseling and Psychotherapy* for a detailed discussion of several family sessions.) In this family there is an enmeshment among members. They lack a clear sense of their individuality and roles in the family. Families such as this one are prone to conflict and confusion, and the behavior of one member or unit, in this case both Ruth and John, immediately affects the other members of the family.

Ruth and John are learning new behaviors. She is learning not to maintain her role as peacemaker, and he is gradually learning to be more supportive of her. As a result, the other family members are being forced to learn to deal with one another. The children have been increasing the conflict among themselves and with Ruth to bring her back into her previous role as mediator. In family therapy terms this involves prompting a return of the family (Ruth) to the former status.

### You Continue Working With Ruth

1. If you were seeing Ruth in individual counseling, would you suggest that she involve her family in the therapeutic process, at least to a minimal extent? Why or why not?

2. If you suggested a family therapy session to Ruth, what would you most hope to accomplish?

3. To what extent do you see it as essential to deal with Ruth's concerns from a systemic perspective? What value, if any, do you see in dealing with the environmental factors (especially family influences) related to Ruth's struggles?

4. How would you deal with Ruth if she were resistant to the idea of including any of her family members in her therapy?

5. How might you proceed in dealing with Ruth's parents and the role she feels they have played in her life? How important would it be to focus on working through her attitudes and feelings toward her parents? Do you think this can be done symbolically (through role playing), or is it necessary for Ruth to deal directly with her parents? In what ways might you want to work with Ruth's family of origin?

6. Refer to *Case Approach to Counseling and Psychotherapy* (Chapter 12) for a comprehensive illustration of a family therapist (Mary Moline) who works with Ruth from a systemic perspective. What are some positive outcomes for Ruth from this approach?

7. See the *CD-ROM for Integrative Counseling* (session on emotive focus) and analyze my attempt to incorporate family systems ideas in Ruth's counseling (dealing with her husband, John). What might you have done differently if you were counseling Ruth?

## QUIZ ON FAMILY SYSTEMS THERAPY

### A Comprehension Check

Score _____ %

**Note:**  Refer to Appendix 1 for the scoring key.

**True/false items:**  Decide if the following statements are "more true" or "more false" as they apply to the perspective of family systems therapy.

T (F)  1. The trend today is toward reliance on a single theory of family therapy rather than using an integrative approach.

(T) F  2. The emergence of feminist and post-modern perspectives has moved the field of family therapy toward more egalitarian, collaborative, and co-constructing relationships.

T (F)  3. Experiential family therapy relies on the expert use of directives aimed at changing dysfunctional patterns.

(T) F  4. A multilensed approach to family therapy is best supported by a collaborative therapist–client relationship.

(T) F  5. Conducting an assessment is one of the phases of the mutilensed perspective in family therapy.

(T) F  6. Understanding family process is almost always facilitated by "how" questions.

(T) F  7. In terms of assessment, it is useful to inquire about family perspectives on issues inherent in each of the lenses.

(T) F  8. The multilensed process of family therapy is similar to the "blueprints for therapy" as proposed by a meta-frameworks model.

(T) F  9. The teleological lens is concerned with the study of final causes, goals, endpoints, and purposes.

(T) F  10. Reframing is the art of putting what is known in a new, more useful perspective.

**Multiple-choice items:** Select the *one best answer* of those alternatives given. Consider each question within the framework of approaches to family systems therapy.

_B_ 11. Which of the following family therapy models makes the most use of genograms, dealing with family-of-origin issues, and detriangulating relationships?

a. Adlerian family therapy
b. Bowenian multigenerational family therapy
c. structural family therapy
d. strategic therapy
e. experiential family therapy

_E_ 12. Which of the following approaches most often employs a co-therapist model, makes use of self-disclosure and use of the therapist's self as change agent, and frequently uses confrontation?

a. Bowenian family therapy
b. Adlerian family therapy
c. structural family therapy
d. strategic therapy
e. experiential family therapy

_D_ 13. Which of the following is *not* a key general movement of the multi-lensed approach to family systems therapy?

a. forming a relationship
b. conducting an assessment
c. hypothesizing and sharing meaning
d. conducting empirical research to evaluate outcomes
e. facilitating change

_A_ 14. Differentiation of the self is the cornerstone of which theory?

a. Bowenian family therapy
b. Adlerian family therapy
c. social constructionism
d. strategic therapy
e. experiential family therapy

_B_ 15. Which of the following lenses addresses these questions: What goals do you have for yourself and for other people in the family? What purposes do you seem to have for how they behave?

a. internal family systems
b. the teleological lens

c. sequences
d. the organization lens
e. the developmental lens

_C_ 16. What lens raises these kinds of questions: How does a typical day go? Are there processes and patterns that characterize current or past transitions for the family? What routines support your daily living?

a. internal family systems
b. the teleological lens
c. sequences
d. the organization lens
e. the developmental lens

_d_ 17. What lens deals with these questions: Are the parents effective leaders of the family? How do the children respond to parental leadership? Is the process of leadership balanced or imbalanced? Does it lead to harmony or conflict?

a. internal family systems
b. the teleological lens
c. sequences
d. the organization lens
e. the developmental lens

_d_ 18. What lens most addresses these questions: Where is the family in the family life cycle, and how are they handling transitions? What relational processes have been established over time and how have they changed through transitional periods?

a. internal family systems
b. the teleological lens
c. sequences
d. the developmental lens
e. the multicultural lens

_E_ 19. What best defines the focus of family therapy?

a. Most of the family therapies tend to be brief.
b. Family therapy tends to be solution-focused.
c. The focus is on here-and-now interactions in the family system.

d. Family therapy is generally action-oriented.

e. all of the above

_C_ 20. Which of the following is *not* one of the eight lenses of family systems therapy discussed in this chapter?

a. the gender lens

b. the multicultural lens

c. the cognitive behavioral lens

d. the process lens

e. the developmental lens

_B_ 21. Which of the following roles and functions would be most atypical for a structural family therapist?

a. joining the family in a position of leadership

b. giving voice to the therapist's own impulses and fantasies

c. mapping the underlying structure of a family

d. intervening in ways designed to transform an ineffective structure of a family

e. being a stage director

_E_ 22. Which of the following is least associated with experiential family therapy?

a. It is an interactive process between a therapist and a family.

b. It focuses on the here-and-now.

c. Techniques grow out of the spontaneous reactions to the present situation in therapy.

d. It stresses the subjective needs of the individual in the family.

e. It is the therapist's task to plan a strategy for solving the problems of each family member.

_A_ 23. Directives and paradoxical procedures are most likely to be used in which approach to family therapy?

a. strategic family therapy

b. Adlerian family therapy

c. multigeneration family therapy

d. experiential family therapy

e. structural family therapy

_A_ 24. Which approach to family therapy stresses the importance of returning to one's family of origin to extricate oneself from triangular relationships?

a. Bowenian family therapy

b. Adlerian family therapy

c. structural family therapy

d. strategic therapy

e. experiential family therapy

_C_ 25. Which approach to family therapy stresses unlocking mistaken goals, investigating birth order and family constellation, and re-education?

a. Bowenian family therapy

b. structural family therapy

c. Adlerian family therapy

d. strategic family therapy

e. experiential family therapy

# Integration
# and Application

**15** An Integrative Perspective

**16** Case Illustration: An Integrative Approach
in Working With Stan

# Chapter 15

# An Integrative Perspective

In this chapter most of the exercises are designed to help you make some comparisons among the various therapy approaches, to help you see a basis for the integration of several approaches, to encourage you to think of the aspects you like and dislike about each therapy, and to give you some practice in applying specific therapies to various client populations.

 ## APPLICATIONS OF THEORETICAL APPROACHES TO SPECIFIC CLIENT POPULATIONS OR SPECIFIC PROBLEMS

As a basis for review and to help you compare and integrate the approaches, I am presenting a list of specific clients, problems, or situations. Decide which of the approaches or techniques you would be likely to use in each case. There is no one "right technique" for these cases, and in some cases you might want to employ several techniques. Keep in mind that the purpose of these exercises is to stimulate your thinking in applying the theories and techniques you have studied to specific cases.

1. Roger, at age 33, is extremely inhibited. He finally seeks out therapy because he is in so much pain over his fears of talking to others or being in public. Roger is very nonverbal and gives only skimpy details; he obviously wants direction and help in conquering his severe inhibitions. During the initial interview he appears extremely uncomfortable and strains whenever he is expected to talk.

   a. Select a technique that you are likely to use in this case. _____
   _____
   _____
   _____

   b. Why did you choose this technique? _____
   _____
   _____

2. Jim is a 40-year-old engineer who says he has gone to many encounter groups and has had a good deal of therapy. He says: "In spite of all this group stuff and head shrinking, I still don't seem to be able to get past the insight level. I see a lot of things I didn't see before, and I understand more why I'm the way I am, but I still don't seem to be able to use what I know to make changes in my life. I'm still troubled by the same old hang-ups, and so far I haven't been able to do much about resolving them."

   a. Select a technique that you are likely to use with Jim. _____
   _____

b. Why did you choose this technique? _____

3. An adolescent girl is having extreme difficulty coping with stress and the demands of school. Penny has many fears of failing, of not being liked by other students, and of being seen as "different," and she suffers from headaches and physical tenseness. She says she would like to lead a "normal life" and be able to go to school and function adequately. She is afraid that unless she can deal with these stresses, she will "go crazy."

a. Select a technique that you think is most appropriate for this case. _____

b. Why did you choose this technique? _____

4. A married couple, Diane and Scott, present themselves for marriage counseling. Scott did not particularly want to come in, but he is willing to give things a try. He basically feels that life is fine, the marriage is all right, and there are no major problems with their children. In short, he likes his life, except he wishes that *she* could be more at peace, and that she would stop bugging him! Diane feels pretty discouraged about life. Her kids do not appreciate her, and surely her husband does not recognize or appreciate her. She feels that she has to be both the mother and the father at home, that she has to make all the decisions, and that Scott will not listen to her. She wants to feel heard by him.

a. Select an approach that you think is most appropriate for this case. _____

b. Why did you choose this approach? _____

5. Fran is returning to college now that her children are in high school. She says: "I feel as if I don't know who I am anymore. At one time I knew what my purpose was, and now I just feel confused (and scared) most of the time. I like going to college and doing something for myself, and at the same time I feel guilty. I ask myself what I'm trying to prove. The most recurring feeling I have is that it's wrong for me to be enjoying college and doing this just for me."

a. Select an approach that you think is most appropriate for this case. _____

b. Why did you choose this approach? _____

6. The client, Yvonne, specifically wants to work on her dreams. She says that they are frequent and powerful and that she wants to learn what they are telling her about what is going on in her life.

   a. Select an approach that you think is most appropriate for this case. _____

      _____

      _____

      _____

   b. Why did you choose this approach? _____

      _____

      _____

      _____

7. Joan comes in for crisis counseling. This young woman complains of chronic depression and is frightened by the frequency of her suicidal thoughts and impulses. She attempted suicide several years ago and was committed to a state mental hospital for a time. She fears being "sent up" again, because she does not know how to cope with her bouts of depression.

   a. Select a technique that you think is most appropriate for this case. _____

      _____

      _____

      _____

   b. Why did you choose this technique? _____

      _____

      _____

8. The clients are a group of elderly people on a ward of a state mental hospital. Most of them are senile and have little capacity to relate to one another. They are typically people who feel lost, abandoned, and depressed, and they have lost much of the meaning in their life. The program director would like some form of therapy aimed at enabling these patients to learn to make contact with one another and to encourage them to talk about their feelings and their experiences.

   a. Select an approach that you think is most appropriate for this case. _____

      _____

      _____

      _____

   b. Why did you choose this approach? _____

      _____

      _____

      _____

9. Herb comes to therapy to help work through his feelings about his divorce. He feels that the divorce was his fault and that if he had been different his wife would not have left. He keeps bemoaning the fact that she left him. He feels devastated to the extent that he can hardly function. He is preoccupied with getting her back.

   a. Select a technique that you think is most appropriate for this case. _____

      _____

      _____

      _____

b. Why did you choose this technique? _____

_____

_____

10. Jake, who is middle-aged, is seeking therapy because he wants to learn how to deal with his anger. As long as he can remember, he has felt anger toward someone: his mother, his wife, his children, his boss, and his few friends. He says that he is frightened of his anger and of what he might do, so he keeps it all bottled up. He reports that as a child he was always given the message that anger is a bad emotion and that you should surely never show angry feelings. Jake also realizes that he fears getting close to people, and he would like to explore his fear of intimacy as well as his fear of his anger.

a. Select a technique that you think is most appropriate for this case. _____

_____

_____

_____

b. Why did you choose this technique? _____

_____

_____

These exercises make good discussion material for small groups in class. In addition to comparing and discussing their selections, my own students have found it valuable in these small groups to get some practice in role playing. One of the students might assume the identity of a given client while another student functions as a counselor by using a particular technique that is a part of one of the theories. This activity may last about 10 minutes; then others in the group give the "counselor" their reactions, and another student may work with the client using a different approach. This combination of practice and discussion typically works well.

# WORKING WITH RUTH FROM AN INTEGRATIVE PERSPECTIVE

In this section I will give a concise presentation of the 13 sessions with Ruth that I demonstrate in the *CD-ROM for Integrative Counseling.* For each session with Ruth, I provide a brief description of my thinking regarding integrating concepts and techniques from the various theoretical orientations. Then I raise questions for you to think about regarding how you might pursue work with Ruth from an integrative perspective in each session.

## Session 1: Beginning of Counseling

When we begin, I am mainly interested in structuring the therapeutic relationship. My hope is that Ruth will have enough information after our first session to decide if she wants to continue with me and that she will be able to make informed decisions about her therapy. I listen to Ruth's story and try to get a sense of what is bringing her to counseling at this time. We explore her expectations pertaining to the therapeutic venture. As much as possible, I want to demystify the therapeutic process, which I do by teaching her how to get the most from her work with me. It is really important that Ruth reflect on what she wants to talk about in our sessions and that she learns how to be an active participant in her counseling. The informed consent process and teaching about how counseling works is not something that is finished after the first session; rather, these issues are revisited throughout the duration of our work together.

During our initial session, several theories may influence the direction I take. I think the person-centered approach is an excellent foundation for initiating the counseling process. I need to understand Ruth as fully as possible and create a climate whereby she will feel free to talk about those matters that are of deepest concern to her. From the feminist orientation, I am guided by presenting adequate information to Ruth so that she can decide if she wants to continue working with me, and if so, what she most wants to accomplish.

1. How would you begin your work with Ruth? What would you most want to accomplish by the end of the first session?
2. Feminist therapists stress the role of educating clients about the therapy process. What kind of teaching would you want to do during the early phases of therapy? How would you go about making Ruth a collaborative partner?

## Session 2: The Therapeutic Relationship

Regardless of the theoretical orientation, the client–therapist relationship is of paramount importance to the therapeutic outcomes. Both the existential and person-centered approaches place primary emphasis on the therapeutic relationship as the vehicle for change. I attempt to establish a collaborative relationship whereby therapy becomes a partnership. Both the narrative and solution-focused therapies view Ruth as an expert in her own life, and my role as her therapist would be as a consultant. I ask Ruth to reflect out loud about her reactions to our last session. She admits that counseling is all new to her; she is not used to being the focus of attention nor is she used to looking at herself. She is somewhat concerned about sharing herself in personal ways and worries that she will feel exposed if she reveals "too much." As Ruth talks about her vulnerability, it is essential that I be nonjudgmental and that I listen to her fears. Trust will be the foundation of our working relationship.

In deciding how you would establish a working relationship with Ruth, consider these questions:

1. What value do you place on the quality of your relationship with Ruth? How important is the client–therapist relationship for you as a determinant of therapeutic outcomes?
2. What life experiences have you had that would most help you in working with Ruth? What personal characteristics might hinder your work with her?
3. Which specific theories do you find most useful to you in conceptualizing the nature of the therapeutic relationship?

## Session 3: Establishing Therapeutic Goals

Ruth makes a list of goals that she would like to explore in her therapy sessions. These are the themes we identified as the target of our remaining sessions:

1. "I just don't trust myself to find my own answers to life."
2. "I'm afraid to change for fear of breaking up my marriage."
3. "It's hard for me to ask others for what I want."
4. "It's hard for me to have fun. I'm so responsible."
5. "I'm afraid to make mistakes and look like a fool."
6. "I've lived by the expectations of others for so long that I don't know what I want anymore."
7. "I'm afraid to tell my husband what I really want with him, because I'm afraid he will leave me."
8. "There's not enough time for me to be doing all the things I know I should be doing."
9. "I'm afraid of my feelings toward other men."
10. "When my children leave, I'll have nothing to live for."

Examine this list of Ruth's statements. What major themes would you focus on in Ruth's life? Show how you would begin working with Ruth with the themes you select. How might you help Ruth clarify her goals for therapy? How would you help her make her goals concrete? How would you assess the degree to which she was meeting her goals?

## Session 4: Working With Diversity

Early in our work Ruth brings up the matter of our differences. One of the areas she is concerned about is our differences in religion. She is wondering if I will be able to understand her. I must be finely attuned to any differences between us that may pose a problem for her, and together we explore the meaning of differences in religion, gender, and life experiences. I do not want to make the assumption that there will necessarily be a gap in understanding because she is a female client and I am a male therapist. I let Ruth determine which of our many differences are salient in our relationship, which we then will discuss fully.

1. As you become aware of differences between you and your client, would you bring up such differences for discussion? How might you handle the matter of Ruth wondering if you will be able to understand her because of whatever differences exist?

2. What kinds of differences—gender, sexual orientation, religious—between you and your client might be problematic for you?

## Session 5: Understanding Resistance

After four sessions, Ruth wonders if therapy is creating more problems in her life than it is solving. Indeed, she hesitated in keeping her appointment. In short, Ruth is afraid that if she changes too much this will cause real problems with her husband and children. From my perspective, it is essential that we explore resistance, not fix it or simply get around it. Gently challenging resistance can open up new vistas for the client. I do not want to judge Ruth's behavior, but I do want to point out what I see her doing and ask her to reflect and comment on certain of her behaviors. When she wonders if she should continue or quit therapy, I do not want to respond defensively. Instead, my hope is that she will make her own decision. Even though she may be frightened of the prospects of remaining in therapy because of transformations in herself, Ruth can challenge her fears and move forward. She also has the potential to decide that she does not want to risk changing that much at this point in her life, and she could decide to terminate therapy.

1. How do you think you would respond to Ruth telling you that she is thinking of quitting therapy because of her fear of what will happen if she continues changing?

2. How do you see resistance? And how might resistance in your clients affect you?

3. Which theories are helpful to you in understanding and conceptualizing resistance?

## Session 6: Cognitive Focus

In this session Ruth discloses her belief that she must be perfect at everything she does. Ruth is a performance-oriented person, and the demands she puts on herself in living up to external standards are leading her toward exhaustion. I find value in getting Ruth to reflect on her beliefs and how these beliefs affect how she feels and what she is doing. I introduce a cognitive role-play situation, which leads to a realization of how tired she is because of all the ways she burdens herself. Working within the framework of cognitive behavioral therapy, Ruth and I explore specific messages she continues to tell herself. We look at alternative beliefs, ones that will allow her to be freer and less bound by perfectionistic goals.

Although I value dealing with how clients think about life, I do not narrowly stay with identifying and challenging self-talk and core beliefs. Thinking, feeling, and behaving are interactive aspects, and these three dimensions can be blended in the work of a single session. I may begin by suggesting a cognitive role play with Ruth where we might deal mainly with some of her faulty beliefs or self-talk that tend to get her into trouble. As we engage on the cognitive level, Ruth is likely to experience feelings about her awareness of what she tells herself. Thus, we can shift to doing some experiential work or a role play dealing with emotional issues. We may end the session by discussing how beliefs and feelings often influence the way we behave.

1. Would you be more inclined to focus on Ruth's feelings? her thought processes and other cognitive factors? her ability to take action as measured by her behaviors?

2. What specific concepts from the cognitive behavioral therapies would you draw on in working with Ruth's perfectionism and her other faulty beliefs?

## Session 7: Emotive Focus

Ruth mentions that she would like to talk about her relationship with her husband, John. She feels depressed when she thinks about their relationship. I ask Ruth to pay attention to what she is experiencing in the here-and-now as she is talking about what is missing in her marriage. She feels unappreciated and unloved. I suggest a role play that entails Ruth talking to me as John. As she talks to me (as her husband) in the present tense, Ruth becomes aware of her feelings of sadness and cries. I think it is important to allow clients to experience whatever they are feeling and to allow those feelings to deepen. I try not to shift her to a thinking or behavioral focus, but encourage her to stay with whatever she is aware of and express this. A Gestalt therapy perspective is extremely useful in facilitating Ruth's exploration of a range of feelings. At this point it is not useful to make interpretations, to give advice, or to suggest solutions. Instead, it is therapeutic to simply move with the moment-by-moment awareness of the client. From the existential perspective, I am attempting to enter her world and see reality as she does. Paying attention to whatever Ruth is experiencing in her body is an important direction for us to follow. Although she is not accustomed to recognizing bodily signs, by asking her to notice some of her movements or subtle bodily shifts, she becomes better able to identify the meanings of bodily sensations.

1. What therapeutic approaches are useful for you in dealing with the emotional dimension of counseling?

2. What value do you see in asking Ruth to stay with her present awareness and express what she is feeling moment by moment?

3. Given the fact that you are limited to brief therapy with Ruth (about 13 sessions), how inclined are you to encourage her to identify, express, and explore a range of feelings? Do you see ways of dealing with the emotive dimension and still work both cognitively and behaviorally?

## Session 8: Behavioral Focus

The prior session was an emotional one, so I ask Ruth at the beginning of this session if she reflected on last week or had any afterthoughts. Ruth admits that she feels a bit embarrassed over making herself that vulnerable. She wrote in her journal about the sadness she feels about her relationship with John and her children. Then she initiates a discussion of her weight. Ruth admits that she does not exercise, that she does not have much energy, and that she does not feel good about her weight or how she looks. I choose to focus on the behavioral dimension, but this does not exclude working with beliefs she has about her weight or her feelings about being overweight.

Drawing on behavior therapy and reality therapy, I strive to help Ruth assess the contributing factors to her concern over her weight. Once Ruth and I agree that getting involved in an exercise program is something she really wants, I function as a teacher and a consultant in helping her develop a behavioral plan. Simply wanting to feel better, have more energy, and lose weight will not translate into actual changes. I teach her about the importance of formulating an action plan, which we collaboratively devise together. I also suggest that she find a support system to encourage her to stick to her commitments. In addition, we discuss how essential it is that Ruth monitor and record her progress in carrying out her plans.

1. If you are counseling Ruth and she informs you that she wants to work on concerns about her weight, how would you proceed? What behavioral methods would you use?

2. Besides working from a behavioral slant on themes such as weight and exercise, what possibilities do you see of bringing a cognitive and emotive dimension into this work?

3. What value do you see in homework and practicing outside of the session?

## Session 9: Integrative Focus

Because Ruth is an integrated being, it makes sense to work with her from an integrative focus. I very much like the ideas of Arnold Lazarus as expressed in his approach to behavior therapy known as multimodal therapy, which begins with a comprehensive assessment of a client on all dimensions of human functioning. After making this broad-based assessment of Ruth's current functioning, we can then identify a number of specific target goals in different areas. It is possible to deal with a wide range of feelings, thoughts, and actions from a holistic framework. Here I find Adlerian theory most useful in providing a holistic perspective. Also useful are some concepts and techniques of both solution-focused brief therapy and narrative therapy. These approaches provide a foundation for building on Ruth's strengths and resources, as well as assisting her in revising her life story.

At this point, ask yourself how you would proceed with Ruth. I encourage you to think of the process of developing a counseling style that fits you as an ongoing project. Certainly it is not a task to be accomplished quickly. It entails far more than picking bits and pieces from theories in a random and fragmented manner. As you take steps to develop an integrated perspective, you might ask: Which theories provide a basis for understanding the cognitive dimension? Which theories help you understand the feeling dimension? And what about the behavioral dimension? As you are aware, most of the 11 therapies you have studied focus primarily on one of these dimensions of human experience. The task is to wisely and creatively select therapeutic procedures that you can employ in working with a diverse population.

## Session 10: Understanding Transference and Countertransference

Transference can be an especially useful tool in the counseling process. Clients will project a diversity of feelings, and they will oftentimes react to you as they reacted to other significant figures in their life. In Ruth's case, she saw some of her father in me. She felt that she could not please her father, and she reports mixed feelings of love and hate toward him. She expresses that in some ways she feels that she cannot please me or meet my expectations. In working with transferential reactions, it is important not to get defensive. I allow Ruth to express a range of feelings. Once she has done this, she can sort out aspects that are projections based on past experiences from real reactions. Whenever there is transference of a client onto the therapist, there is the possibility that this will touch on the therapist's personal issues. Countertransference is the other side of the coin, which needs to be monitored by the therapist if the therapy is to proceed. Of all the theories, I find the psychoanalytic approach to be the most useful in conceptualizing ways of understanding and working with transference and countertransference.

1. If you are engaged in short-term therapy with Ruth, to what extent will you be interested in exploring transference reactions? What will you do if Ruth's reactions to you trigger some of your own feelings?

2. Reality therapy and rational emotive behavior therapy pay little attention to transference. What are your thoughts about this?

## Session 11: Exploring the Past

The past is an important path to the here-and-now. I tend to pay attention to what clients report in the here-and-now and listen for evidence of unfinished business from the past. I am indebted to Gestalt therapy with its emphasis on how stuck points from the past tend to show up in present functioning. I don't need to ask Ruth to recount lengthy stories about her early childhood experiences to adequately understand how her past is influencing her presently. Instead, I look and listen as Ruth is talking about reactions she is having toward her father. In a Gestalt manner, I ask Ruth to stay with whatever comes to her awareness and identify this. After she reports an event that happened when she was a child, I shift the emphasis from Ruth merely reporting an event to living that event. I suggest that she become the age she was and talk directly to her father (using me as her symbolic father). Ruth has many concerns from her childhood. Rather than talking about these events and the feelings associated with them, I find it much more powerful to suggest experiments whereby Ruth can relive and reexperience these earlier situations. Even in time-limited therapy, I find value in attending to the interweaving of the past and the present. By attending to the present, salient events from the past are illuminated and provide a fruitful avenue of exploration.

1. How much interest would you have in working with Ruth's past life experiences? her current issues? her future aspirations and strivings? Which of these areas do you favor? Why?

2. How comfortable would you be in drawing on Gestalt interventions as a way of working with past experiences? What other theories would you find useful in linking Ruth's past and present?

3. What ideas might you borrow from both solution-focused brief therapy and narrative therapy in assisting Ruth in getting a clearer picture of what kind of future she wants?

## Session 12: Working Toward Decisions and Behavior Change

As we move toward the final phase of our work together, Ruth identifies some early decisions she made and becomes increasingly aware of new possibilities. Ruth has discovered a pattern in decisions she has made and how those decisions have a continuing influence in her life today. She learned that sexuality was bad and wrong, that she should be in the service of others, and that she should keep a tight rein on her feelings lest she lose control. Because she has been willing to take what she has learned in the counseling office to the outside world, Ruth is able to make new decisions that are more functional. She also notices changes in her actual behaviors. She put her newly learned assertive skills into action to get into a fitness class that was full. Ruth is getting better at identifying old messages and self-defeating self-talk, and she is learning how to talk back to these critical voices. The key is not to discard early learnings but to help clients revise early decisions.

Ruth even brings up the matter of termination, which we talk about for some time in this session. Together we begin to explore plans for where she can go from here. Therapy is a new beginning rather than an answer to all of life's problems. Here I would draw from approaches such as narrative therapy, solution-focused therapy, and existential therapy in encouraging Ruth to reflect on ways she would like to continue the process of redesigning herself and what kind of life she would like 5 years hence. Again, I would draw from cognitive behavioral approaches in helping Ruth restructure some of her basic beliefs and develop further plans as a way to reach her new goals.

1. Would you orient Ruth's therapy more toward insight or toward action? What balance might you seek between the cognitive aspects and the feeling aspects?
2. What theories would you find useful in working with Ruth's decisions?
3. How would you intervene to get Ruth to critically evaluate some of the messages that influence what she does today? How might you help her to evaluate the degree to which her early decisions are still serving her well at this point in her life?

## Session 13: Evaluation and Termination

Termination is a process. We use the final session to review some significant points in the past 12 sessions and to discuss what was most helpful to her in her therapy. We talk about future therapy possibilities, such as getting into a counseling group, getting into family therapy, or getting involved in a number of projects that she feels are therapeutic for her. It is important that Ruth look specifically at what she learned, how she learned these lessons, and what can she do to build on these learnings now that formal therapy is over. From the narrative approach, I use the technique of writing a letter to Ruth in which I summarize many of her strengths and accomplishments that became evident in our work together. Ruth discovered that she is a person with various abilities, resources, and insights which she can draw upon in dealing with both her present and future concerns. Through our therapeutic partnership, Ruth has been able to free herself of many of her problem-saturated stories that restricted her level of satisfaction. She was able to come a long way toward co-constructing an enlivening alternative narrative. At this point, Ruth believes that she has expertise in many areas of her life. As she leaves formal therapy and enters into the next stage of her personal work, Ruth will be able to resist internalizing inadequacy and will be more able to externalize and challenge the cultural prescriptions that have constrained the life she wants to create. She now has confidence in herself and knows she can draw upon her courage and resourcefulness in dealing with future challenges. I also leave the door open so that Ruth will feel free to come in for future sessions should the need arise.

At this point, consider the partnership that you and Ruth formed and summarize the highlights of your work together.

1. Reflect on how you might make the determination of when Ruth was ready to end therapy? How could you fully include her in this process?
2. If you were to write Ruth a letter in which you wanted to remind her of her major accomplishments, what would you most want to say to her? What value do you see in writing Ruth a letter that would give her your perspective on the changes you have noticed in her?
3. What therapeutic approaches would you rely upon in assisting Ruth to bring closure to her therapeutic experience? What specific techniques are you likely to use?
4. What would you want to do to ensure that although her therapy with you is ending this is merely the beginning of new possibilities for her?

## An Exercise: Themes in Ruth's Life

A few of the major themes that have therapeutic potential for further exploration are revealed in statements Ruth has made at one time or another in her therapy sessions. These statements include:

- "You seem so distant and removed from me. You're hard to reach."
- "In spite of my best attempts, I still feel a lot of guilt that I haven't done enough."
- "I just don't trust myself to find my own answers to life."
- "I'm afraid to change for fear of breaking up my marriage."
- "It's hard for me to ask others for what I want."
- "I feel extremely tense, and I can't sleep at night."
- "All my life I've tried to get my father's approval."
- "It's hard for me to have fun. I'm so responsible."
- "I've always had a weight problem, and I can't seem to do much about it."
- "I'm afraid to make mistakes and look like a fool."
- "My daughter and I just don't get along with each other."
- "I give and give, and they just take and take."
- "I've lived by the expectations of others for so long that I don't know what I want anymore."
- "I don't think my marriage is the way it should be, but my husband thinks it's just fine."
- "I'm afraid to tell my husband what I really want with him because I'm afraid he'll leave me."
- "I fear punishment because I've given up my old religious values."
- "I wear so many hats that sometimes I feel worn out."
- "There's not enough time for me to be doing all the things I know I should be doing."
- "I'm afraid of my feelings toward other men."
- "When my children leave, I'll have nothing to live for."

Look over this list of Ruth's statements and select the ones that you find most interesting. Here are three suggestions for working with them:

1. For each of the themes you select, show how you would begin working with Ruth from each of the 11 perspectives.
2. If you prefer, take only two contrasting approaches and focus on these.
3. You might want to attempt to combine several therapeutic models and work with Ruth using this synthesis.

After reading about my integrated way of working with Ruth in this chapter, work with a few of Ruth's statements in small groups, using role playing and discussion. One person can "become" Ruth while others in the group counsel her from the vantage point of several different therapeutic perspectives. Practicing a variety of approaches will assist you in discovering for yourself how to pull together techniques that you consider to be the best.

## Concluding Comments

Knowing the unique needs of your clients, your own values and personality, and the theories themselves is a good basis for beginning to develop a theory that is an expression of yourself. Building your personalized orientation to counseling is a long-term venture, so be patient with yourself as you continue to grow through your reading, thinking, and experience in working with clients and through your own personal struggles and life experiences.

In this brief section on the values of an integrative perspective, it is not possible to do justice to this approach. For some further reading on applying an integrative perspective in working with Ruth, see Chapter 13 in *Case Approach to Counseling and Psychotherapy*. This detailed discussion brings the theoretical approaches together and shows how to develop your own therapeutic style. In this chapter I also present my integrative approach to working with Ruth. In addition, my book, *The Art of Integrative Counseling*, has as its primary purpose assisting students in thinking about ways to construct their own therapeutic style. Chapter 16 of *Theory and Practice of Counseling and Psychotherapy* deals with applying an integretive approach to working with Stan. Many of the techniques I describe in working with Stan could also be applied to Ruth's case.

## QUESTIONS AND ISSUES: Guidelines for Developing Your Personal Style of Counseling

In reviewing the various approaches to psychotherapy, apply the following questions to each theory. Comparing your own thinking on the underlying issues with the positions of the various therapies can assist you in developing a frame of reference for your personal style of counseling.

1. Are you drawn to a particular theory because it fits your own worldview, experiences, and value system? Does your theory provide you with confirmation of your views, or does it challenge you to think about new dimensions of the counseling process?

2. What aspects of each theory are most useful to you? Why?

3. If you had to select one theory that comes closest to your thinking, which theory would this be? What is your theory of choice? Explain?

4. What theory that you have studied is most divergent from your own theoretical frame of reference? Explain.

5. Does your theory of choice account for differences in culture, gender, sexual orientation, and socioeconomic status? How relevant is this theory when it is applied to working with culturally diverse client populations?

6. What are the implications of each theory for multicultural counseling? Can you think of any ethnic or cultural groups that are likely to experience difficulties with any of the particular therapy approaches?

7. Are you open to using the methods and techniques of a particular approach in a flexible manner, especially in working with culturally diverse clients? Would you tailor your techniques to the needs of your clients, or would you be inclined to fit your clients to your techniques?

8. To what degree does your acceptance or rejection of a particular theory indicate your own biases?

9. Examine the contemporary popularity of each theory, and attempt to identify factors that contribute to this popularity or lack of it. Consider issues such as efficiency, expense, population served, time involved, and so on.

10. Which theories lend themselves well to time-limited and brief formats? Is brevity an important concern for you? Why or why not?

11. What does each theoretical approach offer you (by way of key concepts) that is most significant in terms of integrating it into your practice?

12. What are the philosophical assumptions underlying each theory? How is the view of human nature of each theoretical approach reflected in the therapeutic goals? in the client–therapist relationship? in the techniques and procedures?

13. What are some unique features of each of the therapies presented? What is the central focus of each approach? What are the significant contributions?

14. What are the limitations of each approach in terms of its theoretical concepts, the therapeutic process, and the applications of techniques to various counseling situations? What are some other limitations with respect to practical aspects such as time involved, level of training necessary, kind of population for which the therapy is effective or ineffective, settings where it is appropriate or inappropriate, and cost? What are some limitations of the approach as applied to multicultural counseling?

15. What are some common denominators among the therapies? To what degree do most approaches share some underlying areas of agreement with regard to goals, therapeutic process, and use of techniques?

16. What approaches can be combined to give a broader, deeper, and more useful way of working therapeutically with people? For example, what are the possible benefits of combining Gestalt therapy and reality therapy? or combining the basic philosophy of the postmodern therapies with Gestalt techniques? or REBT with reality therapy?

17. What are some contrasts between therapies? For example, what major differences exist between psychoanalysis and behavior therapy? between psychoanalysis and existential therapy and behavior therapy? between person-centered therapy and REBT? between narrative therapy and REBT? between reality therapy and person-centered therapy? between solution-focused brief therapy and person-centered therapy?

18. What criteria exist for determining the degree of "successful" outcomes of counseling and psychotherapy in each approach? How specific are the criteria? Can they be measured objectively or observed?

19. Most approaches emphasize the client–therapist relationship as a crucial determinant of the outcomes of the therapeutic process. How does each approach view the nature and importance of the therapeutic relationship? What constitutes an effective collaborative therapeutic relationship?

20. What time frame does each approach emphasize: the past? the present? the future? How do the therapies that focus on the here-and-now account for the client's past and future?

21. How do the various therapies view the issue of the balance of responsibility between therapist and client? To what degree is the client's behavior controlled in the counseling sessions? outside the sessions? What degree of structure is provided by the therapist?

22. What are the advantages and disadvantages of practicing within the framework of one specific theory as opposed to developing a more integrative approach made up of several different therapies?

23. State the position of each of the theoretical approaches on these basic issues:
    a.  the importance of the role of interpretation
    b.  diagnosis as essential or detrimental
    c.  the balance between the cognitive aspects and feeling aspects
    d.  transference and countertransference
    e.  the importance of the client–therapist relationship
    f.  a collaborative partnership in which therapy becomes a joint venture
    g.  insight as a crucial factor
    h.  the orientation of therapy toward insight or action
    i.  the degree to which therapy is viewed as a didactic and re-educative process
    j.  the issue of reality

24. For each therapeutic model assume that you are a practitioner following that approach. How would you approach your work with clients at the initial session? How would you function? What would you focus on with respect to goals and therapeutic procedures?

25. For each approach cast yourself in the role of a client to get a sense of how you might respond to the approach. What would be your goals, role, and experience in the therapy process? How might you react to some of the techniques in each of the approaches?

# SUGGESTED ACTIVITIES AND EXERCISES:
## Developing Your Philosophy of Counseling

Early in the semester I routinely ask my students to write their philosophy of life (and counseling). At that point their views and values toward counseling are fuzzy. The exercise helps them gain a clearer focus on the basic attitudes and issues underlying counseling practice, and it typically generates thoughtful reflection. The material also can provide a variety of resources for discussion in class.

During the final weeks of the course I ask them to write a *revision* of the earlier paper. This time I ask them to integrate what they have learned from their readings in the various theories with their own basic values related to counseling. A *comparison* of the two papers provides excellent summary and integration material at the conclusion of the course, and it helps students determine what they have personally learned during the semester.

I recommend that you write your philosophy of counseling or, at the very least, develop a fairly comprehensive outline of your key ideas on that topic. What follows is offered as a guideline.

1. What is your view of human nature? How is your point of view significant in terms of your philosophy of counseling? What factors account for changes in behavior?

2. What is your definition of counseling? How would you explain to a prospective client what counseling is about at the first meeting?

3. What are some examples of goals of counseling that you view as appropriate? Can you list any goals that you consider inappropriate?

4. What are some of the most important functions of a counselor? How would you define your own role as a helper?

5. What do you think are the essential characteristics of an effective relationship between the client and the therapist? How important is this relationship as a factor for change?

6. What makes for a therapist's excellence? What distinguishes a mediocre therapist from an outstanding one?

7. What is one value you hold that you see as influencing your work as a counselor? How might this particular value influence you as a helping person?

8. How do cultural variables influence the counseling process? To what extent are you clear about the values of your culture and how they might influence your work as a counselor?

9. What life experiences of yours will help you work effectively with a wide range of clients? What struggles or crises have you effectively faced in your life, and how did you deal with them? What experiences have you had with people whose cultural values are different from your own?

10. What gives you a sense of meaning and purpose in life? How is your life's meaning potentially related to your need to help others?

11. Why are you selecting work in one of the helping professions? What is in it for you personally? What needs of yours are being met by being a helper?

12. To what degree are you doing in your life what you would want for your clients? What are you doing in your own life that will enable you to be an agent of change for your clients?

13. Now that you have studied the various theories, what steps could you take to begin to formulate your own orientation to counseling?

14. What key ethical concerns do you have about the practice of counseling? How would you go about resolving an ethical dilemma that you might face?

15. Can you think of some limitations in your own life experience that might hinder your ability to understand and relate to certain clients? How might you overcome some of your personal limitations so that you could counsel a wider range of clients more effectively?

## QUESTIONS FOR REFLECTION AND DISCUSSION

1. There appears to be a growing trend toward eclecticism and integrative perspectives. What do you think this movement signifies? What are the advantages and disadvantages of this trend?

2. If you were asked in a job interview to state your theoretical orientation, what would you say? Be sure to describe what you mean by your preference. (For example, if you would say, "I am eclectic," clearly spell out what theoretical concepts will guide the techniques you employ.)

3. Taking the key concepts of all 11 approaches that you have studied, how could you classify these concepts under the three separate headings of thinking, feeling, and behaving?

4. Again, assume that you were asked in a job interview to state your view of the goals of psychotherapy. In what ways could you categorize the 11 therapy systems in terms of goals under one of the three areas of focus: thinking, feeling, and doing?

5. What is your view of your role and function as a therapist? How would you answer this question in an interview by bringing several theoretical perspectives together?

6. How essential is the client–therapist relationship to therapeutic outcomes? Specifically, what do you think you would do to create the relationship with your clients that you deem ideal?

7. Assume that you are still in the interview situation. You are told that in this agency the clients come from diverse socioeconomic and cultural backgrounds. Explain which approaches might be most helpful to you in effectively working with a multicultural population.

8. Which of the 11 theories of counseling provides you with the best frame of reference for understanding yourself? Which basic ideas from these theories stand out as especially useful for you?

9. What are a few common denominators of all the therapeutic approaches?

10. What are some of the advantages of functioning within the framework of a single theory, as opposed to having an integrative perspective? What are some disadvantages of adhering to one theory?

# Chapter 16

# Case Illustration:
# An Integrative Approach
# in Working With Stan

 ## QUESTIONS FOR REFLECTION AND DISCUSSION

1. As you anticipate meeting Stan for the first session, what might you be thinking and feeling? From what you know of him after reading how each of the therapies was applied to his case, what will be some of your main focal points as you begin working with him?

   a. What therapeutic approaches might you draw from in helping Stan formulate goals that will guide his therapy?

   b. How might you enlist his involvement in collaboratively developing goals for therapy?

   c. What background information might you seek as a foundation for working with him? Which therapies might you draw from in doing this assessment of his current functioning?

2. Show how you might proceed with Stan by combining concepts from various theories. Give some idea of how you would work with him if you could meet with him 6 to 12 times. Attempt to integrate techniques and concepts that suit your personal style, and show how you could draw on several of the models in a balanced way.

3. Describe how in working with Stan you might pay attention to the factors of thinking, feeling, and doing. How could you develop a series of counseling sessions that would encourage him to explore his feelings, develop insight, put his problems into a cognitive perspective, and take action to make the changes he would most like to make?

4. In conceptualizing Stan's case and in thinking about a treatment plan (or approaches you might take with him), consider some of the following questions:

   a. How much direction and structuring do you see him as needing? To what degree would you take the responsibility for structuring his sessions?

   b. What major themes would you be likely to focus on in his life?

   c. How would you modify your interventions to fit a brief therapy framework?

   d. How much might you be inclined to work toward major personality reconstruction? How inclined would you be to work toward specific skill development and problem-solving strategies?

   e. What values do you hold that are similar to Stan's? How do you expect that this similarity would either get in the way of or facilitate the therapeutic process?

   f. Assume that Stan is an ethnic minority client. Think of the ways in which you might modify your techniques. What special issues would you want to explore with him if he were an African American? Native American? Latino? Asian American?

   g. What ethical issues do you think may be involved in working with Stan's case?

h. How might you structure outside-of-therapy activities (homework, reading, journal writing, and so forth) for Stan? Thinking about his case, can you come up with suggestions of activity-oriented homework assignments for him?

i. In working with Stan, how much interest would you have in his *past* experiences? How might you work with some early childhood issues? What interest would you have in his *current* functioning? Would you have a concern about his *future* strivings and aspirations? How might you work with him on his expectations?

j. Might you be inclined to focus on his *thinking* processes and his belief systems (cognitive dimension)? his *feelings* associated with his experiences (emotional dimension)? his ability and willingness to *do* something different and to *take action* (behavioral dimension)? Which dimension do you think you would make the focus of therapy? Why?

5. In thinking about termination of Stan's therapy, show what criteria you might use to determine when it would be appropriate. Consider a few of these issues:

a. Would you, as Stan's counselor, suggest termination? Would you wait until he brought up the matter?

b. Consider each of the various therapeutic approaches. When would he be ready to stop coming in for counseling? What are some different standards to determine his readiness for termination, depending on various theories of therapy?

c. What might you do if you thought he was ready to terminate but *he* did not feel ready quite yet? What if he wanted to stop coming to sessions and you were convinced that he had many more issues to explore that he was avoiding and that he was somewhat frightened about continuing therapy?

d. What ideas do you have for evaluating overall therapy? How might you assess his level of change? How would you measure the outcomes of your work together?

## ADDITIONAL CASES FOR PRACTICE

Show how you would work, using an integrative approach, with the situations presented in the following six brief cases. These cases are designed to give you some additional practice in applying concepts and techniques from the various approaches to specific situations. I suggest that you use the material I have provided merely as a point of departure. You can flesh out each case yourself by creating additional data. The following questions are useful to apply to each of the vignettes.

1. What ethical and clinical issues does each case represent? What is your assessment of each of these key issues? What value issues arise in each case? How might your values affect the way in which you intervene?

2. Which theoretical approaches would be most helpful to you in counseling the clients involved in each case? What specific concepts would be useful? What techniques and procedures are you likely to employ?

3. What is your assessment of the core of the problem involved in each scenario? Show how you would proceed, and give your rationale for the interventions you would expect to make.

4. In each vignette, what are some special considerations relative to factors such as differences in ethnicity, cultural values, socioeconomic status, religious values, sexual orientation, lifestyle characteristics, and sex-role and gender expectations?

### 1. A Husband Betrayed by His Wife

The Reverend Joshua Hunter, an African American Baptist minister in his late 30s, lives with his wife and children in a small town in North Carolina. About a month ago his wife told him that she had been having an affair for over a year and intended to ask for a divorce. At first Joshua was totally shocked and went into denial. He thought to himself that he must be having a horrible dream. As reality hit him, he experienced a range of emotions. He is seeking counseling because he says that he cannot cope with his feelings and is just not able to function and get through a day. In counseling he tells you:

> I feel so humiliated and shamed in front of all those who respected me. It's hard to face anyone. With all this going on, I just don't know how I can continue in the ministry in my town. It's hard to understand why this happened to me, because I've always tried to be the best husband and father that I could be. I know I was gone a lot, with all the work that needed to be done in the parish, but it's so hard to understand why she is doing this to me. As hard as I try to put this crazy thing out of my mind, it's just impossible to do so. All day long, and even much of the night, I keep ruminating about all she told me. As a God-fearing man I just don't know what to do next.

## 2. A Lesbian Confronting Her Parents

Gail is seeking counseling because she feels a strong need to tell her parents about her true identity as a person and her lifestyle. Her parents are strictly religious people who are highly intolerant of homosexuality. For most of her life Gail struggled with hiding the feelings she had for other women. She tells you that she has been living a lie so as not to be disowned by her mother and father. She says, however, that from her adolescence she has known deep down that she is a lesbian but was not able to actually admit it to herself until her junior year at college. She then went on to graduate school and got a master's degree in social work. She is involved in a long-term relationship, and the two women have been considering taking steps to adopt a child. If this happens, there will be no way that she can continue hiding her sexual orientation. Although she counsels others, she is coming to you for counseling because she wants to clarify her priorities and make some key decisions about taking the risk of confronting her parents. She wants their approval and acceptance of the person who she is, yet she finds herself resenting them when she thinks of how they are likely to relate to her decisions.

## 3. A Man With a Disability Searching for Meaning and Spiritual Identity

Herb suffered a spinal-cord injury when he was cutting trees and one of them fell on him. For a time after the accident, he continually asked himself, "Why did this have to happen to me?" He tells you that for the first 2 years after he became a paraplegic, he fantasized about suicide a great deal. He had been very active, and to be confined to a wheelchair for the rest of his life was more than he thought he could bear. It has been 5 years since his injury, and he says he has a better outlook on life than he had then, but he still goes into periods of depression and wonders what the meaning of his life is, especially when he considers all the physical activities that he loved so much that he cannot do any longer. A close friend urged Herb to get into counseling to work on his dissatisfaction and help him find a new direction in his life. He tells you that he would really like to discover a way to feel worthwhile again, and he seems somewhat inspired when he thinks of the accomplishments of some of his physically disabled friends. He says: "If they can overcome odds, even in sports, maybe I could too. It's just that I get discouraged, and then it seems like such hard work to get myself into gear. I'm so much hoping that I can find this motivation in counseling."

## 4. A Woman Struggling With Her Cultural Background

Dr. Deborah Wong is from a second-generation Chinese family. She tells you that even though she has lived in the United States all of her life, her Chinese roots are deep, and she has many conflicts over whether she is Chinese or American. Sometimes she feels like neither. Deborah has distinguished herself in her profession, and she holds a highly responsible position as a pediatrician. She feels married to her work, which she says is the thing she can do best in life. She has not made the time to cultivate intimate relationships with either sex, and she tells you that she very much feels as if she is "missing out" on life. She has always felt tremendous pressure to excel and never to let her family down. She feels as if she is in a competitive race with her older brothers, with whom her parents have always compared her. No matter how hard she works or what she accomplishes, she always feels a sense of inadequacy and experiences "not being enough." With some mixed feelings she is seeking counseling because she wants to feel "sufficient as a person." Although she enjoys her profession, she'd like to learn to take some time for herself. She also wants to develop a close relationship with a man. Yet whenever she is not working, she experiences guilt.

### 5. A Man Grieving Over the Loss of His Wife

At age 74 Erving says he has been totally lost ever since his wife, Amanda, "left" him after her long battle with lung cancer. A hospice worker strongly encouraged him to participate in counseling to work through his grief reactions. During her illness the hospice group was of tremendous help to both Amanda and Erving. After her death, however, he felt strange when he'd go to a hospice group meeting. He tells you:

> Over 90 percent of the group members are widows, and I keep thinking that I wish it had been me who died instead of Amanda. Even though it has been over a year since her death, I still feel lost and struggle to get through each day. I'm so lonely and miss her so much. They say it takes time, but I don't seem to be getting any better. Nothing seems very worthwhile anymore, and without her in my life I can't find anything I really like doing. I never had many friends. Amanda was really my only friend, and now that she's gone, it doesn't seem that there is any way to fill this huge gap in my life.

He would like to get over feeling regret at what he didn't say to her as well as what he didn't do with her when she was alive. He'd like to resolve feeling so guilty that he is alive while she is gone.

### 6. A Woman Who Wants Her Marriage and Her Affair

Loretta and Bart come to you for marriage counseling. In the first session you see them as a couple. Loretta says that she can't keep going on the way they have been for the past several years. She tells you that she would very much like to work out a new relationship with him. He says that he does not want a divorce and is willing to give counseling his "best shot." Loretta comes to the following session alone because Bart had to work overtime. She tells you that she has been having an affair for 2 years and hasn't yet mustered up the courage to leave Bart for this other man, who is single and is pressuring her to make a decision. She relates that she feels very discouraged about the possibility of anything changing for the better in her marriage. She would, however, like to come in for some sessions with Bart because she doesn't want to hurt him.

- What would you be inclined to say to Loretta based on what she has told you privately?
- Would you be willing to work with Loretta if her aim was to continue her affair and keep her marriage? Why or why not?
- How would your views on extramarital affairs influence the interventions you made with Loretta and Bart?
- Would you encourage Loretta to divulge what she told you privately in a later session with Bart? Why or why not?
- Would the element of "the other man" pressuring Loretta to make a decision have a bearing on your intervention in this case?

# Scoring Key for Chapter Quizzes

| Item Number | Chapter 4 Psychoanalytic Therapy | Chapter 5 Adlerian Therapy | Chapter 6 Existential Therapy | Chapter 7 Person-Centered Therapy | Chapter 8 Gestalt Therapy | Chapter 9 Behavior Therapy | Chapter 10 Cognitive Behavior Therapy | Chapter 11 Reality Therapy | Chapter 12 Feminist Therapy | Chapter 13 Postmodern Therapy | Chapter 14 Family Systems Approaches |
|---|---|---|---|---|---|---|---|---|---|---|---|
| 1 | F | T | F | F | T | F | F | T | F | T | F |
| 2 | T | T | T | F | T | T | T | T | T | T | T |
| 3 | T | F | T | T | F | T | F | F | T | F | F |
| 4 | F | F | F | F | F | T | T | F | F | T | T |
| 5 | T | T | T | F | T | T | F | F | T | F | T |
| 6 | F | F | F | F | F | T | F | F | T | F | T |
| 7 | F | F | T | T | T | T | F | F | T | T | T |
| 8 | F | T | F | F | F | F | T | T | F | T | T |
| 9 | T | T | F | F | F | T | T | T | F | T | T |
| 10 | T | F | T | T | T | T | T | F | F | F | T |
| 11 | D | D | E | E | E | B | C | E | A | A | B |
| 12 | B | B | D | B | E | A | C | B | D | C | E |
| 13 | C | B | C | E | B | B | A | D | C | C | D |
| 14 | B | D | B | A | A | A | D | B | A | C | A |
| 15 | C | E | A | E | A | B | A | E | D | A | B |
| 16 | C | C | D | D | D | B | D | B | B | D | C |
| 17 | A | D | A | D | B | E | B | B | B | B | D |
| 18 | B | B | E | D | E | B | C | B | B | A | D |
| 19 | C | B | D | D | C | D | E | B | A | E | E |
| 20 | C | D | C | E | D | E | C | E | D | D | C |
| 21 | C | B | B | D | E | D | C | D | C | A | B |
| 22 | C | E | B | B | C | B | B | A | E | B | E |
| 23 | B | A | C | E | A | A | E | B | C | B | A |
| 24 | E | E | B | E | D | C | D | D | B | D | A |
| 25 | A | C | D | B | E | D | B | C | B | B | C |

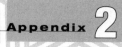

# Other Books and Videos
# by the Author

Here is a list of other books that my colleagues and I have authored or co-authored, and some educational student videos as well, that might be of interest to you. These books and videos are published by Brooks/Cole Thomson Learning, Belmont, CA 94002.

Corey, G. (2005). *Case Approach to Counseling and Psychotherapy,* 6th ed.
Demonstrates how theory can be applied to specific cases using the theories that correspond to chapters in *Theory and Practice of Counseling and Psychotherapy.* Readers are challenged to apply their knowledge of these theories to the case of Ruth. Also, a proponent of each theory writes about his or her assessment of Ruth and demonstrates his or her particular therapeutic style in counseling Ruth. I then show how I might intervene with Ruth by staying within the general framework of each of these theories, and also in an eclectic, integrated fashion.

Corey, G., & Haynes, R. (2005). *CD-ROM for Integrative Counseling.*
This CD-ROM interactive educational program brings theory to life for the case of Ruth. Showing my own integrative style in counseling Ruth, I draw on the thinking, feeling, and behaving perspectives, highlighting the value of working with a singular theme from all three modalities of human experience.

Corey, G. (2004). *Theory and Practice of Group Counseling,* 6th ed. (and *Student Manual,* 6th ed.).
A comprehensive group counseling textbook that describes 10 contemporary theories of group counseling and highlights techniques applicable to therapeutic groups.

Corey, G., Corey, M. S., Callanan, P., & Russell, J. M. (2004). *Group Techniques,* 3rd ed.
Describes ideas for creating and implementing techniques for use in groups. Gives a rationale for the use of techniques in all the stages in a group's development.

Haynes, R., Corey, G., & Moulton, P. (2003). *Clinical Supervision in the Helping Professions: A Practical Guide.*
This is a book for those who are interested in learning how to become a supervisor. The book deals with topics such as roles and responsibilities of supervisors; models of supervision; the supervisory relationship; methods of supervision; ethical, legal, and multicultural issues in the supervisory process; managing crisis situations; and evaluation issues.

Corey, M. S., & Corey, G. (2003). *Becoming a Helper,* 4th ed.
Many topics of concern to students studying in one of the helping professions are discussed here. Some of the issues explored are examining your motivations and needs, becoming aware of the impact of your values on the counseling process, learning to cope

with stress, dealing with burnout, exploring developmental turning points in your life, and ethical issues.

Corey, G., Corey, M. S., & Callanan, P. (2003). *Issues and Ethics in the Helping Professions*, 6th ed.
A combination textbook and student manual, this book contains self-inventories, open-ended cases and problem situations, exercises, suggested activities, and discusses a variety of ethical, professional, and legal issues facing practitioners.

Corey, G., Corey, M. S., & Haynes, R. (2003). *Ethics in Action: CD-ROM*.
This self-study program is aimed at exploring ethical decision making, the role of values in the counseling process, and managing boundary issues and multiple relationships. The video role-play segments and the exercises for interactive learning can be used along with either *Becoming a Helper* or *Issues and Ethics in the Helping Professions*.

Corey, M. S., & Corey, G. (2002). *Groups: Process and Practice*, 6th ed.
This book outlines the basic issues and concepts of group process throughout the life history of a group. These basic concepts are applied to groups for children, adolescents, adults, and the elderly.

Corey, G., & Corey, M. S. (2002). *I Never Knew I Had a Choice*, 7th ed.
This self-help book for personal growth deals with topics such as the struggle to achieve autonomy; the roles that work, gender roles, sexuality, love, intimacy, and solitude play in our lives; the meaning of loneliness, death, and loss; and how we choose values and find meaning in life.

Corey, G. (2001). *The Art of Integrative Counseling*.
This brief supplementary book is an expansion of Chapters 15 and 16 in *Theory and Practice of Counseling and Psychotherapy*.

Corey, G., Corey, M. S., & Haynes, R. (2000). *Evolution of a Group Video*: *Student Video and Workbook*.
This 2-hour self-study video-workbook package demonstrates group process in action and illustrates techniques for all the stages of a group. This video is also designed to be used in conjunction with *Theory and Practice of Group Counseling*, *Groups: Process and Practice*, and *Group Techniques*.

For a copy of the latest Brooks/Cole Thomson Learning Human Services, Counseling, and Social Work Catalog, contact:

**Wadsworth Publishing Company**
10 Davis Drive
Belmont, CA 94002
Telephone: (650) 595-2350
Web site: www.wadsworth.com

NOTES

NOTES

## TO THE OWNER OF THIS BOOK:

I hope that you have found *Student Manual for Theory and Practice of Counseling and Psychotherapy,* Seventh Edition, useful. So that this book can be improved in a future edition, would you take the time to complete this sheet and return it? Thank you.

School and address: _____

_____

Department: _____

Instructor's name: _____

1. What I like most about this book is: _____

_____

_____

2. What I like least about this book is: _____

_____

_____

3. My general reaction to this book is: _____

_____

_____

4. The name of the course in which I used this book is: _____

_____

5. Were all of the chapters of the book assigned for you to read? _____

   If not, which ones weren't? _____

6. In the space below, or on a separate sheet of paper, please write specific suggestions for improving this book and anything else you'd care to share about your experience in using this book.

_____

_____

_____

_____

_____

_____

TAPE HERE.
DO NOT STAPLE.

TAPE HERE.
DO NOT STAPLE.

FOLD HERE

**THOMSON**

**BROOKS/COLE** ™

## BUSINESS REPLY MAIL
FIRST-CLASS MAIL    PERMIT NO. 34    BELMONT CA

POSTAGE WILL BE PAID BY ADDRESSEE

Attn: *Counseling/Amy Lam*

BrooksCole/Thomson Learning
10 Davis Dr
Belmont CA 94002-9801

FOLD HERE

OPTIONAL:

Your name: _____ Date: _____

May we quote you, either in promotion for *Student Manual for Theory and Practice of Counseling and Psychotherapy,* Seventh Edition, or in future publishing ventures?

Yes: _____ No: _____

Sincerely yours,

*Gerald Corey*

TAPE HERE.
DO NOT STAPLE.